Ethnic Preference
and
Public Policy
in
Developing States

Ethnic Preference
and
Public Policy
in
Developing States

edited by
Neil Nevitte and Charles H. Kennedy

Lynne Rienner Publishers, Inc.
Boulder, Colorado

Published in the United States of America in 1986 by
Lynne Rienner Publishers, Inc.
948 North Street, Suite 8, Boulder, Colorado 80302

Library of Congress Cataloging-in-Publication Data

Ethnic preference and public policy in developing states.

    Bibliography: p.
    Includes index.
    1. Ethnic groups—Government policy—Developing
countries. 2. Developing countries—Ethnic relations.
3. Developing countries—Politics and government.
4. Developing countries—Economic conditions—Regional
disparities. I. Nevitte, Neil. II. Kennedy, Charles H.
JF1063.D44E87 1986   323.1'09712'4   86-13505
ISBN 0-931477-89-1

Distributed outside of North and South America and Japan by
Frances Pinter (Publishers) Ltd, 25 Floral Street,
London WC2E 9DS England. UK ISBN 0-86187-672-5

Printed and bound in the United States of America

Contents

Tables

Acknowledgments

This volume grew out of the presentations of a panel organized for the Annual Meeting of the American Political Science Association in Washington, D.C., in September 1984. In editing this volume and conducting the panel, we received assistance from a number of organizations and individuals. We wish to acknowledge their help.

The Department of Political Science, University of Calgary, and the Department of Politics, Wake Forest University, provided important logistical support throughout the project. Also, a number of individuals provided assistance with the preparation of the manuscript. As in any enterprise of this sort, skillful secretarial assistance is essential. We were lucky to have such assistance from Judy Powell and Cecile Calverley at the University of Calgary and Elide Vargas at Wake Forest University. Norman Hill and Jean Seeman at Wake Forest provided important technical assistance, and the Research and Publications Fund of the Graduate School of Wake Forest University provided financial assistance during the final stages of manuscript preparation.

Finally, we would like to thank the contributors, both those who presented their papers (which they then revised for this text) at the Annual Meeting of the American Political Science Association and those who prepared chapters especially for this volume. All the contributors shared their insights with a spirit of openness and good will, they listened patiently to ponderous editorial queries and suggestions, and they responded promptly to all of our requests.

Neil Nevitte
Charles H. Kennedy

1

The Analysis of Policies of Ethnic Preference in Developing States

NEIL NEVITTE / CHARLES H. KENNEDY

State policies of preference for one group are contentious because they engage fundamental questions about fair access to or just distribution of valued resources. The use of the state to confer special advantages on particular groups is hardly a novel theme. The divisive potential of such preferential treatment has been realized across such historically significant divisions as citizen versus slave, the propertied versus the propertyless, black versus white, Catholic versus Protestant, and the enfranchised versus the unenfranchised. What is more novel, at least from a Western perspective, is the conscious deployment of preferential policies as a strategy for regulating social conflicts. For example, affirmative action or compensatory legislation is widely regarded as a tool for regulating, and rendering more benign, contemporary social divisions grounded in age, gender, physical disability, and sexual preference. Given the sheer variety of preferential policies, the diversity of relevant social divisions, and the vast historical sweep of the evidence, it would be a herculean task to develop a comprehensive explanation of how preferential policies affect social conflict in general. The contributors to this volume, however, have a more modest goal: to examine how a special type of preferential policy, policies of ethnic preference, work to affect communal conflict in a particular setting, that of developing states.

There are sensible, practical reasons for limiting the scope of any study. The central problem becomes more accessible, the analysis more focused and manageable, and the chances of making some advance, though it may be a modest advance, are improved. But after the legitimate practical reasons are set aside other more crucial questions emerge. For example, what is the rationale for delineating a problem in a particular way? What sort of approach is germane to the analysis of the problem? What are the prospects of learning general lessons from the analysis of a limited subset of cases? The purpose of this chapter is to address these questions, and more particularly, to expose the volume's theoretical supports in order to identify the strengths and limitations of the analytical approach. By way of conclusion this chapter draws attention to central themes common to the analyses of different contributors and suggests what implications flow from the collective efforts of the contributors.

Focus: Theoretical Considerations

To delineate the scope of any inquiry requires that two sorts of analystical decisions be made. The first has to do with focus, i.e., establishing the range of the phenomenon to be explained. The second has to do with approach and the decision of how the phenomenon in question is to be explained. The decision to limit the range of inquiry to one type of social division, ethnicity, in effect identifies the principal unit of analysis—the ethnic community. Ethnic community is commonly defined as a collectivity within a larger society that claims common ancestry, a shared past, and shared subjective cultural identifications.

Such a definition stresses the importance of identification and thus emphasizes the subjective qualities of ethnicity, but membership in an ethnic community is not entirely voluntaristic or a question of individual choice. Although the individual is not constrained by ethnic group membership in the sense that gender characteristics are involuntarily predetermined, ethnic identifications cannot be readily shed, and membership in ethnic communities cannot be abandoned at will. The constraints on ethnic group membership, however, are not merely subjective. As moral economists, social anthropologists, and others have pointed out, ethnic communal solidarity also involves a network of social, economic, and moral as well as cultural relationships.[1] Thus, communal solidarity is reinforced by the interaction of instrumental and psychic factors. Two important consequences flow from this observation. First, the costs of exit from an ethnic community are extremely high, and thus, ethnic identity and communal membership tend not to be bargainable. Second, to adopt the ethnic group as a primary focus of analysis does not mean that economic, class, or status factors are preempted or precluded from consideration. On the contrary, the starting assumption in this volume is that ethnic groups, like other groups, have interests and that those interests embrace economic, status, and class factors as well as the religious and linguistic hallmarks of cultural groups.

The focus on ethnicity is further circumscribed by a second distinction, between developing states and Western states, and attention is limited here to a consideration of policies of preference and intercommunal ethnic conflict in developing states.[2] There are several reasons for suggesting that contextual factors shape the deployment of policies of ethnic preference in developing states in ways that are qualitatively different from comparable policies in the developed West. First, in developing states ethnicity is frequently a principal axis of political conflict. Indeed, as will be apparent from all of the cases in this volume, the levels of interethnic communal rivalry are often sufficiently high as to threaten regime stability. In some instances, ethnic rivalries threaten the very foundations of the state itself. In this context the search for strategies to manage such conflicts is a "high stakes" enterprise because the failure to develop conflict regulating solutions holds critical consequences.

A second set of contextual factors unique to developing states may explain why this is so. As indicated at the outset, policies of preferences revolve around the distributional issue of how to allocate scarce resources. There is no sense in which developing states enjoy economic surpluses or the magnitude of resources commonly available for allocation in developed Western states. Nor, given the typical dependence on primary resource exports, the value of which fluctuates dramatically on world markets, and given the structure of the international economic system, can developing states realistically cling to the prospects of a Western-type economic expansion that ostensibly will alleviate allocative problems.[3] Just as the resources for allocation are scarce, so can the interethnic competition for those limited resources be expected to be intense.

The concept of resources, of course, is not limited to economic goods; it extends also to what may be broadly referred to as organizational capacity, and in this respect, too, there are fundamental differences between developing and Western states. Compared to Western states, most developing states, in fact all of those states considered in this volume, have a limited organizational capacity. Organizational capacity is limited not only by a relative shortage of skilled administrative and political personnel, but also by relatively weak institutional structures and norms. The difference between ethnic conflict in developing and Western states is one of kind and not degree because the impact of the contextual factors is not merely additive; rather it is magnified by the interaction of each factor with the others. Any allocative decision is difficult in an environment of weak institutional structures and norms. But those decisions are even more difficult in that environment when there is crippling economic scarcity and an absence of significant other crosscutting social divisions that could countervail or moderate ethnic communal identifications.[4]

The reason developing states have weak organizational capacity exposes another difference between developing and Western states. Developing countries have achieved political independence only relatively recently and as a consequence have limited experience with autonomous institutions. Moreover, the contemporary character of those institutions was forged in, and inherited from, the crucible of the colonial experience. As J. S. Furnivall and others have shown, the type of colonial experience is of considerable importance to historically grounded explanations of the performance of recently autonomous regimes.[5] Essentially, comparative analysts have a choice as to how to incorporate the "colonial heritage" variable into explanations of postcolonial regime performance. One strategy is to compare states with different types of colonial experiences, say British and French ex-colonies, and to include variations of the colonial experience into the explanations of the preformance of new states. The alternative approach, and the one adopted here, is to compare the regime performances of those countries that share similar, in this instance, British, colonial heritages. This approach imposes a form of analytical control on (variation in) "colonial heritage," but it does not deflect attention away from the significance of the colonial experience itself.[6]

In the 1960s a conventional, and now mostly bankrupt, developmentalist perspective held the view that new states had much to learn about their developmental path and prospects from Western experience. By extension, some might be tempted to suggest that new states could learn a great deal about managing ethnic conflict from Western experience also. It is not very clear, however, precisely what lessons could be learned from Western practices in this respect. Indeed, we have argued that ethnic conflict in developing states is qualitatively different from that found in the West, and that difference suggests an intriguing alternative possibility—that the West may learn a great deal about the dynamics of managing ethnic conflict from the experience of developing states. This is so because in developing states ethnic conflicts are most central, the search for solutions most urgent, and the resources that can be brought to bear on those solutions most limited.

Theoretical Approach

The choice of approach presents a major dilemma for any crossnational analysis. The wide variety of candidate theoretical approaches familiar to most social scientists range from straightforward description of the particular on the one hand to global generalization on the other.[7] Studies of the particular are criticized for being merely descriptive and for having an atheoretical preoccupation with the unique. The search for a global generalization that calls for synthesis and abstraction in turn, can be challenged on the grounds that general theories are rootless, inapplicable, and unrecognizable because they attenuate reality. In fact, of course, description is a necessary first step in any analysis. All comparativists confront the issue of how description feeds theory and how to settle the trade-off between the general and particular. The problem of finding a middle ground is multiplied in collaborative enterprises such as this one, notwithstanding the fact that the project's focus has already been limited in significant respects.

One way of dealing with this problem is to allow collaborators maximum freedom, leaving to them the decision of which approach to adopt. The major difficulty with this strategy is evident in the fragmentation of the final product, which, seen as a whole, does not maximize the collective potential of the contributors. Although the resulting case studies may be of high quality, they tend to "stand on their own." Lack of a common approach increases the chances that case studies will spin in different orbits and will not address each other. Editors are left the tortuous and often tortured task of bringing case studies together, usually under the guise of a concluding, untested "pretheory" or framework to which the contributors do not reply. The strategy adopted in this instance is somewhat different: it is not only to limit the focus but also to start with a common approach -- one that develops a public choice perspective within an exchange theory framework.[8] The contributors, each of whom is an experienced comparativist with considerable expertise in particular countries, were asked to address the public choice framework presented in the next chapter and they were invited to explore its utility. In essence, their efforts amount to an approximate test of the framework.

It is worth emphasizing that the contributors were asked to address the framework; they were encouraged to reach their own conclusions about the extent to which the framework provides a useful window on the cases of ethnic preference policies with which they are most familiar. There was no strident, and necessarily fruitless, search for unanimity, nor were participants called on to enthusiastically embrace the framework or to swallow it whole and reify it. The essays in this volume represent an assessment of the utility of one approach. Significantly, none of the contributors abandoned it wholesale. Notwithstanding the unusually large constraints placed on them, contributors exhibited a high degree of professionalism and entered into the spirit of the enterprise by offering constructive criticism. Modifications are suggested, areas of agreement stressed, and weaknesses are identified. This, it seems to us, conforms with the notion of an intellectual dialogue.

The Western emphasis of most empirical crossnational research probably reflects the greater accessibility and reliability of Western data. But the conceptual advantages of adopting a policy approach apply equally to Western and developing states. The approach fixes attention on a single policy issue as the primary object of analysis and explicitly asks that three kinds of questions be addressed. In this instance they are:

First: What are the origins of policies of ethnic preference? Or, what are the forces that drive them onto the public agenda?

Second: What do governments hope to achieve through the implementation of such policies? How do they work?

Third: Do the policies achieve what is intended? What are the costs of such policies?[9]

In sum, the first set of questions addresses the causes of policies; the second set calls attention to goalsetting; and the third set identifies the significance of evaluating goal attainment with an eye to policy improvement. To take on a policy approach, then, shifts the analytical center of gravity away from the traditional concerns of how, for instance, institutional and constitutional/legal factors "shape" minority relations toward a systematic search for the dynamics that drive policies and affect their chances of success. In a sense, a policy perspective regards institutional and constitutional/legal factors as epiphenomenal except insofar as they have a direct bearing on the origins, implementation, and consequences of the policy in question. But it would be misleading to speak of the policy approach because no single unifying approach prevails. At the level of practical application, policy approaches are middle range analytical guides at best. It is useful, then, to turn to a discussion of the particular approach that serves as a reference point for this volume. The intention is to render more concrete the preceding generalizations about policy perspectives by highlighting some essential elements of the framework that is fully developed in the following chapters.

Frameworks have been referred to as a *déformation professionelle*. Many are stillborn, and most are lifeless, unused because they lack a dynamic ingredient. The framework advanced by Donald Rothchild (Chapter 2) injects a dynamic element at the start by squarely focusing on the idea that ethnic groups have interests. The idea is extended in an important way by the suggestion that ethnic groups can be seen as but one variety of interest group. This connection opens a theoretical gate because explanations of ethnic group behavior are no longer confined to relatively barren land; they are free to roam in the richer pastures of interest group theory. Like other interest groups, ethnic groups can be seen as utility maximizers engaged in exchange relationships with other ethnic groups, exchange relationships wherein each actor seeks greatest advantage in the battle for scarce resources.[10]

These initial core ideas are the point of departure from which the framework is developed, but even at this stage, it is evident that the approach has significant theoretical consequences and advantages. The first is that the approach openly acknowledges the relational aspects of intercommunal behavior. This point is congruent with conventional relational conceptions of power. Intercommunal behavior is relational precisely because it involves the expression of power. This premise suggests that the character of the exchanges, like all expressions of power, is affected by the number of participants.[11] It also implies that what is pertinent to the outcomes of exchanges is the relative, not absolute, distribution of resources and capacities that interest-maximizing ethnic groups can bring into play.[12]

A second general advantage of the approach is that it acknowledges that the state is a central actor, not merely a passive bystander or neutral referee, in the exchanges between contending ethnic groups. The state is active not only in the sense that it participates in structuring those exchange relationships, but also in the sense that it, too, has interests not the least of which is a minimal interest in its own continuity. As such, the state requires a measure of public support, even under conditions of limited accountability, in its search for legitimacy. As the contributions to this volume illustrate, these questions can hardly be regarded as secondary. When the principal lines of political conflict revolve around ethnic divisions, the issues of which group control the state and how state authority is exercised, particularly with regard to policies of preference, become crucial. As Rothchild emphasizes, policies are the tangible objects of exchange.

A third general point worth emphasizing is, in fact, a response to an anticipated challenge to the approach, to wit: The focus on interests, exchange relationships, and resources of ethnic groups diminishes the significance attached to historical experience. A concern with interests, though, is not fundamentally ahistorical. Indeed, Barrington Moore, Charles Tilly, and others have given a clear demonstration of how a historical appreciation of shifting interests, alliances, and discontinuities can provide valuable insights into contemporary exchange relationships.[13] The utility of these insights is not unique to Western states. Rothchild begins with the premise that the historical encounter with colonialism was decisive in shaping the political, social, and economic capacities of ethnic groups in the postcolonial era. Indeed, a comparative reading of the non-African cases presented in this volume (most particularly Premdas, Chapter 7) extends the same general point in suggestive ways.

All policy frameworks are guided by the desire to explore policies systematically through a search for the most analytically important dimensions and to identify useful distinctions within those dimensions. Rothchild, drawing from his wide knowledge of African politics, structures a framework around seven basic dimensions. They are (1) identifying patterns of exchange relations; (2) distinguishing between the character of ethnic group demands; (3) specifying the societal conditions that affect the load on the state; (4) specifying a range of outcomes; (5) distinguishing between types of state responses; (6) evaluating alternative decision processes; and, finally, (7) comparatively evaluating nine conflict-regulating strategies. Constructing a framework in one context and applying it to others is a chancy proposition at best; it would be rare for a framework to emerge from that test untouched. But to be valuable, an approach does not have to account for everything. If if identifies demonstrably crucial questions, combines the relevant variables in suggestive ways, and thus indicates rewarding avenues of inquiry, it has done its job.

Findings

The aim of this chapter was to set the theoretical and methodological stage for the volume by addressing general questions of focus and approach. This concluding section does not restate those questions. Instead, it shifts gears and takes the opportunity to comment on two substantive issues that emerge as recurring themes in the following chapters. The first theme concerns the evident significance of the bureaucracy and of postsecondary education as the institutional sites of preferential policy battles. The second issue returns to the theme of the relationship between the colonial experience and postcolonial policies of ethnic preference.

Every contributor to this volume, in particular the chapters authored by Gordon Means (chapter 4) and Charles Kennedy (chapter 3) observes that bureaucracies are intimately involved with policies of preference. Even a brief reflection on why this might generally be the case makes it clear that bureaucracies in developing states experience enormous tensions between demands, expectations, and organizational capacities. To proceed any distance at all toward a credible explanation of these tensions it is necessary to abandon the expectation that these institutions conform to the classical Weberian ideal of what a modern bureaucracy should be.[14]

The first point to be made in this context is that bureaucracies are not neutral, and given their responsibility for the direction of state-sponsored development, it may be unreasonable to expect them to be so. Developing states are differentiated from their Western counterparts not only by the fact that the available resources are relatively scarce, but also by the pattern of resource distribution. Typically, the bureaucracies hold a significant proportion of the human, organizational, and other resources essential to the coordinated functioning of political communities. To the extent that the bureaucracy is both a significant resource node (some would say drain) and the principle distributor of resources, it is hardly surprising that the bureaucracy itself becomes an attractive target of the redistributive demands of contending ethnic communities. What is problematic is the extent to which the bureaucracy can be simultaneously an effective instrument of integration and an arena in which preference policies get full play.

Part of the explanation for why bureaucracies are not neutral or apolitical is rooted in the colonial experience. It is frequently argued that in the colonial phase, bureaucracies were relatively highly developed—to the extent that in the immediate postcolonial period they stood as one of the few deeply rooted structures with a national reach and overarching responsibilities. The fact that bureaucracies are typically surrounded by weak executive, legislative, and judicial political structures at a time when "development" is a national priority has important consequences. "Development" requires the planning, coordination, and execution of strategies. It places a premium on the cohesive organizational capacity of the bureaucracy as well as its reservoir of skill, and thus, it increases the chances of direct bureaucratic involvement in political decisionmaking. At the same time, the extension of bureaucratic involvement into those realms enhances bureaucratic power, often at the expense of the development of executive, legislative, and judicial institutional autonomy. Bureaucracies are an attractive target for contending groups not simply because they are reservoirs of relatively limited resources, but because bureaucracies occupy a crucial place in the power structure and operate across an extended field of activity.

It has been argued that the prospect of achieving responsible bureaucratic neutrality is tied to the status position of the higher civil service.[15] That status position is improved and bureaucratic efficiency advanced by strict adherence to meritocratic recruitment. The use of ethnic quotas in recruitment, then, actively undermines that status and the neutrality of bureaucracies, if not their efficiency. The use of quotas to gear upward mobility is not limited to the bureaucracy; it extends to the educational system also. To the extent that education provides a gatekeeping function for the middle class, educational quotas operate not only to shape the character of the recruiting pool from which the bureaucracy draws, but also to shape the character of the evolving middle class. Historically, it has been the middle class that acts to limit bureaucratic expansion (see Milne, Chapter 5).

The decision to limit the scope of the analysis to those developing states that experienced British colonialism recognized both the significance of the colonial experience and wide variation in European colonial practices. A close reading of the case studies in this volume, and indeed the vast literature on comparative colonialism, reveals profound variance even within British colonial experience. It also indicates significant commonalities. The policy approach structures the search for commonalities through a particular line of questioning. Who are the actors? What are their interests? To what extent and in which areas are the actors' patterns of interests congruent or conflictual? And, how does the distribution of resources contribute to, or constrain interest maximizing strategies?

In this context the prevailing interest of the British colonial actor was straightforward: to maintain power in a cost-effective manner. This maintenance was conditioned by such resource constraints as limited manpower and information. The confluence of such interests and constraints led to a consistent set of policies pursued in most arenas of British colonialism.[16] One was to insist on the predominance of the English language in administration, a second to favor the recruitment of "generalist" European administrators (for the most part, recent products of English public schools) to staff critical administrative posts. From the perspective of this volume, however, the most important policies concerned the interplay of British interests with the interests of indigenous subjects. Given manpower constraints, the British were forced to recruit large numbers of clerks, soldiers, informants, and collaborators to staff relevant posts within the colonial administration. Ideally, such recruits would be loyal, literate in English, and competent in the relevant sphere of employment. In practice what developed was an expedient recruitment policy wherein British colonial administrators recruited differentially from particular segments of the colonized population. The selection of one group over others (e.g., Tamils in Sri Lanka, see Oberst, Chapter 6) in effect constituted an incipient policy of preference during the colonial phase. Such incipient policies conferred differential advantage to particular groups, improving their status in relationship to other groups. This improved level of status found institutional expression in the bureaucracy.

Historically, the bases of such original preference have been diverse, encompassing an ethnic group's geographical proximity to centers of British activities (Bengali, Gujarati, and Tamil preference in pre-1857 India)[17]; perceived levels of loyalty to British rule (discrimination against Bengalis after 1857 for alleged complicity in the Indian Revolt)[18]; educational attributes, including but not limited to, knowledge of English (preference for mission school-educated Tamils in Sri Lanka)[19]; physical or racial characteristics (the designation of the so-called "martial races" of northern India—Pathans, Punjabis, and Sikhs)[20]; and so on. The central question is not whether these distinctions were valid or whether they had anything to do with merit. The important point rather relates to the consequences of these policies—especially how these recruitment practices affected the relative interests and eventually, the capacities of different ethnic communities for sustained collective action.

The interests and strategies of the other major actor (the subjects of colonial rule) were structured to a great extent by the presence of the British. From the perspective of utility maximizing groups, the primary goal of indigenous populations confronted with the reality of British rule was to maximally increase relative levels of authority within British administration with the ultimate long range goal of displacing the British. The most important constraints limiting the accomplishment of this end were associated with organizational weaknesses. First, British policy placed restrictions on the expression of political demands and the development of autonomous indigenous political institutions. Second, the bulk of distributional benefits within the colonial system were controlled by the British. Third, the ethnic groups nominated and selected by the British to share in the structures of government had little incentive to challenge the font of their benefits. Finally, groups excluded from the interchange (with few exceptions) were imperfectly mobilized to express their interests. Typically, relatively favored groups enjoyed increased levels of authority within British-led bureaucracies. On this issue the interest of the colonists and colonized converged. The British proved eager to minimize administrative costs by devolving authority to indigenous groups, and preferred groups developed an increased stake in the status quo and in developing increased organizational capacities.

The exit of the British radically altered the structures of such interests, but significant continuities remained. Indeed, the legacy of colonial policies of preference proved resilient at least in the short term. The newly independent elites continued to utilize political institutions inherited from the colonial period and significantly the bureaucracy retained a considerable measure of *esprit de corps* in the years immediately following independence. Notwithstanding such continuities, by independence the fairly inchoate ethnic milieu encountered by the British at the outset of their colonial experience had been transformed into environments in which several distinct ethnic groups were mobilized to express their communal demands in the context of incipient nation-states. The capabilities of such ethnic groups varied due to size, relative positional representation in state institutions and organizational capabilities—the latter two factors largely a function of British colonial policy.[21] But most crucial, the departure of the British raised the stakes of interethnic outcomes. In the colonial phase, preferential recruitment practices resulted in the disproportionate representation of members of favored ethnic groups in mid-level civilian and military posts. With independence, they were catapulted to the pinnacle of state power.

The resultant dynamics of interethnic competition in the postcolonial environment is structured by the interaction of relatively advantaged and relatively disadvantaged ethnic groups. The former wish to maintain their relative advantage; the latter to redress their relative disadvantage. Typically, in the years immediately following independence, the former translate their positions of relative advantage into policies of ethnic preference conducive to such ends. Policies of preference are adopted which have the net consequence of maintaining favored ethnic group dominance. As our case studies demonstrate (particularly Sri Lanka, Guyana and Pakistan), early postindependence policies have the appearance of success: There is little overt evidence of ethnic group conflict. But such appearances can be deceptive. The period of quiescence is shattered when relatively disadvantaged groups "discover" their relative disadvantage and take steps to redress their grievances. Indeed the lull before the storm may be explained as necessary for the relatively disadvantaged groups to develop some threshold of organizational capacity to enable them to realistically challenge the system maintained by the dominant ethnic group. It is this confrontation between organizational near-equals which produces maximal and persistent interethnic conflicts.

Notes

1. For a review see Joel S. Migdal, *Peasants, Politics and Revolution* (Princeton, N.J.: Princeton University Press, 1974) esp. chapters 1-3.
2. This, of course, does not mean that there is no utility in comparing policies of preference in "developed" and "less developed" states. See for example Myron Weiner and Mary F. Katzenstein, *India's Preferential Policies: Migrants, the Middle Classes and Ethnic Equality* (Chicago: University of Chicago Press, 1981), 136-153.
3. Among the more compelling treatments of this issue are found Fernando Enrique Cardoso and Enzo Faletto. *Dependency and Development in Latin America* (Berkeley: University of California Press, 1979); and Peter Evans, *Dependent Development: The Alliance of Multinational, State and Local Capital in Brazil* (Princeton, N.J.: Princeton University Press, 1979).
4. The seminal study was Samuel P. Huntington, *Political Order in Changing Societies* (New Haven, Conn.: Yale University Press, 1968).
5. J. S. Furnivall, *Colonial Policy and Practice: A Comparative Study of Burma and the Netherlands East India* (Cambridge: Cambridge University Press, 1968).
6. Adam Przeworski and Henry Teune, *Logic of Comparative Social Inquiry* (New York: John Wiley and Sons, 1970); and Donald Campbell and Julian Stanley, *Experimental and Quasi-Experimental Designs for Research* (Chicago: Rand McNally, 1968).
7. For an overview of these concerns see Sidney Verba, "Some Dilemmas in Comparative Research," *World Politics* 20 (October 1967): 111-127; and Robert T. Holt and John E. Turner, eds., *Methodology of Comparative Research* (New York: Free Press, 1970).
8. For a brief review of this approach see Anthony Heath, "Exchange Theory," *British Journal of Political Science* 1, no. 1 (July 1971): 91-120.
9. For a general discussion of this approach see Arnold Heidenheimer, Hugh Heclo and Carolyn Teich Adams, *Comparative Public Policy: The Politics of Social Choice in Europe and America* (New York: St. Martin's Press, 1983); Stuart S. Nagle, *Public Policy: Goals, Means, Methods* (New York: St. Martin's Press, 1984); and B. Guy Peters, "Comparative Public Policy," *Policy Studies Review* 1 (August 1981): 183-197.
10. A systematic early treatment of this theory is found in Mancur Olson, *The Logic of Collective Action: Public Goods and the Theory of Groups* (Cambridge: Harvard University Press, 1971).
11. An early and still useful treatment of this is found in Thomas C. Schelling, "Bargaining, Communication, and Limited War," *Journal of Conflict Resolution* 1, no. 1 (March 1957): 19-36.
12. Robert Goodin and John Dryzek, "Rational Participation: The Politics of Relative Power," *British Journal of Political Science* 10, no. 3 (July 1980): 273-292.
13. See Barrington Moore, Jr., *The Social Origins of Dictatorship and Democracy: Land and Peasant in the Making of the Modern World* (Boston:

Beacon Press, 1966); and Charles Tilly, ed., *The Formation of National States in Western Europe* (Princeton University Press, 1975).

14. For a general discussion see Joseph La Palombara, ed., *Bureaucracy and Political Development* (Princeton, N.J.: Princeton University Press, 1963), esp. chapters 1-2.

15. Fritz Morstein Marx, "The Higher Civil Service as an Action Group in Western Political Development" in ibid., pp. 62-95.

16. Obviously the literature pertaining to British colonialism is vast. A good starting point for the non-specialist is Stanley Wolpert, *A New History of India* (New York: Oxford University Press, 1982), esp. chapters 1-22; and Geoffrey Moorhouse, *India Britannica* (London: Paladin, 1983). A fascinating approach to British colonial social practices and interactions with subject peoples is provided by Charles Allen's, *Tales of the Dark Continent: Images of British Africa in the Twentieth Century* (London: McDonald, 1982); and *Plain Tales of the Raj* (London: McDonald, 1981).

17. See V. Subramaniam, "Coastal Colonialism and the Derivative Middle Class Values as a Cause of Regional and Caste-Tribal Disparities of Representation in India and Africa." Paper presented at the American Political Science Association Meeting, Washington, D.C., September 1982.

18. Wolpert, pp. 233-238.

19. See chapter 6.

20. For instance over one-third of the recruits to the British Indian Army during World War II were Punjabis, Pathans, or Sikhs. Calculated from Stephen P. Cohen, *The Pakistan Army* (Berkeley: University of California Press, 1984), 41-42.

21. For a more detailed comparative analysis of the lasting impact of colonial "domination" of minority groups see Donald L. Horowitz, *Ethnic Groups in Conflict* (Berkeley: University of California Press, 1985), 147-171.

2

State and Ethnicity in Africa:
A Policy Perspective

DONALD ROTHCHILD

The applicability of policy analysis to the study of contemporary interethnic conflict in Africa rests upon a recognition that, in part at least, we are dealing with interest-defined groups and elites. It is this stress upon the political, economic, and social interests of categorical groups and their elites within the state, as opposed to their historical loadings or their intangible psychological or cultural "essence,"[1] that makes a public choice approach feasible. To the extent that overt, tangible interests—rather than an abstract sense of unique, fixed, and total identities—are involved, ethnic groups can be regarded as utility maximizers who are responsive to the political exchange process. Obviously, concessions essential to a direct or tacit exchange among groups and between these groups and the state becomes extremely difficult where antagonistic rivals view the impact of their exchanges in possibly damaging, zero-sum terms, and such seemingly intractable situations are in evidence the world over (i.e., in Northern Ireland, Lebanon, South Africa). Yet, in many of the less dramatic instances of state-ethnic and interethnic relations (Zambia, Ghana, Kenya, Nigeria, Sudan) the moral links and informal norms and understandings necessary to an exchange of interests are in fact present. It therefore becomes possible to contend that "one of the striking characteristics of the present situation is indeed the extent to which we find the ethnic group viewed in terms of interests, as an interest group."[2]

This perspective implies a shift in emphasis from the culturally based conflict that frequently marks non-African interethnic encounters to conflict that involves collective struggles in the marketplace for an increased group share of scarce political, economic, and social resources. Politicization occurs as a result of two overlapping factors: the interests of elites and group competition for scarce resources. In either case, the distributional aspect in African ethnicity makes a policy focus, with its stress on social exchange, increasingly relevant at this time. Where a substantial coincidence occurs between the identity of a cultural or social group and the identity of the administrative unit (i.e., the subregion), a policy framework is especially germane.

In an environment of evident scarcity, an approach that links public choice to the configuration of political and economic resources in each African state may contribute to a more rational and constructive state decisional process. Policy analysis concentrates on the alternative courses of action that a state's decision makers may pursue in order to achieve desired politicoeconomic objectives. It combines analysis with prescription and offers partially autonomous state elites practical insights into the range of available options and their anticipated consequences.

The aims of policy analysis, as summarized by Warren F. Ilchman and Norman T. Uphoff, are to assess "the comparative efficiency of policy alternatives" and to provide "some means of formulating priorities."[3] To achieve these purposes three main ways of addressing policy issues may be chosen. First, the policy analyst may select an institutional approach and examine the consequences for ethnic groups that follow from the adoption of certain public formulas and rules. Second, the analyst may settle on a cost-benefit or cost-effectiveness approach, thereby attempting to relate public expenditures to political system outputs affecting ethnic interest. Or third, the analyst may fix on a political-systems approach and focus broadly on the interaction between state institutions and society.

Such a systematic framework for policy analysis subsumes an examination of seven stages of the policy process: the definition of the problem; the assemblage of information; the promotion of policy alternatives; the state elite's choice of alternatives; the implementation of policy; the appraisal of policy effectiveness; and the policy revision or termination. Given constraints on the availability of data, a political-systems framework, with its concern for the dynamic interplay between state and society, currently seems to offer the greatest scope for comprehensive examination of ethnically related policy issues. Even so, the commonality of concerns implicit in these three policy approaches is apparent, and this overlap facilitates an eclectic effort at organizing the available information.

In Africa, the modern-day problem of interethnic conflict is very much a product of historical experience. To be sure, variations in natural resources, climate, cultural values, missionary contacts, and proximity of both markets and transportation centers contributed to racial and ethnoregional (the nexus between the subregional unit and ethnic people) disparities.[4] In addition, contextual variables such as the number and size of groups, the distribution of wealth, and the pattern of group recruitment to the economy and polity also affect the nature of the encounter. But no single factor has proven more significant as a cause of uneven development and inequality than the experience with colonial overrule. This overrule concentrated administrative, military, communications, trade, and industrial activity on the privileged urban core of what became a relatively advantaged subregion, and thus, imperial power facilitated the growth of central capacity and structured core-periphery roles and relationships.

These disparities, and resulting ethnoregional cleavages, widened noticeably in the later years of colonial overrule. The consolidation of external hegemony brought with it an entrenchment of bureaucratic control, economic dominance, and social and cultural patterns that (consciously or unconsciously) marked off the relatively advantaged urban core from the relatively disadvantaged hinterland periphery. In time, something amounting to a core political culture took hold.[5] The ascendant state elite (largely expatriate, with significant indigenous infusions by the time that self-government approached) felt justified in making authoritative decisions on the allocation of scarce resources to the territory as a whole. The consequences of these decisions, with their adverse impact on the great majority of people living in the less advantaged areas, gave rise to much of today's grave imbalances in the distribution of resources among the racial collectives and subregional units. The somewhat unplanned policies of colonial decision makers seem frequently to have paid little heed to the fundamental and inescapable connections between center and periphery and to have fostered the growth of economically privileged and politically powerful urban cores boasting life-styles only possible when buttressed by a process of asymmetrical ethnoregional exchange.[6] Thus, enclave values and life-styles emerged among the relatively privileged elite of advantaged subregions and linked this cluster of peoples more closely to its counterpart in the metropole than to the relatively disadvantaged in the urban center or the hinterland areas surrounding it.[7]

The resulting structure of external linkage and unequal interethnic exchange was firmly set in place by the time of the transfer of power to African hands. As a consequence, the structure of interethnic relations has proven to be more and more repugnant to the doctrine of equality put forth by African spokesmen during the years. This antagonism of structure and doctrine poses a major challenge to those engaged in state and nation building, and hence to policy analysts. Clearly, state elites cannot pass onto others the ultimate responsibility for establishing and implementing choice strategies in their own societies. All that the policy analyst can meaningfully contribute to this decision process are recommendations on a framework in which rational, effective, and constructive (morally self-realizing) choice can take place. But such a contribution is not to be minimized, especially if it points to innovative and life-affirming mechanisms of conflict management (i.e., in the sense of setting out the terms and costs of interaction).

This chapter contents itself with describing the policy process as it relates to state-ethnic and interethnic relations, leaving to subsequent examination the specific issues of trade-offs between competing objectives and the costs and benefits of particular hegemonial and what I will call "hegemonial exchange" mechanisms. In the latter case, these are decision systems that combine a hierarchically organized one- or no-party system with formal and informal norms and rules allowing for reciprocal behavior (including political exchanges) among state and ethnoregional elites in top executive, legislative, and party institutions. In doing so, ethnoregional (rather than racial) relations are emphasized largely because these are regarded as a more long-standing challenge to state elites engaged in regulating conflict.

The Efficacy of a Policy Approach

Comprehensiveness both distinguishes policy analysis from other schools and underscores its potential for including the insights of other approaches. In this regard, variations and connections to two major schools of thought (the modernization-penetration and the internal colonial frameworks for analysis) are well worth our attention. In diverse ways these other schools highlight the structural differences and inequalities persisting in core-periphery relations in developing countries. As descriptions of the ethnoregional and interracial imbalances resulting from Africa's contact with the powerful forces of colonialism, the policy approach can add little to these explorations. What it can do, however, is to go on from where these two schools leave off to examine more fully (1) the relationship between collective demands and public policy outputs and outcomes, (2) the asymmetrical exchange process frequently in evidence, and (3) the full range of policy options available to state elites for problem-solving actions. As Rajni Kothari declares, "It is necessary . . . to consider and interpret the problem of relationship between center and periphery in a dynamic way, with special attention to the changing character of both the center and the periphery."[8] This dynamic aspect, embracing an ongoing and bidirectional or multidirectional encounter, seems all too often ignored in analyses of racial and ethnoregional relationships.

In the eyes of the penetrationists, center-periphery contacts essentially involve unidirectional message and power flows from the core to the hinterland. Thus, Gabriel A. Almond refers to "the penetration of the informal and intermittent structures of political communication by the specialized mass media," and Joseph La Palombara asserts that "in its broadest sense, penetration means conformance to public policy enunciated by central government authority."[9] Unlike "modern" societies, center-periphery relations in "transitional" societies, according to the modernization-penetration school, are marked by problems in establishing an effective central presence throughout the domain of the state. Hence, the "crisis" of center-periphery relations is largely that of inadequate central capacity. For the penetrationists the remedy is therefore clear: Improve the state's capacity to diffuse values to the periphery and the society will move toward a more effective administration of development.

Leaving aside the issue of culture-boundedness implicit in this modernizing process, let us concentrate solely on the precision with which this description of message flows conforms to Africa's real-world experience. In Ghana, the economic and political dependence of the hinterland on the center did give rise to some social and cultural penetration, both in the colonial and postcolonial years. John Dunn and A. F. Robertson, for example, see considerable continuity over time in the movement of messages from Accra to Ahafo in the hinterland, resulting in social and cultural change in such activities as education, religion, health, and sanitation.[10] This infusion of central values was only partially effective in penetrating the diffuse networks of the periphery, and then most likely when a process of adaptation took place between central requirements and local culture. In commenting on a sanitation program in Goaso during the colonial period, Dunn and Robertson offer an insightful description of the way central extension of influence and peripheral response interacted with one another:

> The compound of paternalism and anality was hardly likely to establish a commanding sway over the allegiance of the Ahafo population. But the Ahafos have in the event taken from the experience of this five-year colonial sanitary crusade what it was in due course instrumentally convenient for them to have taken. Ahafo today does not exhibit a Scandinavian obsession with the domination of dirt. But in a tropical forest environment which remains recalcitrant to cleanliness, . . . the Ahafos have kept their environment within levels of pollution which their indigenous culture would scarcely have insisted on but which have in fact made possible a healthier and more agreeable life.[11]

Therefore, externally inspired efforts to alter behavior patterns proved to be influential to the extent that culturally defined groups in the periphery accommodated and utilized them. The process at work was by no means a unidirectional one, however; in the end the adaptive social and cultural features that allowed for new adjustments after transmission tended to survive. Certainly, we can learn much from the penetrationist analytical construct about the nature of central domination and extraction, the resources and apparatus of state power, and the process of message flows from the center to the periphery. At the same time, we must be on guard against the assumed dichotomy between the traditional and the modern as well as the assumed unidirectional nature of message and power flows.

In general, the modernization-penetration school suffers, perhaps unconsciously, from a lack of concern with the channeling of messages from the hinterland to the center. Those adopting such an approach presume a need for an extension of central influences and policies outward to the periphery: The more effective the center is in gaining compliance for its regulations, the more likely the territory's success in attaining its modernization objectives. The goals of those adopting a modernization-penetration orientation seem clear, and the challenge they face is reduced to the acquiring of sufficient central capacity to achieve these ends. Not only are largely Eurocentric end values implicit in such a worldview but the proposed means for political development may well prove to be self-defeating. Rather, in real-world African situations an eye to the multisided interactional process is indispensable, not only to achieve a full understanding of what transpires but also to be able to offer a detached assessment on the stages of policy implementation, appraisal, and revision.

In contrast with the penetrationists' optimism about the possibility of transforming the hinterland through a unidirectional flow of authoritative communications and regulations, the internal colonial school takes a decidedly pessimistic view of the chances of transforming the structure of colonialist roles and relationships. Whereas the penetration school assumes that a process of acculturation will follow from the diffusion of core values to the outlying parts, the internal colonialism school does not regard center-periphery contact as necessarily sociational in its consequences. From an internal colonialist perspective, writes Michael Hechter, "the 'backwardness' of peripheral groups can only be aggravated by a systematic increase in transactions with the core. The peripheral collectivity is seen to be already suffused with exploitative connections to the core, such that it can be deemed to be an internal colony. The core collectivity practices discrimination against the culturally distinct peoples who have been forced onto less accessible inferior lands."[12] Although Hechter does envisage the possibility of central state action to transfer resources from the core to the periphery,[13] in general he sees persistent, even widening, inequality, dependence, and cultural distinctiveness in the relationship between dominant center and subordinate subregions and peoples at the periphery.

It is important to note that the observers utilizing an internal colonial approach are a diverse set of analysts and, not surprisingly, come to varied findings on the rigidity of this structure as well as the possibilities for meaningful change.[14] Nevertheless, they tend to be alike in resting their thesis on the class conflicts they find in capitalist relationships.[15] They reach roughly similar conclusions about the salience of cultural distinctness, unequal exchange, and structural dependence in the relation of the periphery to the national core as well as to the international metropole. Thus, a dual system of exploitation exists in which the human and material resources of the hinterland are distributed in such a way as to benefit mainly the bourgeoisie of the center and the privileged national core, with only marginal benefits for the periphery. Domestic ethnoregional relations are depicted as analogous to colonialism. Thus, the critical element in a colonial relationship (i.e., the domination of one culturally distinct collectivity by another) is evident in domestic center-periphery contacts. To be sure, this theory recognizes that the elite of the hinterland may be coopted into the ruling class; nevertheless, the system is marked by mechanisms of collective subordination, stereotyping of the relatively disadvantaged collectives, and peripheral underdevelopment.

As was true for the penetrationists, the internal colonial theorists depict message flows as unidirectional—from the center to the peripheral parts. The purpose of these communications is essentially exploitative, for the center exercises hegemonic authority in such a way as to extract and distribute scarce resources in terms of dominant core interests. In Africa, such a model conforms aptly to center-periphery relations in the Union of South Africa. In that country, the white center does indeed utilize the paraphernalia of the state to systematize communal control over the other racial groups in its midst as well as the spatially separated Africans confined to homelands or other reserved areas. Nevertheless, the South African experience, with its interrelated policies on separate development and the Bantustans, is something of a special case, more applicable to vertically than to horizontally stratified societies. Present-day egalitarian values represent a fundamental challenge to the validity of such vertically stratified arrangements, fitting more comfortably with societies that decline to rank collectivities on a hierarchical basis. In horizontally stratified societies, as Donald Horowitz points out, "parallel ethnic structures exist, each with its own criteria of stratification."[16] Such equality, in principle at least, between ethnoregional entities does not conform nicely with the structural inequality implicit in the internal colonial model. In these situations, uneven development reflects a broader process of economic development at work and not a systematic exploitation of one ethnoregional section by another.

Certainly if anything marks ethnoregional encounters it is the diversity of their resource bases and styles of regulating intergroup relations. Exploitation and oppression of the periphery by the center are not equally present in each situation. Each case must be examined against the backdrop of its own history; to view the situation solely from the standpoint of conflicting class interests is to distort reality. Furthermore, because the internal colonialist theory is unable to specify the relationship between class exploitation and the ethnoregional domination characteristic of internal colonialism, Harold Wolpe has concluded that while the internal colonial thesis purports to rest on class relations of capitalist exploitation, in fact, it treats such relations as residual. That is to say, the conceptualization of class relations, which is present in theory, is accorded little or no role in the analysis of relations of domination and exploitation which are, instead, conceived of as occurring between "racial," "ethnic," and "national" categories. To this extent, the "internal colonial" thesis converges the conventional race relations theory (in particular, the theory of plural society), and...suffers from the same analytical limitations as the latter.[17]

Clearly, a contradiction exists in the internal colonialist model between a recognition of class differences within the collective and the affirmed presence of distinct, homogeneous racial or ethnoregional groupings in confrontation with one another. Such a contradiction can be solved by minimizing either the conflicts among classes within collectives or the extent of center-periphery cleavages. Either course, however, would seem to be fundamentally harmful to the neat convergency of ethnicity and class that underlies the internal colonial model.

The diversity of ethnoregional encounters also raises some questions regarding the model's accuracy as a description of horizontally stratified societies. For instance, the center may include more than one key urban cluster, the capital city may not be the wealthiest or most powerful locality, and the core may encounter too great a resistance in the autonomous peripheral areas to allow for unrestrained oppression or exploitation. The challenges of Katanga, Eritrea, Biafra, Front for the National Liberation of Chad (FROLINAT), and National Union for the Total Independence of Angola (UNITA) (buttressed by external power) to the unity and integrity of the state symbolize the capacity of the autonomous collective to stand against the impingement of the center. Similarly, Zambia's central government must be cautious in its dealings with relatively advantaged Cooperbelt Province if it is to be in a position to extract sufficient resources for state purposes. If anything, the African state is marked by its fragility and "softness," not by its overbearing nature. Hence, a genuinely descriptive model must adapt to the horizontal stratification of moral equals and not insist in all instances on a dominant-subordinate relationship.

Surely, there is a changing, dynamic quality to center-periphery relations that is not reflected in internal colonial analyses. Core areas do not necessarily remain stationary and fixed centers of wealth and power; nor do peripheral regions automatically stay poor and disadvantaged. They shift over time, responding irregularly to changing economic, social, and cultural factors. The emergence of Lagos vis-à-vis Ibadan in the twentieth century may be matched by the rise, in the political and administrative spheres at least, by Abuja in the twenty-first. Canberra, Brasilia, Bonn, and Washington, D.C. are precedents for just such a transition. In Chad, moreover, the control over Ndjamena secured by northern Muslim forces led by Goukouni Queddai's army in 1979, and in 1982 by the rival forces of Hissene Habre, represented a reversal in twentieth century north-south relations; the once dominant Sara now became "the stubborn periphery."[18] If it were not for an international political culture that no longer permits the range of "imperial" strategies of state building allowed in the early modern period of European development, a further reversal might well become evident. Libya could conceivably emerge as a potential state-building core, extend its domain southward, and consolidate its hold over an enlarged political community.[19]

The appearance of these new centers of power and influence involves a further complication of core-periphery message flows. But what is important to note here is that the direction of messsage flows has never been a uniform and unidirectional process. If a main line of communication linked Ahafo and Accra, this should not blind us to a tridirectional communications process, which also took place in colonial times. Within Ahafo, a significant number of chiefs (the Mimhene and a number of like-minded authorities) retained a strong affinity with Ashanti. By looking to Kumasi "as an alternative intermediate point of communication," these pro-Ashanti chiefs added a complicating, third channel for the movement of messages in Ghana.[20] Obviously, this three-way pattern of message flows contributes an element of irregularity to the process of transmitting messages from the center to the periphery, and vice versa. Yet it is precisely because such a complex organization of message flows corresponds to reality that we gain an appreciation of how numerous and varied are the interacting points of influence in the current African context.

Thus, no static and enduring one-to-one relationship between a particular center and a particular periphery adequately describes what, in Africa at least, is a shifting, irregular, and often highly accommodative process. To be aware of very genuine rural-urban or ethnoregional disparities in one period of time is by no means to predict the perpetuation of these inequalities far into the future. Theory must avoid too rigid a determinism and be flexible enough to fit the reality of changing intergroup or interunit capacity, influence, and consciousness if it is to prove an effective explanatory tool for our purposes.

In brief, a realistic description of center-periphery encounters must meet at least two critically important tests. First, it must allow for considerable situational variance: What is applicable to Sékou Touré's Guinea where the center tends to permeate the periphery without permitting effective autonomous response (the abolition of chieftaincy weakened the mobilization of ethnic demands in that country) is hardly relevant to contemporary Ghana where an autonomous local dimension remains a part of an interactional process as variegated as it is complex. Second, such a description, if it is to be accurate, must emphasize the relational nature of power. Modification—

even transformation—can be anticipated in the years ahead. Patterns of socioeconomic opportunity seem likely to alter: also the way in which elites act to mobilize ethnoregional consciousness or to distribute scarce resources can be expected to wax and wane in response to new values, priorities, and circumstances. Because the course that each center-periphery encounter will take cannot be predetermined in an assured manner, an eye to the dynamic interplay of the encounter itself becomes indispensable to effective interpretation.

At this point, a wide range of possible approaches—political psychology, conflict theory, organizational theory, economic trade analysis, and so forth—can contribute to an understanding of the interactional process at hand. We choose policy analysis because of the effective manner in which it brings together the disciplines of political science and economics. By relating societal (and extrasocietal) inputs to decisional outputs made by state elites, the policy framework offers insight into the dynamics of political exchange. In addition, the consequences of policy decisions and implementations are studied, both from the standpoint of state and ethnic group goal achievement as well as systemic coherence (i.e., the regularized patterns of interaction between these centers of power and influence). Although such a comprehensive focus may lack the neatness and clarity of other analytic frameworks, it seems worthy of pursuit because it clarifies the process of political interactions and throws light on public formulas for reducing the intensity of interethnic conflict.

Interethnic Conflict and Policy Analysis

Political conflicts among groups and leaders can be expected to emerge where competing collectives seek contradictory outcomes.[21] It is necessary to distinguish at the outset between conflict as a normal, social behavior and conflict as a hostile, and sometimes highly destructive, type of encounter. In the former case, conflict involves the attempt to secure competing interests and can be kept, if the state remains sufficiently responsive to ethnoregional demands, at moderate levels of intensity; the interaction is sociational in that it contributes to group formation, the reaffirmation of group identity, and the maintenance of boundary lines against other groups in the social system.[22] Collaboration on issues of common concern may well lead to mutually beneficial outcomes. The latter case goes beyond the maximization of interests to include feelings of antagonism and resentment. In certain instances, where the state elite is unwilling to implement moderate demands and where the rules regulating interaction are not observed—and are even dismissed—conflict may become unmanageable and perhaps lead to irreconcilable cycles of ideological polarization, terrorism, and counterterrorism.[23] Highly intense encounters involving underlying belief systems and values remain ever possible (as in Armenia, Nazi Germany, Zanzibar, Burundi, Rwanda, Algeria, South Africa, Uganda).

Yet a comprehensive overview of ethnoregional relations must also focus on the group-preserving as well as the group-destroying functions of conflict. In such a situation the policy analyst appears as something of a divided personality. The detached investigator must be fully attuned to the wide range of alternative policy outcomes present in each interethnic encounter; meanwhile, the problem-solver must endeavor to prescribe rational courses of action. Those utilizing a policy approach, therefore, must engage in open-ended inquiry while at the same time remaining ever ready to recommend lines of action likely to result in constructive outcomes.

If a policy approach to interethnic relations is oriented toward the rational and the life-affirming (Kenneth Kaunda's man-centered perspective),[24] it follows that in the final analysis such a theoretical framework is not entitled to assert its "scientific" merits. Rather, policy analysis seeks comprehensiveness and rational problem-solving—the creation and maintenance of an order in which conflicting interests may establish mutually beneficial relationships, not rigid forms of hierarchy buttressed by the coercive power of the state. Ever realists, the policy analysts dismiss as utopian the prospect of a world without interethnic conflict. Such a disclaimer leads them to limit the problem for investigation to that of how interethnic conflict can be reduced to, or maintained at, manageable levels by public authorities seeking policies of simultaneous benefits for major interethnic interests. It is to this central problem that we now turn.

Group Demands

The extensiveness of the literature on conflict-producing situations makes it necessary for us to concentrate on those factors that affect core processes of hegemony and hegemonial (or coercive) exchange (political exchange that takes place within the hierarchically organized one- or no-party system). Among such general explanations of interethnic conflict are the identity crisis;[25] the communications revolution;[26] social mobilization;[27] and the fragility of political institutions. Obviously each has an environmental impact on the ultimate interactional process.[28] But because these explanations lack problem specificity, they cannot serve as full explanations of each conflict situation.

Let us focus, then, on the conflict-creating circumstances that tend toward interactions of a hegemonial and hegemonial exchange type. Although each particular ethnic encounter is best understood in terms of its own special nuances, it seems useful to distinguish in a general manner between those conflict-producing circumstances that are negotiable and those that are not. Overlaps between these categories are apparent. For example, a disintegrating stratification system or a collective sense of relative deprivation might at times be amenable to symbolic or material exchanges; nevertheless, these examples are classed among the situations contributing to hegemony because of the complex and sometimes precarious negotiating process entailed. Similarly, where negative remembrance or a sense of superiority has an effect on highly visible ethnic group-social class (i.e., Milton M. Gordon's "ethclass") difference, the moral links indispensable to a bargaining relationship may be undercut.[29] The major conflict-producing situations are grouped according to their processual categories as follows:

1. General: identity crisis; communications revolution; social mobilization; fragility of political institutions.
2. Hegemony: fear of minority status; negative remembrances and images; sense of superiority; breakdown in stratification patterns; collective sense of relative deprivation; fear of state disintegration.
3. Hegemonial Exchange: ineffective norms of reciprocity; disparities in recruitment; inequitable resource allocations; disproportionate political power; highly visible ethclass differences; lack of adequate constitutional protections.

In general, those conflict-producing situations that give rise to hegemonial interactions are likely to emphasize the subjective side of relations while those likely to occasion hegemonial exchange encounters tend to stress the objective side of relations. The difference between these two types of interactions is useful in determining which conflicts among ethnic groups can be expected to prove negotiable and which intractable, thereby requiring that they be resolved, in part at least, by means of centralized state mechanisms of control and suppression.

Journalistic impressions to the contrary, Africa exhibits a wide range of conflict-creating situations, leading both to hegemonial exchange and hegemonial state relationships. Repetitious journalistic accounts of the excesses of hegemonial practices as well as the behavior and attitudes of groups contributing to such practices can obscure a comprehensive view of the highly variegated types of processes at work.

One suspects, however, that if cross-national multivariate analysis were to link societies to the variables of ideological and distributional politics, multiethnic societies in Africa would doubtlessly score higher than their European counterparts in the frequency of their emphases on distributional issues. To be sure, scarcity of resources, opportunities, and power by no means account for all conflict among ethnic peoples in Africa. Thus, intense differences, not easily negotiable, occur about issues of group status, particularly where established stratification patterns appear to be crumbling

(Rwanda, Burundi, Fernando Poo, Zanzibar)[30] and where a shift toward majoritarian participation is interpreted as a threat to a dominant minority section (Rwanda, Burundi, Zanzibar, Rhodesia, South Africa). South Africa's Minister of Foreign Affairs Roelof Botha expressed the sentiments of many among the dominant sections in vertically stratified societies: "We cannot negotiate on our own destruction, either now or tomorrow."[31] Not only does status reversal tend to be a nonnegotiable subject, but claims to superiority or moral ascendancy[32] and misperception of reality by group opinionmakers (which leads to negative remembrances or images about rival sections of the population)[33] both lack the necessary tangibleness for exchange relationships. In addition, in prerevolutionary Zanzibar a strong sense of comparative deprivation on the part of the African people on that island became a major source of state instability.[34]

Although it is essential to remember these subjective sources of conflict, it is important at the same time to keep in mind the objective side of these relationships. The extent to which collective rivalries take place over tangible differences opens up a significant dimension for an effective politics of mutual adjustment. Particularly in horizontally stratified societies, which bring morally equal sections together under an accepted state system, distributional conflicts may come to be of greater moment than those involving ideology, status reversal, or a strong sense of relative deprivation. Thus, scarcity or a disproportional allocation of values—in employment opportunities, high status positions, fiscal resources, or political apportionments—becomes rooted in a sometimes sharp, but still negotiable, conflict among ethnoregional sections.

If, in new states, the problem of economic scarcity seems frequently to be intractable, the issues embodied in claims to proportional allocations and recruitment policies lend themselves, within definite limits, to political exchange outcomes.[35] Where a sense of moral community exists, political exchange may help to regulate poignant disputes about imbalances of opportunity between relatively advantaged and relatively disadvantaged peoples. In numerous situations (for example, Zambia, Sierra Leone, Benin, Zaire) where slow economic expansion has exacerbated intense ethnoregional competition, the relatively advantaged seek to maintain their privileged position (in occupations, housing, education, amenities, access to decisionmakers) in the face of concerted demands for equal distribution—or redistribution—by the relatively disadvantaged majority. Thus, the great value confrontations of postindependence Africa about need and deprivation in extractive and allocative policies (Nigeria, Sudan, Zaire),[36] equity and productiveness in the allocation of scarce economic and fiscal resources (Ghana, Zambia), merit and proportionality in recruitment policies (Kenya, Liberia),[37] central representation in the legislative body based on population or on parity among the subregions (Nigeria),[38] and centralization versus decentralization of power and responsibilities (Sudan) have all provoked controversy while at the same time remaining open to informal, and even formal, intergroup exchanges.

To be sure, the strains resulting from such conflicts cause African leaders to pull back, for the most part, from putting genuine polyarchical systems (i.e., those allowing for open public contestation) into effect; yet even in the absence of competitive party policies, African leaders have managed to develop the means for a creative exchange relationship among the spokesmen for sectional interests. For instance, an analysis of public expenditure patterns during recent years in Nigeria and Kenya shows extensive use of the proportionality principle in these countries. This analysis suggests that dominant political elites in such states are, in certain instances at least, willing to enter into quiet exchanges with elites at the periphery, allocating resources according to the proportionality principle to assure support and compliance for state regulations on the part of ethnoregional elites and people in the hinterland.[39]

I have differentiated between the types of conflict-creating situations and indicated how these lead to a further distinction between our core processes of hegemony and hegemonial exchange; it is necessary now to focus on the specific demands that ethnoregional interests make on governments. Such demands inject a dynamic quality into the political process, requiring state elites to set policies that respond to or suppress these claims coming from the domestic (or, at times, the external) environment. Certainly, the task of these decisionmakers is as great as in any time in history. Not only is the period marked by increasing group self-awareness, but the more assertive style these groups have adopted in presenting demands to public authorities makes the task of reconciling legitimate group claims with available political, economic, and social resources a challenge of great dimensions.

Even though relatively little systematic research has been done on collective demand patterns in Africa, it seems possible, nonetheless, to distinguish between the types of claims advanced in both hegemonial and hegemonial exchange contexts. Central to this contrast is a distinction between negotiable and nonnegotiable demands. Whereas negotiable demands accept the legitimacy of competing interests and acknowledge the need for mutual gains formulas within the existing state system, their nonnegotiable counterparts perceive their interests in zero-sum terms and, at times, may come to question the validity of the state itself. The implications of this distinction may well be far-reaching. Certainly, where political actors assume demands to be negotiable (and this may vary as the context of each encounter shifts), the possibility of using reconciliatory mechanisms in an effective way seems practicable. However, the impact of nonnegotiable demands on the mechanisms of conflict management is very different. To the extent that the nonnegotiable demand is perceived as fundamentally threatening to state viability, it seems likely to provoke a counterreaction aimed at strengthening central control. In the latter situation, institutions become entrenched and thereby deny reciprocity in political relations—at least until such a time as their viability erodes and interest group leaders come to prefer a return to informal or formal norms of exchange.

Negotiable and nonnegotiable demands are evident in both horizontally and vertically stratified societies. As might be expected, where moral equality is accepted among ethnoregional actors, demands in horizontally stratified situations tend to cluster around power-sharing, recruitment, and distributional issues, not the more subjective—and more emotionally laden—ones of identity, survival, or status. Moreover, contrary to popular impressions on "rising expectations" in the rural areas, demands in the periphery tend to be minimal, reasonable, and attainable—at least for the present. Thus, surveys administered or processed by this author in Kenya, Zambia, and Ghana revealed that villagers, particularly in the more isolated communities, were the least aware of their disadvantaged condition and made only modest demands on government.[40] Those who did communicate their wishes sought such improvements as the building of clinics, roads, and schools as well as programs for adult literacy, community and homecraft centers, and marketing facilities. The 1973 Ghana surveys showed that respondents in the less advantaged subregions were less likely than their more advantaged counterparts to demand a wide range of expensive services or amenities and more likely to prefer central government action and leadership. When asked what they disliked about their present life situation, respondents in relatively deprived Northern and Upper Regions pointed to such immediate dissatisfactions as lack of sanitation, high cost of living, and inadequate law enforcement, not the wide range of expensive and difficult-to-satisfy demands (e.g., hospitals, educational facilities, large markets) sought by their counterparts in the relatively advantaged areas. Thus, the demands made by the people in the neglected parts of the three surveyed countries seemed limited, particularly in light of the uneven development that had worked so manifestly to their disadvantage. Such modest requests on their part open the way—for the time being, at least—to political exchange relationships of an interethnic and state-ethnic nature.

The margin for political exchange relationships in vertically stratified societies (colonial Kenya, Zambia, Rhodesia) is not nearly so wide. In colonial times, the dominant minority sections in these societies frequently denied the principle of racial equality, and after the transfer of power had taken place, they used their economic power to insist on supportive economic and social policies as the price for their continued participation in the life of these countries. In November 1978 some members of Zambia's small but highly productive expatriate commercial farming community predictably threatened that they would cease their operations or burn down their farms unless the

Zambian government forced Zimbabwean guerrillas to end their harassment.[41] To the extent that security could be assured, a return to conflict-regulating rules could be expected to ensue and, within these parameters, interest-determined relationships could again be anticipated. In such circumstances, a process of tacit exchange affecting specific issues seemed likely to take place between African-run state institutions and the spokesmen for the numerically small but economically powerful racial interests. As has been shown for postindependence Kenya, minority racial groups pressed demands on such issues as property rights, citizenship, the allocation of fiscal resources, and the pace for implementing Africanization programs.[42] Such a process of implicit transactions took place in quiet, behind-the-scenes encounters and showed that public authorities were prepared to make concessions (albeit unwritten) as evidence of their backing for the expatriate-dominated business community. The significance of these informal bargains in determining the rules by which public and private authorities can establish and maintain an ordered relationship is not to be underestimated.

Yet to argue that the analyst must not overlook the negotiating dimension in contemporary Africa is by no means to keep the presence of powerful nonnegotiable demands in the background. A lack of power dispersion, shared values, or economic or administrative capacity may all contribute to the failure of political exchange relationships and may take the shape of "a dialectic without possibility of synthesis, without possibility of a higher unity."[43] Where the state seeks to consolidate political power in a hierarchically organized governmental or party system or where ethnoregional groups divide over political and economic principles, not interests, it becomes extremely difficult to manage conflict by means of formal rules or informal political exchanges. Hence, antagonistic conflict may emerge between state and ethnoregional actors, leading in extreme cases to irreconcilable division and violence.

In horizontally stratified societies, ethnoregional demands for the self-determination of territorial units "which themselves originate in arbitrary colonial divisions"[44] (Biafra, Katanga, Eritrea, Southern Sudan) or for irredentist reunifications (Bakongo, Ewe, Greater Somalia) do not readily lend themselves to mutual adjustment procedures. Because self-determination is identified here with the sole outcome of state independence (the external sense) and could lead to the fragmentation of the state itself, these demands necessarily amount to a radical assertion of the rights of internal ethnoregional groups.

Certainly, nonstate, ethnoregional collectives have what is tantamount to group rights in certain specified political, economic, and social areas.[45] Nevertheless, a claim to a right of secession involves a more far-reaching demand than those dealing with representation, language laws, the distribution of licenses, recruitment into the army or civil service, or preferences on admission to schools and universities. It involves a claim to group survival and must, if it is to be regarded as a valid one, be supported by evidence that a people as a whole lack physical security or the possibility for development within the larger community.[46] This is precisely what was argued by Tanzania's Julius Nyerere at the time his government recognized Biafra. For Nyerere, secession "was declared because the Ibo people felt it to be their only defense against extermination." In a truly Lockean statement of the "social contract" between a nonstate people and the state, he contended as follows:

> Surely when a whole people is rejected by the majority of the state in which they live, they must have the right to life under a different kind of arrangement which does secure their existence. . . . When the machinery of the state, and the powers of the Government, are turned against a whole group of the society on the grounds of racial, tribal, or religious prejudice, then the victims have the right to take back the powers they have surrendered, and to defend themselves.[47]

In a manner similar to the principles embodied in the U.S. Declaration of Independence, then, secession was not justified by "light and transient causes," but only where the security of an ethnoregional people was fundamentally threatened. Such a "right" to self-determination represents the ultimate in the nonnegotiable demand. When used in an externalist sense, concessions and adjustments no longer suffice, and a breaking of linkages is deemed unavoidable. With rival state and ethnoregional actors irreconcilably opposed, conflict becomes intense and potentially destructive and a shared community seemingly impossible.

Certainly, intractable conflict seems built into the vertically stratified society from its very outset. In these situations, the margin for political exchange relationships is always narrow. Because such societies deny egalitarian values and rely essentially on hierarchically organized control to maintain the system, it is not surprising that they become the source of powerful nonnegotiable demands—both from majority racial groups at the bottom of the hierarchy and vulnerable minority elements at the top. Decades of African nationalist struggle against colonial domination and racial oppression attest to the strength of majority African determination to wrest political and economic power from the European colonizer. In Frantz Fanon's words, "the colonial context is characterized by the dichotomy which it imposes upon the whole people."[48]

At the time of the struggle, at least, the colonized demanded a transformed world in which they would be assured genuine decolonization: freedom, equality, participation, and so forth. It is precisely because such a broadly conceived decolonization is considered by the dominant minority to be directly threatening to its well-being that the demands of the colonized are generally viewed as repugnant and incompatible. The racial minority's perception of threat brings on a reciprocity of nonnegotiation (Algeria, Angola, Mozambique). In a process characterized by Leo Kuper as "ideological escalation," the opposing parties perceive (or misperceive) their situation in terms of antagonistic intergroup conflict.[49] For the dominant minority section, it is assumed that rival interests are fundamentally threatening to the dominant group's physical, cultural, or social survival, making any compromises on its part likely to produce new calls for concessions by determined adversaries. Hence, the minority perceives its realistic choices in terms of two stark alternatives: suppression or exodus.

Barry M. Schutz's survey data of white Rhodesian attitudes collected during the relatively calm period of 1968-1969 has shown that this perception of political reality is at work among these dominant racial minorities well in advance of the point of an irreversible decision. Among "middle-level" Rhodesian Front (RF) activists, a large number of respondents looked on 1965 and/or the Unilateral Declaration of Independence (UDI) as the "moment of nationhood," indicating, Schutz concludes, "a propensity on the part of the RF respondents to identify nationhood with their own rule." At the same time, 43 percent of this survey group admitted that they had considered leaving Rhodesia prior to 1969; these respondents attributed such ideas mainly to their fears of the return of a liberal (white) government to power or fears of conditions arising that would be conducive to an African political takeover.[50] Although a second survey group, the white residents of a Salisbury municipality, were somewhat less inclined to equate UDI with nationhood and to give the imminence of a liberal white or African-run state as a reason for considering departure from the territory, there remains a link between discontinued European control and their planned departure as well. The European community's demands for political and economic control under these circumstances represents a nonnegotiable form of interaction. In the absence of moral linkage across groups, the European community's "essentialist" perceptions make genuine political exchange relationships extremely difficult and tenuous.

The State's Decision Process

How are partially autonomous but by no means disinterested state authorities to cope with these various ethnic demands originating in the environment? As an action agency engaged in allocating values, the state as the institutionalization of public power may pursue three main courses: (1) design significant policy initiatives in its own right; (2) convert demands into public policies; or (3) resist societal demands and delay raising ethnic claims to a level requiring a political response.[51] Although my main concern is with comprehensive choice and the processing of demands, it is important also to recognize that many demands are never processed by state authorities, either because they are not pressed with sufficient intensity or because state elites, conscious of their corporate self-interests, block off access channels to these ethnoregional interests. State elites—civilian as well as military—have in various instances effectively resisted the pressures of ethnoregional intermediaries. In addition, they have also proposed political systems designed, in part at least, to depoliticize conflict and obstruct change. In the case of Ghana's 1977 Union Government scheme, the Acheampong regime made a determined effort to create a nonparty representative system whose central objective was to forestall a wide gamut of effective civilian demands on state authorities.[52] A side effect of Ignatius Kutu Acheampong's strategy of purposive depoliticization would clearly have been a reduced sensitivity on the part of the military-led state to the claims of ethnoregional interests.

Although these suppressed demands are an important aspect of the social environment and therefore must be taken seriously, my main focus must be on incremental and synoptic kinds of public choices. In either case, state authorities have chosen to define their problem in policy terms and to begin examining and promoting policy alternatives. Thus, irrespective of whether one views the state as manager or controller or, alternatively, with a Marxist or non-Marxist philosophical perspective, it is possible to view the state as inseparably linked to the larger policy process. Certainly, the two concepts of a class state and a partially autonomous state capable of some measure of purposeful action on its own are by no means mutually exclusive. Ralph Miliband, in an important reconstruction of Marx's thought, reconciles them in the following way: "The state is indeed a class state, the state of the 'ruling class.' But it enjoys a high degree of autonomy and independence in the manner of its operation as a class state, and indeed must have that high degree of autonomy and independence if it is to act as a class state."[53]

Marxists and non-Marxists can find common ground with regard to the active and partially autonomous role of the state vis-à-vis international and, to a lesser extent, domestic class pressures. Where Marxists and non-Marxists tend to disagree is on the extent to which the class consciousness of the dominant political elite necessarily distorts public policy, particularly in capitalistically oriented countries. Are states and their instrumentalities no more than protagonists of class interests, or can they come to represent a countrywide constituency? As the state elite allocates value authoritatively and implements public policies on economic development and on the regularizing of relations among groups and between these groups and the state, can the dominant political elite be expected, even if only intermittently, to rise above narrow class interests and accept the limitations of community-wide organizing principles?

There also is another important dimension to the debate about the state's capacity for meaningful autonomous action. To the extent that the African state is a political superstructure having only a limited relationship to the rural productive process, as Goran Hyden contends,[54] then its efforts to transform the nature of production or to modify intergroup relationships may appear as movement without significant consequence. Obviously, states vary enormously in the extent and nature of their active roles on the African scene; nevertheless, in paying heed to the problems of policy implementation, we must take the state's limited capacity fully into consideration in order to gain an appreciation of what claims can be made on the state as well as what demands the state can realistically make on ethnoregional peoples, especially those living in the periphery.

At this point, I can begin to probe the ways in which the partially autonomous state converts divergent demands into public policies; in the next section of the chapter, I discuss the state as policy initiator. If at times the state's role as a processor seems more weighty than its role as policy initiator, this reflects the "softness" of state institutions under contemporary African circumstances. Paradoxically, the modern African state is overcentralized and consumes extensive resources, yet is fragile and lacks the ability to carry out its ambitious programs. If this is not the place to examine the causes for the state's softness,[55] it is nonetheless important to note that the impact of such limitations on state initiative is to incline decision elites away from meaningful commitments and toward incrementalist choices largely reflecting the most insistent demands of society and of the state institutions themselves.

Let me comment then on comparative decisional methods for coping with the demands advanced by ethnoregional groups. Paralleling and generally related to our categories of nonnegotiable and negotiable demands, we see two basic types of decision processes—hegemony and hegemonial exchange—in evidence in contemporary African states. Hegemony and hegemonial exchange can be distinguished in terms of their interactional processes and consequences. Broadly speaking, hegemonial state systems, which view open conflict as threatening and possibly unmanageable, seek to control conflict from the top downward; hegemonial exchange state systems, which tend to perceive conflict as ubiquitous but manageable, are based on a mutual adjustment of conflicting interests on the part of multiple authorities. The former regulates the various types of ethnic conflict by strengthening the control that authoritative institutions at the center exercise over the subregions; the latter manages conflict by means of reciprocal exchange obligations among state and ethnoregional leaders at the center of the political system. As an ideal type, hegemonial exchange is a form of state-facilitated coordination within the parameters of the single- or no-party arrangement in which a somewhat autonomous central state actor and a number of considerably less autonomous ethnic-based interests engage, on the basis of informally understood norms and rules, in a process of mutual accommodations. Within the partially closed political systems of contemporary middle Africa, hegemonial exchange allows for tacit exchanges of interests, frequently applying the proportionality principle in resolving such contentious issues as political coalition formation, political recruitment, resource allocation, and constitutional protections.

Hegemonial state systems in Africa are elite-dominated, bureaucratically directed political orders characterized, for the most part, by limited public accountability. The level of mass participation tends to vary according to choice strategies on development and external linkages;[56] those governments (often Marxist) that pursue a "transformation" strategy are more likely than their "accommodation" or "neocolonial" and "reorganization" counterparts to provide forums (albeit controlled) for public expression of grievances and commitments.[57]

Although some state-ethnic reciprocity is present in these various hierarchical political orders in the relationship between rulers and ruled, an essential attribute of all such state systems is their potential for low-cost decisions and regulations.[58] Because leaders can often contain the least pressing ethnoregional demands, suppress formal oppositions, and set, but not implement, public policies at relatively low cost, they need invest only limited resources in decisionmaking. This strategy sometimes works to the benefit of these relatively noncompetitive, centrally dominated political systems, for it strengthens their capacity for containing interethnic conflict and for overriding divisive ethnoregional claims. Where the hegemonial state system actually succeeds in isolating and constraining racial and ethnoregional challenges, it is possible to say that the state system performs efficiently (i.e., managing conflict at low cost) although perhaps not effectively (i.e., managing conflict in the best possible way). Hegemony regulates interethnic conflict by controlling and dispersing it, but such a system fails, in some instances, to establish the moral linkages indispensable to an ongoing relationship.

In the long run, then, the costs of a hegemonial decision process are not to be underestimated. These costs may include low responsiveness to legitimate group demands, lack of reliable information throughout the system, failure to encourage new local leadership, and a general ineffectiveness in promoting interethnic political exchange and in establishing cooperative procedures for conflict regulation. In brief, the intensity of ethnoregional conflict may make frequent recourse to hegemonially determined decision processes likely (Angola, Ethiopia, Mozambique, Tanzania, Guinea).[59] Yet such approaches are often not sufficiently flexible and alert to the intricacies of political exchange and social interpenetration to create lasting informal norms and rules for the constructive management of conflict. To use Charles Lindblom's apt phrase, as applied originally to command economies, these hegemonial modes of implementation sometimes "look like all thumbs, no fingers," although, as he quickly adds, "the thumbs are nevertheless powerful."[60]

In contrast, hegemonial exchange state systems allow a broader range for open conflict and collaboration among decisionmakers. Information is more widely shared, the avenues for communicating demands are more readily accessible, and state elites exhibit greater sensitivity to the resource claims put forward by ethnoregional strongmen in the cabinet or party central committee. Political exchange takes place in an environment of heightened public participation on the part of the "politically relevant strata of the population" in intraelite bargaining and intergroup reconciliation.[61] The assumption that interaction will facilitate the growth of a shared community lies at the core of this exchange. Social learning in the form of political experience will, it is hoped, lead to the development of moral linkages among groups and among individuals; this learned relationship will permit a creative process of conflict to occur—at least within bearable limits.

By diffusing decisional authority and putting their faith in pragmatic (or nonideologized) politics, hegemonial exchange state systems tend to raise the cost of decisionmaking.[62] The process of hegemonial exchange enables a relatively large number of authorities to participate in efforts to work out mutually acceptable policies. In such a complicated undertaking, where joint movement toward an overarching goal requires concessions by all rival parties, the difficulties of developing informal communications networks and reaching acceptable compromises are evident. Hence, the costs of decision in the negotiation of satisfactory outcomes is likely to prove relatively high. The concessions necessary for agreement place the ethnoregional brokers in a situation of double jeopardy. Not only must such brokers convince their local constituents to give up one value to secure another, but they must repeat this process in their bargaining encounters with their central state-ethnic partners. Provided that the contending ethnoregional intermediaries can accomplish this two-sided task simultaneously, the system is likely to prove effective as well as efficient. In all circumstances, however, the various state-ethnoregional actors can only achieve such an outcome if they are prepared to invest considerably more resources in the decisionmaking process than their hierarchically oriented counterparts are prepared to do.

In order to make a hegemonial exchange state system operate effectively in the long term, it is essential that major societal interests compete for scarce resources according to widely understood informal rules of relationship. No doubt the existence of such conditions as relative social equality, high socioeconomic levels, and broad educational opportunities acts to facilitate stable hegemonial exchange relationships, but, as shown by such cases as Jomo Kenyatta's Kenya and Félix Houphouet-Boigny's Ivory Coast, they are not indispensable to decisional processes built on the reconciliation of mutual benefit. Asymmetrical political exchange encounters are always possible—

provided that the various state-ethnoregional actors perceive their interests to be at least minimally benefited by the relationship. Thus, the concession of subregional autonomy to ethnoregional claimants in the Sudan and Nigeria was in part an attempt to allay minority fears in an effort to promote the unity of the country as a whole. In this situation, the political elite's consensus about systematic rules and procedures proved indispensable to an ongoing bargaining encounter. Hence, the statement made by Lieutenant General Olusegun Obasanjo, Nigeria's head of state, at the time he announced a return to party politics, was no mere truism. "From now on," declared Obasanjo, "let the game of politics be played according to the laid-down rules. Let all players be good sportsmen. No matter the result of the competition, let all players remain friendly and without bitterness look forward to another competition."[63]

By lending an air of regularity to the political system, such rules, whether formal or informal, reduce uncertainty on the part of various political actors, thereby encouraging exchange practices.[64] In other words, hegemonial exchange state systems recognize and accept the legitimacy of social pluralism. What they attempt to do is to channel conflict arising from diversity of interests along predetermined paths. To be sure, such an organizing principle may involve substantial decision costs for the participants, but so long as the possibility of a mutually advantageous social relationship is in the offing, such costs are considered bearable. Indispensable to this process of channeling conflict is a willingness on the part of key state-ethnoregional actors to proceed on the basis of understood procedures. Hence, the way in which demands are presented and then converted by the state's decisionmakers into public policies must conform to the prescribed norms and values of a hegemonial exchange system.

As will be evident in a discussion of strategies and policies in the next section, this predisposition for interactions grounded on hegemonial exchange relations is carried over into the organizing principles that state elites seek to apply. In part, public formula strategies would seem to be influenced by the character of public demands. Past experience indeed suggests a link between nonnegotiable demands—hegemonial decision processes—hegemonial instruments for applying nonreciprocal policy on the one hand (Idi Amin's Uganda, Ethiopia, Rhodesia, South Africa, Northern Ireland, Lebanon) and negotiable demands—hegemonial exchange decision processes—exchange mechanisms for reciprocal policy application on the other (Ghana, Kenya, Malaysia, Scotland, Belgium, the Netherlands). Thus, where nonnegotiable demands are made for autonomy and secession by means of military or terrorist actions, the likelihood of hegemonially imposed solutions, particularly on the part of regimes already inclined toward hegemonial decision processes, seems substantial. By contrast, negotiable demands advanced within the system for distributional benefits have a better chance of being dealt with by means of political exchange procedures and programs, especially where regimes are predisposed toward hegemonial exchange decision processes. Hegemony and hegemonial exchange can be viewed as "process(es) that form volitions as well as process(es) for making policy respond to them."[65] As a consequence, *all aspects of the policy process represent interlinked and reinforcing activities* and underlie the fragility of such complex relationships as well as accounting in part for their ongoing dynamic.

State Policies for Managing Conflict

The Dimensions of Choice

The partially autonomous African state not only resists and processes demands —it also makes demands of its own. Certainly, an evident scarcity of fiscal and institutional resources acts to limit the state's coercive capacity and initiative, particularly in the assemblage of reliable data, the implementing of policy, and the monitoring of results. Yet a constriction on public choice by no means precludes an active role for state elites in defining their problems, promoting policy alternatives, choosing alternatives, revising policy, and, to a lesser extent, undertaking the other stages of the policy process. Thus, even though certain state decisions appear structured by international and domestic forces in the environment, collective choice on rules and processes for managing state-ethnic relations (for example, in resource allocation, coalition formation, and recruitment policies) is still not precluded.

Hence, in putting forth a typology of conflict-regulating strategies and implementing policies, I wish to emphasize that state elites in postcolonial Africa can have considerable maneuverability. They are not necessarily limited to neutral roles, merely responding to international and domestic pressures, but can, in certain circumstances at least, be designers, organizers, and movers of policy. As a political class with a vested interest in the state itself, this dominant elite is responsible in part for the expansion of state activity into all spheres of public life. The application of formal and informal rules to guide the political behavior of ethnoregional interests is no exception here. Although broad patterns on hegemony and hegemonial exchange are discernible, I wish nonetheless to avoid a too-restrictive dichotomy and to take note of the many possible combinations and gradations of choice at hand. Both hegemonial and hegemonial exchange systems make use of many of the nine conflict management strategies set out below, with their varying amalgamations of policy instruments. If hegemones have entered into informal reciprocal arrangements with ethnoregional interests, hegemonial exchange systems have not always been loath to impose top-down solutions.

To note the possibility of such an array of suboptimalized choices is to underscore the range of alternatives at the disposal of state elites for determining relevant formulas and policy packages. To contend, as does one well-informed observer on Malaya's race relations, that conflict in that country "could only be avoided by maintaining colonial rule and a laissez-faire exchange market economy," seems as static and fatalistic as it is circumscribed with regard to choice options.[66] The scope for state leadership —for good or ill—must be fully comprehended for it to be available. Two primary ways of structuring interethnic conflict (i.e., hegemony and hegemonial exchange) and nine strategies for coping with interethnic conflict are set out here.

Those strategies normally associated with hegemonic styles of policy application (i.e., subjection, avoidance, isolation, assimilation, displacement) tend to display relatively low levels of political interaction and reciprocity; by contrast, those strategies related for the most part to hegemonial exchange styles of policy application (i.e., sharing, redistribution, protection, buffering) tend to show relatively high levels of political interaction and reciprocity. To be sure, this typology is far from exhaustive. One option, genocide (Amin's Uganda, Burundi, the German campaign against the Hereros and Namas in the early 1900s), has been omitted because, if followed to its logical conclusion, it has the effect of terminating the relationship among groups within the state. Similarly, such forms of encounter as incoherence and transformation have not been included, in part as they lack policy applicability and specificity. Also, in the case of incoherence at least, there is an "absence of any shared forms of tension-management between individuals and groups who stand, nonetheless, in conscious encounter with each other."[67]

Clearly, then, the conflict-regulating scheme adopted here inevitably involves intersecting and overlapping features. This necessarily occurs in any dynamic process that brings together different political actors, decision processes, and policy outcomes. However, avoiding overlaps is less central to our purposes than the delineation of the dimensions of choice. Perhaps knowledge about choice opportunities will enable decisionmakers to design specific policies aimed at enlarging the scope for creative conflictual relations. Enlightened public policy consists of more than a desire to reduce the costs of intense and destructive conflict; it also requires an appreciation of the policy options inhering in each situation that will facilitate the development of lasting intergroup linkages. With this in mind, I will now characterize the nine conflict regulating strategies, moving generally from the most explicitly coercive to the least.

(1) Subjection. A strategy involving the subjection of one ethnic group by another is the very quintessence of a hegemonial approach. The dominant group exercises sufficient control over the political system to achieve its own

self-determination irrespective of the countervailing pulls of rival parties at the periphery. Subjection usually suggests a calculation by the dominant actor that the benefits of thoroughgoing control more than outweigh the political, economic, and psychological costs of pursuing such a policy. Pierre L. van den Berghe, emphasizing the structure of relationships in South Africa, virtually excludes meaningful concessions by the dominant political elite:

> The ruling regime of South Africa is a captive of a system in which a monopoly of political power is a *sine qua non* of maintenance of those economic privileges of the white working class and petty bourgeoisie, and that is why, however pragmatic, flexible, intelligent, and rational the ruling circles of the Nationalist party might want to be, they simply cannot get away with making substantial concessions.[68]

Yet even in the South African case, the particular strategy adopted to apply the coercion option has shown a change of emphasis from time to time. If the basic strategy of control has remained constant, the government has shown considerable subtlety in adapting its forms to meet domestic and, especially, international imperatives.[69]

Because relationships in a situation of subjection are strikingly unequal and intergroup conflicts often intense, a coercive relationship between groups may be regarded as necessary in order to maintain a structure of inequality.[70] Once state elites apply policy instruments to achieve their domination and control, reciprocity between collectives is minimal; genuine power-sharing is precluded; contact is limited and generally circumscribed with ritual; and, partly by design, the responsiveness of the system to public demands is kept at low levels. Although these policy mechanisms frequently reflect the extreme anxieties of minority people in highly exposed and vulnerable situations (South Africa, Burundi, Amin's Uganda), it is not by any means limited to minority domination (Arabs in Zanzibar, Kurds in Iraq and Iran, Arabs in Israel).[71] To be sure, policies of ethnic subjection may allow for participation within the dominant section or sections, even while refusing equivalent rights to the oppressed elements of the population (e.g., South Africa's parliamentary elections); however, such an asymmetrical pattern of group rights does no violence to the principle of ethnic domination as outlined here. So long as the government uses its coercive powers to freeze intergroup inequity in place, the existence of a delimited sphere for public contestation within the dominant group or groups only reinforces the stability of the political system by lending it a specious air of semilegitimacy.

(2) Isolation. Whereas avoidance assumes a relatively cohesive political community in the country as a whole, a strategy of isolation is pursued on

the premise that ethnoregional and racial collectives within the same state lack shared interests, goals, and values. Ties to the larger community are not accepted as legitimate, primary political loyalties being directed to the subcommunity, not to the larger society. Isolation is manifest in such institutionalized relationships as de facto partition (Cyprus, Ireland, Lebanon) and attempted secession (Biafra, Eritrea, Katanga, and the Kurds of Iraq and Iran). However, once isolation is carried to its logical conclusion and two sovereign states emerge and are recognized as legitimate (Pakistan/ Bangladesh), then the encounter is transformed into a new type of relationship.

Where isolation does persist within the state, ethnoregional leaders, irrespective of their majority status, regard conflict as intense and potentially destructive. They therefore seek, by coercive means if necessary, to reduce conflict by separating the contending groups into distinct political systems, each of which then possesses a decisional capacity over certain specified activities in its own right. For John de St. Jorre, partition is one conceivable scenario that may materialize in South Africa. "Partition in closely interwoven societies," he writes,

> . . . is never thought possible until it happens, for the simple reason that it is invariably the result of civil war. No one wants it ideally, no one really accepts it, but it finally occurs because neither side can defeat the other and the alternative is endless bloodshed. . . . Partition will, of course, mean disruption, sacrifice, a harder life for the Afrikaner tribe in a much smaller state. But that is the price they will have to pay for their ethnic exclusiveness, for their continued existence in Africa.[72]

Because of the drastic nature of such separations, a two-sided form of hegemonial interaction, often involving elements of force and coercion, seems well nigh inevitable during the period of de-linkage. Provided the process of separation is not too destructive, however, new types of relationships between separate and distinct identities are not precluded in the years to follow.

(3) Cultural Assimilation. Regimes pursuing a strategy of cultural assimilation employ the power of the state to interpenetrate and absorb politically weaker identities into a dominant core culture. Such regimes can be controlled by a numerically preponderant collectivity or collectivities (Sudan) or by a powerful minority people (the American-Liberian people of Liberia), but in either case a similar impulse toward cultural expansion and incorporation is evident. To be sure, a subtle process of "unconscious assimilation" marks many interethnic encounters;[73] while not unmindful of this process, this essay focuses on cultural assimilation as a conscious choice strategy on the part of a state's decisionmakers. It is their effort to take

deliberate steps to promote core cultures, values, attitudes, and aspirations on a nationwide basis that is of primary concern in this context.

Surely there is a positive, egalitarian dimension to an assimilationist strategy.[74] Nigeria's national service system of the late 1970s and early 1980s, which required every university graduate to serve for a year in a subregion other than his or her own, used state authority as a means of promoting a more united country. Moreover, because the dominant collectivity controls the educational system, it disperses the national language, thereby assuring that the members of all groups are equipped to enter into market exchanges and to compete for skilled positions in the public and private sectors. Full and free ethnoregional representation also requires an extensive facility with the lingua franca, or, as Uganda's former president Milton Obote has warned, whole peoples risk possible isolation from proceedings in the central legislative body that affect them in a fundamental manner.[75] Yet despite these positive aspects, the attempt to mold a relatively uniform national culture and worldview nevertheless entails some potentially heavy costs. Because cultural assimilationist policies use state power to compel the relinquishment of certain cultural traits, they inevitably involve an element of linguistic, religious, and/or value suppression; not surprisingly, such suppression evokes a strong emotional response by politically peripheral peoples. The concern of French-speaking African intellectuals in colonial times with negritude was in part a reaction to France's overbearing assimilationist policies.[76] Outside of Africa, Quebec's René Lévesque has responded in a similar manner to what he views as Anglo-Saxon assimilationist pressures in Canada.[77]

In postcolonial Africa, this dialectic of assimilation-resistance continues to be of considerable relevance. Various regime policies of "Arabization" and "Islamization" in the Sudan have provoked a bitter reaction on the part of the culturally and ethnically distinct peoples of the South.[78] Oliver Albino, describing Southern Sudanese fears in this regard, remarks that

> these differences are taken by the Muslim North as "imperialist influence" calculated to breed hatred between the Arabs and the Africans. Such an attitude and open intolerance by the ruling North makes social harmony impossible. On the contrary, an infamous piece of legislation known as the Missionary Societies Act, 1962, was enacted in order to eradicate Christianity and ensure the spread of Islam.[79]

It is significant that as the Addis Ababa Agreement of 1972 allowed for a measure of relief from these assimilationist pressures [Appendix A(6) gave minority groups guarantees on freedom of religion, conscience, language, and culture], destructive tensions between North and South eased temporarily; however, as Sharia was applied to the whole country in 1983 and Arabic was "emphasized" in southern schools, "at the expense . . . of English and local languages," guerrilla forces in the South mounted military attacks against the Sudanese state.[80]

In Liberia, assimilationist pressures have been in evidence since 1847 when the freed blacks achieved independence status,. The Americo-Liberian population, about 1.5 percent of the total population of the country, automatically secured citizenship until 1944, while the remaining indigenous inhabitants were granted citizenship as they showed themselves to be "civilized." Civilization, which involved the adoption of Western life-styles, the practice of Christianity, and the demonstrated ability to read and write English, was facilitated by participation in an apprenticeship program sponsored by Americo-Liberian commercial or trading institutions or by attending the formal school system. Certainly the way to proven success within the political system lay essentially through acquiring a Western education and life-style. In 1944, citizenship was granted to all the inhabitants of Liberia and participation in government was extended to leaders from hinterland areas. However, assimilationist impulses became stronger, despite apparent misgivings in the periphery, as the core culture had gained an ascendancy over the economic and political centers of the society.[81] As one ambitious young man expressed his dilemma over assimilation:

> Before you will be known by Liberians you should be a member of Civilized Society.
> For this reason if I go to church I always ask in my daily prayer "Hear me crying, oh God, give ear unto my prayer, when my heart is in heaviness. O set me free upon the Rock which is higher than I, for me to see a sort of work during time I shall appear before President of Liberia W. V. S. Tubman."[82]

For this young man, the assimilation-resistance dialogue was internalized.

(4) Avoidance. In pursuing a strategy of avoidance, decisionmakers use the state's coercive powers to restrain direct interethnic conflict. It is precisely because they consider open group struggles to be so gravely threatening that these decision elites seek to protect the political system through the circumscribing and containing of conflict. Such a process of enclosure finds expression in various institutional forms: military-bureaucratic rule, the single-party system, the no-party state, regulations outlawing tribally based party organizations, and so forth. These mechanisms of avoidance tend toward a similar outcome—the insulation of the state and its institutions from the free communication of ethnic interest demands. The state elites, receiving only such messages as they are prepared to entertain and hammering out decisions on sensitive issues in closed meetings, are inclined to reduce troublesome conflict-producing issues to a minimum. The

boundaries they place on ethnic interest encounters represent a purposive effort to avoid the disintegration of the political system.[83] For example, prior to the initiation of Sierra Leone's one-party constitution in 1978, President Siaka Stevens declared that such a hegemonial approach was essential "if the country is not to disintegrate into tribal factions, with all that would imply."[84] For the proponents of no-party government in Ghana and Afghanistan, the elimination of partisan contestation was a means to reduce the harmful divisiveness caused by openly expressed interethnic conflict.[85] Thus, a full awareness of the fragility of the state led numerous African leaders to attempt circumscribing the legitimate arena of politics, even though such a move could impede the process of social learning and thwart the establishment of firm intergroup linkages in the future.

(5) Displacement. A strategy of displacement is limited to efforts on the part of state authorities to transfer an ethnic population permanently from one locale to another in order to transform the nature of the intergroup encounter.[86] The transfer can be to a place inside or outside the country. In this respect, the flight of many of the Fulbe from Sékou Touré's Guinea is not included under this rubric as population transfer was not a consequence of a calculated decision by state leaders. Because such a strategy often involves a state-imposed "solution" to the nationalities problem, a hegemonial approach is usually entailed. However, within the rubric of displacement, a variety of policy instruments have been in evidence. Thus, displacement has been applied on frequent occasions to small urban enclaves (South Africa's Group Areas Act); imposed upon entire nationality groups (USSR); taken the form of local regroupment (Lebanon, Cyprus, Algeria, Palestinian Arabs from Israeli territory, Jews from Ethiopia and from Arab countries); implied assisted repatriation (immigrant workers in Western Europe, nonwhites in the United Kingdom); appeared as disguised or undisguised expulsion (Chinese refugees from Vietnam,[87] Biharis in Bangladesh, Moors and Jews from Spain, Asians in Uganda); and involved formal exchanges of populations across state lines (Greece and Turkey following World War I).

Although an element of state coercion is common to many of these policies, it is nonetheless important to note that political exchange relationships can be present where leaders pursue a displacement strategy. Under an agreement negotiated in 1975 between Bonn and Warsaw, 7,047 ethnic Germans living in Poland's western territories have been permitted to rejoin their relatives in West Germany in the period from 1 January 1976 to 31 July 1977. In exchange for a Polish pledge to allow 125,000 Germans to transfer to the Federal Republic in the four years after the agreement, the German government agreed to make a payment of DM 1,300 million to cover pension and accident insurance claims and to provide a long-term loan of DM 1,000 million. In addition, talks have been held between West German and

Soviet authorities regarding the sensitive question of repatriating some 2 million ethnic Germans living in the USSR[88] On the equally sensitive issue of Jewish emigration from the USSR, Soviet authorities have bridled at any attempt to link the exit of Soviet Jews with U. S. trade pressures (in particular, the Jackson-Vanik Amendment to the Trade Reform Act of 1974).[89] Nevertheless, in something of a tacit bargain, Moscow has allowed a significant outflow of Soviet Jews to take place during critical junctures in Soviet-U. S. relations (i.e., the talks on SALT II in 1978). As of July 1980, nearly 240,000 of an estimated 2 million Soviet Jews had been permitted to leave the country since emigration began in the late 1960s. Finally, one might point to two agreements negotiated between the governments of India and Sri Lanka under which 600,000 Indian Tamil laborers are to be repatriated to India in years to come, while a remaining 600,000 are to be readmitted to Sri Lankan citizenship.[90] Because displacement involves this element of bargaining, it is considered the closest of all the hegemonial approaches to political exchange-type interactions.

(6) Buffering. Where the norms of formalized competition and reciprocity are lacking, the contesting sides can use third-party intermediaries to organize the rules for social interaction. In such situations, interethnic conflict is normally intense and political exchange relations are indirect and intermittent. Because the rules for regulating such conflict tend to be insufficiently determined, the rivals come separately to a decision to make use of an internal or external third-party intermediary to find a minimally satisfactory agreement. As such, a strategy of buffering takes a variety of forms: good offices, conciliation, mediation, and arbitration.

Buffering was commonplace at the time of decolonization in middle Africa. Once the colonial authority became intent on ending its political overrule in these territories, it made an effort to reconcile conflicting ethnoregional and racial interests prior to granting self-government. In Uganda and Kenya, for example, this led to a belated attempt to promote coalition government and quasi-federal constitutional relations.[91] In Namibia, however, the presence of very contradictory demands and preconditions on all sides has made efforts at external buffering more complex and, in the immediate term at least, less successful.[92]

Clearly, buffering can only be effective in managing interethnic conflict where the rival parties are prepared to search for mutually beneficial terms and an acceptable intermediary is willing to undertake the often thankless task of conciliation, mediation, or arbitration. The various spokesmen must bargain within their communities for the right to represent their respective groups at the interethnic bargaining table as well as between one another. The complexity of such a process is shown by the protracted effort to hammer out a settlement of the Namibian dispute, for even with the Lusaka meeting of

May 1984, cochaired by Zambia's president Kenneth Kaunda and South Africa's administrator general in Namibia, Willem Van Niekerk, the Multi-Party Conference and Southwest African People's Organization (SWAPO) representatives found themselves deadlocked over the implementation of U.N. Security Council Resolution 435. Outstanding examples of effective mediation occurred, however, in Zimbabwe and the Sudan. In the former case, Britain's efforts to mediate the dispute received critical support from the frontline states, which pressed the Patriotic Front to negotiate a settlement of political issues at the Lancaster House conference in 1979.[93] In the latter case, a representative of the World Council of Churches chaired successful talks between the Sudanese government and the Southern Sudan Liberation Movement. The uniqueness of this achievement, which led ultimately to the Addis Ababa agreement of 1972, is apparent in light of the difficulty of persuading the Organization of African Unity (O.A.U.) to assume an intermediary's role in the internal disputes of member states (Eritrea, Biafra).

(7) Protection. Where public authorities put policies of group protection into effect, hegemonial exchange relations are direct but intermittent. The core retains unequal political power in relationship to the periphery; however, at its discretion, the core may decide to grant legal and constitutional protections to peripheral groups. Although external actors have pressed for minority guarantees, the decision to make these safeguards a meaningful feature of state policy is ultimately one for state elites themselves. As such, legal protections represent a relatively direct (albeit unequal) form of hegemonial exchange between core and periphery.

Here, as before, it is important to distinguish between the protective policies of colonial and postcolonial regimes. At the time of the transfer of power, the outgoing metropolitan powers frequently extracted minority protections from the newly established African governments as the price of further progress toward political self-government and independence (Kenya, Uganda, Zambia, Ghana, Zimbabwe).[94] Many of these hastily erected guarantees were soon dismantled after independence, and the regimes in power largely shunned further external actor participation in their internal affairs. From this time forward the issue of legal safeguards became matters of domestic predispositon and policy. Some regimes, accommodationist (neocolonial) and transformationist alike, have steadfastly refused to incorporate fundamental rights guarantees in their basic laws.[95] Others have variously inserted protections for individual and group rights into their basic laws, providing for linguistic, electoral, legal, educational, and cultural safeguards. For example, bilingualism has been official government policy in the Cameroun, despite a move to a unitary system of government in 1972; moreover, the Federal Nigerian Constitution of 1979 granted all persons an extensive list of fundamental rights, subject, of course, to qualifications based on defense, public safety, and public morality requirements. Particularly significant for our purposes was a right to freedom from discrimination under the Nigerian constitution. Thus, Article 39 (1) provided:

> A citizen of Nigeria of a particular community, ethnic group, place of origin, sex, religion, or political opinion shall not, by reason only that he is such a person—
> (a) be subjected either expressly by, or in the practical application of, any law in force in Nigeria or any executive or adminstrative action of the government to disabilities or restrictions to which citizens of Nigeria or other communities, ethnic groups, places of origin, sex, religions, or political opinions are not made subject; or
> (b) be accorded either expressly by, or in the practical application of, any law in force in Nigeria or any such executive or administrative action, any privilege or advantage that is not accorded to citizens of Nigeria, of other communities, ethnic groups, places of origin, sex, religions or political opinions.[96]

As shown by this carefully drawn constitutional provision as well as by specific provisions on ensuring the country's "federal character" in making appointments to decisionmaking bodies, the Nigerian state was moving deliberately toward the entrenchment of specific individual and collective rights in its basic law. This represented a significant concession on the part of the state elite, which recognized the link between the reassurance of basic ethnoregional interests in the constitution and the stability of the state itself.

(8) Redistribution. Whereas a strategy of protection instills confidence among the politically disadvantaged by assuring them political, economic, and social rights, that of redistribution represents a more substantial commitment on the part of the relatively advantaged. Redistribution goes beyond concession and suggests a genuine exchange, direct or tacit, between significant domestic political actors: The less advantaged gain much-needed economic resources in exchange for their support and compliance with regime regulations.

In middle Africa, such countries as Nigeria, Ghana, Zambia, and Tanzania have variously allocated substantial resources to the less advantaged subregions for the purposes of economic development, national integration, and regime support. The policy mechanisms used to alter the existing pattern of system allocations include the following: fiscal redistribution (Ghana, Zambia, Tanzania, Nigeria), informal and formal quotas on public service recruitment and scholarships (Nigeria, Malawi, Burundi, Kenya), preferences in distributing contracts (Zambia), siting of industries in the less advantaged areas, and special training and capital assistance programs (Kenya). In all such instances, administrative incentives and controls are instituted that effect a more even distribution of interethnic opportunities. Under conditions of overriding economic scarcity, the scope for redistributive programs is necessarily limited; even so, recently published data from Nigeria and Kenya indicate a greater tendency to use the proportional (and, in some cases, the extraproportional) principle than in the past. The index of variation decreased with respect to Nigeria's road programs during the period from 1975-1976 to 1979-1980 from 1.18 to 0.48, while that country's health program showed a decline in the index of variation from .70 to .51. In Kenya during the 1974-1975 to 1982-1983 period, the hospital programs index decreased from 1.01 to .89 and the education programs from .53 to .45.[97] Such allocative policies suggest a kind of informal hegemonial exchange process at work, which augurs well for constructive conflict relations among state and ethnoregional interests.

Although African countries have not as yet approximated Pakistan's or Malaysia's comprehensive application of preference systems for recruitment to educational institutions and to central, subregional and parastatal organizations, they have taken some initiatives to ensure a more representative selection and admissions process.[98] Nigeria's 1979 constitution included provisions on the "federal character" of the federal civil service and the appointment to federal political and adminstrative positions. The aim was to promote national unity by "ensuring that there should be no predominance of persons from a few States or from a few ethnic or other sectional groups in that government or in any of its agencies" [Sect. 14(3)], and the federal government took steps to comply with the spirit of this provision by including representatives from all states in the federal cabinet. The federal government also acted to set quotas for admission to federal universities and to allocate postgraduate scholarships on a proportional, if not an extraproportional, basis. Its achievements in the latter area are plain to see. Whereas 33.2 percent of the applicants from the eleven states in the federation designated as disadvantaged by the former federal military government (and 46.2 percent in the nine disadvantaged states in the north) received postgraduate awards in the 1980/81 year, only 21.5 percent of those applying from the eight relatively advantaged states were given scholarships. This inclination toward corrective equity was even more apparent in the following year, as 60.9 percent of the applicants from the nine disadvantaged northern states received scholarship awards.[99]

What is less fully appreciated is the continuation of support by the Nigerian military, following its December 31, 1983, coup d'état, for the guideline on "federal character" in central appointments. Upon seizing power, the administration of Major General Mohammed Buhari appointed an eighteen-member federal executive council that included a member from every state except Bendel, and that state was compensated by the selection of a person from the subregion as head of the civil service.[100] The policy of balanced recruitment of subregional interests was abandoned, however, following Major General Ibrahim Babangida's coup d'état of August 27, 1985; his expanded cabinet, heavily weighted with military officers, included two or more members from Plateau, Niger, Oyo, and Ogun states, while leaving Ondo and Bauchi states unrepresented.[101] Other African countries reflecting a geographical balance in high level political appointments range across a continuum from Kenya's, the Ivory Coast's, and Cameroun's hegemonial exchange system to former president Sékou Touré's tight one-party hegemony in Guinea. Unofficial practices of proportionality also have been apparent, moreover, in civil service recruitment experiences in Ghana, Malawi, and various other sub-Saharan countries. In these situations, the soft African state has made a virtue of political necessity. It has frequently responded to the reality of powerful ethnoregional demands for inclusiveness and for fairness in allocations by opting for the seemingly disinterested standard of proportionality.

As proportional and extraproportional guidelines are invoked and minority ethnic peoples and relatively disadvantaged subregions see an increase in their opportunities, the effect of programs based on these principles may be positive in terms of improved interethnic relations. The gap between the relatively disadvantaged and relatively advantaged may narrow somewhat, leading, by stages, toward greater economic, political, and social interdependence. Positive memories of the core group or groups may develop as redistributive programs are implemented sensitively. Nevertheless, the difficulties in carrying redistribution through to its logical conclusion (i.e., substantial equality among ethnic identity groups and subregions) are unwisely minimized. Not only do programs of redistribution encounter resistance from entrenched ethnic and class interests determined to hold onto their privileges,[102] but such programs may also encounter increasing opposition on other grounds: that they make ethnic allegiance more salient in the political process and heighten intraethnic group antagonisms along class lines. Moreover, should the expectations of the relatively disadvantaged outpace the willingness or the ability of the relatively advantaged to reallocate significant benefits—a reaction that might be described as redistrubtor fatigue —redistribution might come to epitomize tokensim or an empty policy ritual for all but the tiny upper middle class elite affected by its provisions. In this event, redistribution, as an alteration in the rules of relationships, could result in increased interethnic tensions.

(9) Sharing. Power-sharing policies, the quintessence of a hegemonial exchange approach, tend only to be relevant in situations where levels of interethnic conflict remain distinctly moderate. Differences are reconcilable in these circumstances, for competition is largely limited to distributional concerns and not usually extended to include matters of basic belief and principle. Nevertheless, the salience of ethnic pluralism requires a continuing

effort on the part of decision elites to ensure that demands do not escalate and that systemic norms of relationship are followed. At heart, the politics of sharing involves a fine-tuned process of feedback geared to the regularizing of reciprocity among groups. By comparison with protection and redistribution, sharing strategies bring relatively equal parties into the political exchange process. In addition, sharing goes beyond the protection of rights and the redistribution of economic resources; it includes group spokesmen in the key area of political decisionmaking.

Even within the parameters of the one- or no-party system, state and ethnoregional actors can enter into informal exchange relationships because they are linked together by well-understood and predictable ties of reciprocity. Such hegemonial exchange models of conflict management avoid adversarial behavior and, instead, channel group interactions along controlled yet cooperative lines. To be sure, ethnoregional strongmen in the cabinet or party national executive continue to strive for the maximization of group interests; however, these encapsulated power struggles tend to be reduced in intensity by the controls placed on public information and by the sense of shared interests emerging over time within the politically dominant class. By quietly agreeing to informal principles of proportionality on such critical issues as coalition formation, elite recruitment, and resource allocation, these state and ethnoregional actors are able to work out informal norms among themselves that, temporarily at least, promote conciliatory behavior under conditions of economic scarcity.

In a more formal sense, this emphsis on joint intergroup participation in the decisional process can also find expression in a variety of policy instruments: executive power-sharing (Nigeria), parliamentary coalitions (Nigeria, Kenya), mutual vetoes (Zimbabwe), regional autonomy (Sudan), and devolution (Ghana, Senegal, Tanzania). Common to all these informal and formal manifestations of sharing is a dynamic process of mutual adjustment. The ethnoregional rivals preserve their separate identities while at the same time cooperating in the search for mutually beneficial outcomes. Provided that group interests overlap and learned social relations have developed, social pluralism does not act as a bar to stable, reconciliational politics.

Further Lines for Policy Research

An examination of the nine strategies for managing interethnic conflict presented above reveals much about the range of choices open to state authorities. However, it tells us little about two related issues: the consequences of choice and the ways of reducing the intensity of conflict. Although these must remain topics for subsequent treatment, it is important to note here the possible contribution that policy analysis can make to these questions.

In an abstract sense, the termination of interethnic conflict is not really a problem at all. As Adolf Hitler demonstrated so dramatically, "final solutions" end domestic interethnic conflicts grimly but decisively. Hence, our challenge is not the elimination of conflict irrespective of cost considerations, but the minimization of destructive encounters between ethnoregional sections. Once feasible policy options are fully understood, the logical next step would seem to be the determination of the costs and benefits resulting from the application of these alternatives. This is not a simple task. In real-world situations, every policymaker finds his or her choices conditioned by the environment and by the nature of the demand process. The policymaker is not free in practice to choose as he or she might wish from among the nine conflict management strategies. Even so, within the parameters of choice, the policymaker can formulate a calculus of likely qualitative costs and benefits attendant to each line of action and then design a policy package that will best reconcile the competing objectives put forth by various interests. In doing so, conflicting claims, values, and objectives must be accommodated. The policymaker may also find that a choice has to be made between the short-term costs and benefits these policies may entail with respect to legitimacy engineering.[103] Inevitably he or she will find that such variables as economic performance, external manipulations, group aspirations, and positive and negative ethnic remembrances and images are part of the policymaking equation.

The results of all this in terms of optimal decisionmaking are no doubt less than completely satisfactory. This is not to cast doubts on the usefulness of setting out priorities and qualitative cost-benefit calculations on the management of interethnic conflict. Information and planning can certainly open up new vistas as to choice opportunities. At the same time, however, it is necesssary to be fully cognizant of the limits of a policy approach. The policy analyst can indeed point the way to improved choices on regulating and redirecting interethnic conflict, but the political actor must remain responsible for the ultimate decisions affecting the course of ethnic interactions in his or her society.

Intertwined with an analysis, broadly conceived, of the costs or benefits of policies is a focus on the prescription of procedures for minimizing interethnic conflict. What recommendations can policy analysts make to promote constructive relations among groups? To be sure, the policy analyst is only equipped to provide a part of the answer to this complex question. Nevertheless, a study of the costs and benefits of alternative courses of state action can offer clues as to each course's likely program-aggravating or problem-solving impact. Certainly, a stress on learning through feedback is indispensable to the life of the political system. The inability of policies to achieve desired objectives ought to be taken as a signal of inadequate performance and lead, in turn, to a creative search for ways of restructuring the interrelationships among competing groups. For example, where the state's refusal to negotiate at a time when demands are reasonable results in ethnoregional violence, a more reconciliational approach may reduce tensions and make the conflict more manageable. Moreover, if the effect of nonnegotiable demands is to complicate the management of group tensions by providing a negative information flow, then the inability of the system to function as desired should act as a sign to group actors that more moderate demands are indispensable to reciprocity among groups.

The inability to establish learned interactional relationships among rival sections may be traceable to the hegemonial decision process itself. Low decision costs associated with hegemonial approaches to decisionmaking may be secured at too high a price in social learning; on the other hand, in certain instances, political leaders may conclude from experience that the high decision costs associated with a hegemonial exchange approach, desirable as the approach may be in promoting interethnic reciprocity, may prove too costly in terms of the competing objective of economic productiveness or decisive central leadership. New problemsolving efforts based on feedback information will not always lead to greater responsiveness on the part of state elites, for the existence of multiple objectives assures, if anything, a constant reassessment of public formulas in order to achieve redefined ends.

What a policy emphasis can offer here—and it is necessarily limited by the nature of its orientation to those decisionmakers and policy analysts thinking in terms of rational and constructive calculations—is a more comprehensive view of the interlinked process as a whole. Where such decisionmakers and analysts are intent on improved performance, this broad-based, and hopefully sensitized approach, may advance new and useful insights into the means of reducing the intensity of interethnic conflicts. To emphasize the qualitative character of many of these judgments is in no way to detract from their significance. In describing policy analysis as the creation and crafting of problems worth solving, Aaron Wildavsky comments most aptly:

> In discovery, analysis as problem solving is more art than craft, more finding new ways than persuading others of their feasibility and desirability. In justification, analysis is more craft than art. Not that I prefer one to the other. Without art, analysis is doomed to repetition; without craft, analysis is unpersuasive. Shifting the frame of discourse, so that different facts become persuasive, suggests that art and craft are interdependent.[104]

Notes

This essay is an updated and extended version of "Inter-ethnic Conflict and Policy Analysis in Africa," *Ethnic and Racial Studies* 9 no. 1 (January 1986). I wish to thank the editor, Dr. John Stone, and the publisher, Routledge & Kegan Paul PLC, for allowing me to reuse these materials. I also wish to express my appreciation to Professors Maure Goldschmidt, Dov Ronen, Ian Lustick, and Ole Holsti for comments on an earlier draft of this essay.

1. Walker Connor, "Nation-Building or Nation-Destroying?" *World Politics* 24, no. 3 (April 1972): 337; and his chapter, "Ethnonationalism in the First World: The Present in Historical Perspective," Milton J. Esman, ed., *Ethnic Conflict in the Western World* (Ithaca, N.Y.: Cornell University Press, 1977), p. 41. Also see Clifford Geertz, "The Integrative Revolution," Clifford Geertz, ed., *Old Societies and New States* (New York: Free Press, 1963), p. 111; and Harold R. Isaacs, *Idols of the Tribe* (New York: Harper Colophon Books, 1977), p. 206.

2. Nathan Glazer and Daniel P. Moynihan, "Introduction," in Nathan Glazer and Daniel P. Moynihan, eds., *Ethnicity: Theory and Experience* (Cambridge, Mass.: Harvard University Press, 1975), p. 7. Also see Walter L. Barrows, "Ethnic Diversity and Political Instability in Black Africa," *Comparative Political Studies* 9, no. 2 (July 1976): 162; and Abner Cohen, *Custom and Politics in Urban Africa* (Berkeley: University of California Press, 1969), p. 192. On Kenya's politicized ethnicity as "merely clientelism writ large," see John S. Saul, "The Dialectic of Class and Tribe," *Race and Class* 20, no. 4 (Spring 1979): 351.

3. Warren F. Ilchman and Norman T. Uphoff, *The Political Economy of Change* (Berkeley: University of California Press, 1969), p. 11.

4. On the overlap between cultural identity and territorial unit, see Brian Weinstein, "Social Communication Methodology in the Study of Nation-Building," *Cahiers d'études africaines* 4, no. 4 (1954): 572-573.

5. Maxwell Owusu describes this core political culture as "a politico-administrative atmosphere." See his book, *Uses and Abuses of Political Power: A Case Study of Continuity and Change in the Politics of Ghana* (Chicago: University of Chicago Press, 1970), p. 121. Also see Robert M. Price, *Society and Bureaucracy in Contemporary Ghana* (Berkeley: University of California Press, 1975), pp. 150-151.

6. For a discussion of asymmetrical transactions, see Donald Rothchild and Robert L. Curry, Jr., *Scarcity, Choice, and Public Policy in Middle Africa* (Berkeley: University of California Press, 1978), pp. 324-328; Samir Amin, *Unequal Development* (New York: Monthly Review Press, 1976), pp. 141-145; and Arghiri Emmanuel, *Unequal Exchange* (New York: Monthly Review Press, 1972), pp. 90-95.

7. On this harmony of interest, see Johan Galtung, "A Structural Theory of Imperialism," *Journal of Peace Research* 8, no. 2 (1971): 84; Colin Leys, *Underdevelopment in Kenya: The Political Economy of Neo-colonialism* (Berkeley: University of California Press, 1975), pp. 8-27; and Frantz Fanon, *The Wretched of the Earth* (New York: Grove Press, 1963), pp. 142-143.

8. Rajni Kothari, "The Confrontation of Theories with National Realities: Report on an International Conference," S. N. Eisenstadt and Stein

Rokkan, eds., *Building States and Nations: Models and Data Resources* 1 (Beverly Hills, Calif.:   Sage Publications, 1973), p. 104.

9. Gabriel A. Almond, "Introduction: A Functional Approach to Comparative Politics," Gabriel A. Almond and James S. Coleman, eds., *The Politics of the Developing Areas* (Princeton, N.J.:   Princeton University Press, 1960), p. 49; Joseph LaPalombara, "Penetration: A Crisis of Government Capacity," Leonard Binder et al., *Crises and Sequences in Political Development* (Princeton, N.J.:   Princeton University Press, 1971), p. 208; and James S. Coleman, "The Concept of Political Penetration," L. Cliffe, J. S. Coleman, and M. R. Doornbos, eds., *Government and Rural Development in East Africa: Essays on Political Penetration* (The Hague: Martinus Nijhoff, 1977), p. 3.

10. On the continuity of central state control values from colonial times to the present, see John Dunn and A. F. Robertson, *Dependence and Opportunity: Political Change in Ahafo* (London: Cambridge University Press, 1973), pp. 154, 345.

11. Ibid., p. 121.

12. Michael Hechter, *Internal Colonialism: The Celtic Fringe in British National Development, 1536-1966* (Berkeley: University of California Press, 1975), p. 32.

13. Ibid., p. 350.

14. See, in particular, Pablo G. Casanova, "Internal Colonialism and National Development," *Studies in Comparative International Development* 1, no. 4 (1965):   27-37;   Robert Blauner, "Internal Colonialsim and Ghetto Revolt," *Social Problems* 16, no. 4 (Spring 1969):   393-408; Cynthia Enloe, "Internal Colonialism, Federalism and Alternative State Development Strategies," *Publius* 7, no. 4 (Fall 1977):   150; Michael Hechter, "Ethnicity and Industrialization: On the Proliferation of the Cultural Division of Labor," *Ethnicity* 3, no. 3 (September 1976):   214-224.   Also see Stokely Carmichael and Charles V. Hamilton, *Black Power: The Politics of Liberation in America* (New York: Vintage Books, 1967), pp. 5-6; and Gwendolen M. Carter, Thomas Karis, and Newell Stultz, *South Africa's Transkei: The Politics of Domestic Colonialism* (Evanston, Ill.:   Northwestern University Press, 1967).

15. Harold Wolpe, "The Theory of Internal Colonialism: The South African Case," Ivan Oxaal, Tony Barnett, and David Booth, eds., *Beyond the Sociology of Development: Economy and Society in Latin America and Africa* (London: Routledge and Kegan Paul, 1975), p. 230.

16. Donald Horowitz, "Three Dimensions of Ethnic Politics," *World Politics* 23, no. 2 (January 1971):   232.

17. Wolpe, "The Theory of Internal Colonialism," p. 230.

18. Samuel Decalo, "Regionalism, Political Decay, and Civil Strife in Chad," *Journal of Modern African Studies* 18, no. 1 (March 1980):   54.

19. I am indebted to Professor Ian Lustick for this observation.

20. Dunn, *Dependence and Opportunity*, p. 35.

21. Kenneth E. Boulding, *Conflict and Defense: A General Theory* (New York: Harper and Row, 1963), p. 5.

22. Lewis A. Coser, *The Functions of Social Conflict* (New York: Free Press, 1956), Chapter 2.

23. On this, see Leo Kuper, *The Pity of It All: The Polarization of Racial and Ethnic Relations* (Minneapolis: University of Minnesota Press, 1977). On Prime Minister Indira Gandhi's refusal to negotiate with Sikh spokesmen

when their demands were "negotiable" and the subsequent escalation of these demands, see James Traub, "The Sorry State of India," *New Republic* 190, no. 22 (June 4, 1984): 19.

24. In elaborating on this concept, Kaunda stressed that government policies must be based on human development rather than material improvement. See Colin Legum, ed., *Zambia: Independence and Beyond: The Speeches of Kenneth Kaunda* (London: Thomas Nelson and Sons, 1966), p. 31. Also see Kenneth D. Kaunda, *Humanism in Zambia and a Guide to Its Implementation,* part 2 (Lusaka: Government Printer, 1974), pp. xii-xvi.

25. Ali A. Mazrui, *Post Imperial Fragmentation: The Legacy of Ethnic and Racial Conflict* 1, no. 2 (Denver, Colo.: University of Denver, Studies in Race and Nations, 1969); Lucian W. Pye, "Identity and the Political Culture," Binder, *Crises and Sequences,* pp. 101-134; Erwin C. Hargrove, "Nationality, Values, and Change," *Comparative Politics* 2, no. 3 (April 1970): 473-499; and Harold Isaacs, "Basic Group Identity: The Idols of the Tribe," *Ethnicity* 1, no. 1 (April 1974): 15-41.

26. Mazrui, *Post Imperial Fragmentation;* Connor, "Nation-Building or Nation-Destroying?" pp. 319-355; Karl W. Deutsch, "Research Problems on Race in Intranational and International Relations," George W. Shepherd, Jr. and Tilden J. LeMelle, eds., *Race Among Nations: A Conceptual Approach* (Lexington, Mass.: Heath Lexington Books, 1970), pp. 123-152; and Karl W. Deutsch, *Nationalism and Social Communication,* 2nd ed. (Cambridge, Mass.: MIT Press, 1966).

27. Karl W. Deutsch, "Social Mobilization and Political Development," *American Political Science Review* 55, no. 3 (September 1961): 493-514.

28. Samuel P. Huntington, *Political Order in Changing Societies* (New Haven, Conn.: Yale University Press, 1968).

29. Milton M. Gordon, *Assimilation in American Life* (New York: Oxford University Press, 1964), p. 51. Although such an impact was evident in Kenya's relationship among races, common interests proved sufficient to allow an effective bargaining encounter to emerge. See Donald Rothchild, *Racial Bargaining in Independent Kenya: A Study of Minorities and Decolonization* (London: Oxford University Press, 1973), Chapter 5.

30. René Lemarchand, "Revolutionary Phenomena in Stratified Societies: Rwanda and Zanzibar," *Civilisations* 18, no. 1 (1968): 47, and René Lemarchand, *Rwanda and Burundi* (London: Pall Mall Press, 1970), Chapter 18.

31. Quoted in *Observer* (London), May 22, 1977, p. 8. Also see *Address to the Nation by the Prime Minister, the Honourable Ian Douglas Smith, M.P., May 20, 1969* (Salisbury: Government Printer, 1969), p. 2. Survey data from South Africa show whites more prepared to allow blacks to take skilled jobs (if white workers' jobs are not threatened by it) than to agree to concessions of political power. See Theodor Hanf, Heribert Weiland, and Gerda Vierdag, *South Africa: The Prospects of Peaceful Change* (Bloomington: Indiana University Press, 1981), pp. 212-213. Also see Lawrence Schlemmer, "Change in South Africa: Opportunities and Constraints," Robert M. Price and Carl G. Rosberg eds., *The Apartheid Regime* (Berkeley: Institute of International Studies, 1980), p. 256, Table 10.

32. See Rothchild, *Racial Bargaining,* Chapter 5.

33. On the critical role of intellectuals in preserving these memories and communicating them to subsequent generations, see Myron Weiner, "Political Participation: Crisis of the Political Process," Binder, *Crises and Sequences,*

pp. 170-172. Their advocacy of secessionist sentiments in Biafra are discussed in K. Whiteman, "Enugu: The Psychology of Secession 20 July 1966 to 30 May 1967," S. K. Panter-Brick, ed., *Nigerian Politics and Military Rule: Prelude to the Civil War* (London: Athlone Press, 1970), Chapter 6. For a European example, note the role of intellectuals in the formation of the Welsh Nationalist Party; see Plaid Cymru, *Royal Commission on the Constitution 1969-1973*, 1, Cmnd, 5460 (London: H.M.S.O., 1973), p. 108.

34. Michael Lofchie, *Zanzibar: Background to Revolution* (Princeton, N.J.: Princeton University Press, 1965), p. 268.

35. "Proportionality," writes Milton J. Esman, "recognizes the group basis of politics in communally divided societies and attempts to achieve rough equity among groups rather than among individuals." Milton J. Esman, "The Management of Communal Conflict," *Public Policy* 21, no. 1 (Winter 1973): 62.

36. See S. Egite Oyovbaire, "The Politics of Revenue Allocation," Keith Panter-Brick, *Soldiers and Oil: The Political Transformation of Nigeria* (London: Frank Cass, 1978), Chapter 8; and Federal Republic of Nigeria, *Report to the Presidential Commission on Revenue Allocation*, 1 (Apapa: Federal Government Press, 1980), pp. 25-31.

37. Donald Rothchild, "State-Ethnic Relations in Middle Africa," Gwendolen M. Carter and Patrick O'Meara, eds., *African Independence: The First 25 Years* (Bloomington: Indiana University Press, 1985), Chapter 4.

38. Kenneth Post and Michael Vickers, *Structure and Conflict in Nigeria, 1960-1966* (Madison: University of Wisconsin Press, 1973), Chapter 4.

39. See Donald Rothchild, "Middle Africa: Hegemonial Exchange and Resource Allocation," Alexander Groth and Larry L. Wade, eds., *Comparative Resource Allocation* (Beverly Hills, Calif.: Sage Publications, 1984), pp. 172-175.

40. Donald Rothchild, "Ethnic Inequalities in Kenya," *The Journal of Modern African Studies* 7, no. 4 (December 1969): 698-699; Donald Rothchild, "Rural-Urban Inequalities and Resource Allocation in Zambia," *Journal of Commonwealth Political Studies* 10, no. 3 (November 1972): 226; and Donald Rothchild, "Comparative Public Demand and Expectation Patterns: The Ghana Experience," *African Studies Review* 22, no. 1 (April 1979): 132-135. On the parallels among these experiences, see Donald Rothchild, "Collective Demands for Improved Distributions," Donald Rothchild and Victor Olorunsola, eds., *State Versus Ethnic Claims: African Policy Dilemmas* (Boulder, Colo.: Westview Press, 1983), pp. 172-198. Also see Anthony Oberschall, "Communications, Information, and Aspirations in Rural Uganda," *Journal of Asian and African Studies* 4, no. 1 (January 1969): 48.

41. Although President Kenneth Kaunda refused to give in to such pressures, he described some of the farmers' complaints as "genuine" and called on them to "keep quiet and wait for the government to deal with their complaints." Quoted in *Christian Science Monitor*, November 14, 1978, p. 2.

42. Rothchild, *Racial Bargaining*, Chapters 1, 13.

43. Leo Kuper, "Some Aspects of Violent and Nonviolent Political Change in Plural Societies," Leo Kuper and M. G. Smith, eds., *Pluralism in Africa* (Berkeley: University of California Press, 1969), p. 156.

44. Crawford Young, "Comparative Claims to Political Sovereignty: Biafra, Katanga, Eritrea," in Rothchild, *State Versus Ethnic Claims*, p. 219.

45. Vernon Van Dyke, "The Individual, the State, and Ethnic Communities in Political Theory," *World Politics* 29, no. 3 (April 1977): 350-357, and his "Human Rights and the Rights of Groups," *American Journal of Political Science* 18, no. 4 (November 1974): 725-741. On the conflict between groups and individual rights, see Ernst Haas, "Human Rights: To Act or Not to Act?" Kenneth Dye, Donald Rothchild, and Robert Lieber, eds., *Eagle Entangled: U.S. Foreign Policy in a Complex World* (New York: Longman, 1979), pp. 174-175.

46. Onyeonoro S. Kamanu writes that "for this rationale to be plausible it must be demonstrated that all other political arrangements capable of ensuring the aggrieved group a measure of self-determination short of outright independence had been exhausted or repudiated by the dominant majority." "Secession and the Right of Self-Determination: An O.A.U. Dilemma," *Journal of Modern African Studies* 12, no. 3 (September 1974): 361.

47. The United Republic of Tanzania, *Tanzania Government's Statement on the Recognition of Biafra* (Dar es Salaam: Government Printer, 1970), pp. 1, 4-5. On the "social contract" theme as the basis for a natural rights doctrine on secession, see Lee C. Buchheit, *Secession: The Legitimacy of Self-Determination* (New Haven, Conn.: Yale University Press, 1978), pp. 51-58.

48. Fanon, *The Wretched of the Earth*, p. 37.

49. Kuper, *The Pity of It All*, p. 254. Also see Alexander Dallin and Gail W. Lapidus, "Reagan and the Russians," Kenneth Oye, Robert Lieber, and Donald Rothchild, eds., *Eagle Defiant* (Boston: Little, Brown, 1983), pp. 206-209; and Robert Jervis, *Perception and Misperception in International Politics* (Princeton, N.J.: Princeton University Press, 1976).

50. Barry M. Schutz, "Homeward Bound? A Survey Study of White Rhodesian Nationalism and Permanence," *Ufahamu* 5, no. 3 (1975): 81-117. On this, also see A. K. H. Weinrich, *Black and White Elites in Rural Rhodesia* (Manchester, England: Manchester University Press, 1973), pp. 69-75; and Cyril A. Rogers and C. Frantz, *Racial Themes in Southern Rhodesia* (New Haven, Conn.: Yale University Press, 1962), chapter 15.

51. David Easton, "An Approach to the Analysis of Political Systems," *World Politics* 9, no. 3 (April 1957): 389.

52 Donald Rothchild, "Military Regime Performance: An Appraisal of the Ghana Experience, 1972-78," *Comparative Politics* 12, no. 4 (July 1980): 462-466. Describing the military as negatively disposed toward political activity, Eric A. Nordlinger writes: "More than any other elite group, military officers view political parties as undesirable agents of disunity." *Soldiers in Politics: Military Coups and Governments* (Englewood Cliffs, N.J.: Prentice-Hall, 1977), p. 56.

53. Ralph Miliband, *Marxism and Politics* (London: Oxford University Press, 1977), p. 74.

54. Goran Hyden, *Beyond Ujamaa in Tanzania* (Berkeley: University of California Press, 1980), pp. 26, 88.

55. Donald Rothchild and Michael Foley, "The Implications of Scarcity for Governance in Africa," *International Political Science Review* 4, no. 3 (1983): 311-326; and Richard Rose and Terence Karran, "Inertia or Incrementalism?" Groth, *Comparative Resource Allocation*, chapter 2.

56. Henry Bienen's warning is appropriate: "Demands and participation must be kept analytically separate. Increased participation need not lead to increased effective demands." *Kenya: The Politics of Participation and Control*

(Princeton, N.J.: Princeton University Press, 1974), p. 194. Cf. Huntington, *Political Order in Changing Societies*, pp. 78-80, 222, 398.

57. On choice strategies, see Rothchild, *Scarcity, Choice, and Public Policy*, pp. 112-142. For a discussion of the stabilizing effects of mass political participation and one-party dominance in pluralistic societies, see Robert W. Jackman, "The Predictability of Coups d'Etat: A Model with African Data," *American Political Science Review* 72, no. 4 (December 1978): 1273-1274.

58. James M. Buchanan and Gordon Tullock, *The Calculus of Consent* (Ann Arbor: University of Michigan Press, 1971), p. 72.

59. Nelson Kasfir, "State Formation and Social Contract Theory: Rwenzururu and the Southern Sudan" (Paper presented to the African Studies Association, Denver, November 6, 1971), p. 17.

60. Charles E. Lindblom, *Politics and Markets* (New York: Basic Books, 1977), p. 75. On the trade-off between short-term political stability and economic development and state autonomy, see Percy C. Hintzen and Ralph R. Premdas, "Guyana: Coercion and Control in Political Change," *Journal of Interamerican Studies and World Affairs* 24, no. 3 (August 1982): 352.

61. Deutsch, "Social Mobilization," pp. 497-498. For a Third World but non-African example of these processes, see Lloyd D. Musolf and J. Fred Springer, *Malaysia's Parliamentary System: Representative Politics and Policymaking in a Divided Society* (Boulder, Colo.: Westview Press, 1979), Chapter 7.

62. Cynthia H. Enloe, *Ethnic Conflict and Political Development* (Boston: Little, Brown, 1973), pp. 81-82.

63. *West Africa*, October 2, 1978, p. 1935.

64. On the role of international "regimes" in facilitating cooperation, see Robert O. Keohane, *After Hegemony* (Princeton, N.J.: Princeton University Press, 1984), p. 244.

65. Lindblom, *Politics and Markets*, p. 136.

66. Alvin Rabushka, *Race and Politics in Urban Malaya* (Stanford, Calif.: Hoover Institution Press, 1975), p. 99.

67. Manfred Halpern, *Applying a New Theory of Human Relations to the Comparative Study of Racism* (Denver, Colo.: University of Denver, Race and Nations Monograph Series, 1969), p. 14. Also see his "Changing Connections to Multiple Worlds," Helen Kitchen, ed., *Africa: From Mystery to Maze* (Lexington, Mass.: Lexington Books, 1976), esp. fns. 12 and 13, pp. 43-44.

68. Pierre L. van den Berghe, "A Response to Heribert Adam," Rothchild, *State Versus Ethnic Claims*, p. 149.

69. On the nuances in control strategies, see Ian Lustick, *Arabs in the Jewish State* (Austin: University of Texas Press, 1980); and Heribert Adam and Hermann Giliomee, *Elite Power Mobilized* (New Haven, Conn.: Yale University Press, 1979).

70. That is, unless what Jacques J. Maquet describes as "the premise of inequality" is accepted by rival parties. See his *The Premise of Inequality in Ruanda: A Study of Political Relations in a Central African Kingdom* (London: Oxford University Press, 1961), pp. 160-172. Also see Philip Mason, *Patterns of Dominance* (London: Oxford University Press, 1970), pp. 11, 21, Part 3.

71. Cf. M. G. Smith, "Institutional and Political Conditions of Pluralism," in Kuper, *Pluralism in Africa*, p. 38.

72. John de St. Jorre, *A House Divided: South Africa's Uncertain Future* (New York: Carnegie Endowment for International Peace, 1977), pp. 133-134.

73. Daniel J. Crowley, "Cultural Assimilation in a Multiracial Society," *Annals of the New York Academy of Science* 83, Article 5 (January 18, 1960): 851.

74. David D. Laitin, "The Political Economy of Military Rule in Somalia," *Journal of Modern African Studies* 14, no. 3 (September 1976): 466.

75. Milton Obote, "Language and National Identification," *East Africa Journal* 45, no. 1 (April 1967): 4-5. Also see Ali A. Mazrui, *Cultural Engineering and Nation-Building in East Africa* (Evanston, Ill.: Northwestern University Press, 1972), pp. 99-100.

76. Of course, in part it was also an expression of Africa's authentic cultural distinctiveness. See Ruth Schachter Morgenthau, *Political Parties in French-Speaking West Africa* (Oxford: Clarendon Press, 1964), p. 14. Also see Ezekiel Mphahlele, "The Fabric of African Cultures," *Foreign Affairs* 42, no. 4 (July 1964): 624.

77. René Lévesque, *An Option for Quebec* (Toronto: McClelland and Stewart, 1968), p. 14. On resistance to assimilationist tendencies in Yugoslavia, see Dennison Rusinow, *The Yugoslav Experiment 1948-1974* (Berkeley: University of California Press, 1978), pp. 134-135.

78. Philip Abbas Ghabashi, "The Growth of Black Political Consciousness in Northern Sudan," *Africa Today* 20, no. 3 (Summer 1973): 35.

79. Oliver Albino, *The Sudan: A Southern Viewpoint* (London: Oxford University Press, 1970), p. 109. Also see Abel Alier, "The Southern Sudan Question," Dustan M. Wai, ed., *The Southern Sudan: The Problem of National Integration* (London: Frank Cass, 1973), p. 20.

80. The Addis Ababa Agreement was reprinted in *Grass Curtain* 2, no. 3 (May 1972); also see Dunstan M. Wai, "Geoethnicity and the Margin of Autonomy in the Sudan," Rothchild, *State Versus Ethnic Claims*, p. 319.

81. See Jane J. Martin, "How to Build a Nation: Liberian Ideas About National Integration in the Later Nineteenth Century," *Liberian Studies Journal* 11, no. 1 (1969): 25, 29-30, 39-42; Martin Lowenkopf, *Politics in Liberia: The Conservative Road to Development* (Stanford, Calif.: Hoover Institution Press, 1976), pp. 3, 87, 147-149, 172; and Merran Fraenkel, *Tribe and Class in Monrovia* (London: Oxford University Press, 1964), Chapter 6.

82. Quoted in Fraenkel, *Tribe and Class*, p. 205.

83. On purposive depoliticization as applied to "open" societies, see Arend Lijphart, *The Politics of Accommodation: Pluralism and Democracy in the Netherlands* (Berkeley: University of California Press, 1968), pp. 129-130; and Eric A. Nordlinger, *Conflict Regulation in Divided Societies* (Cambridge, Mass.: Harvard University Center for International Affairs, 1972), p. 26. With respect to "closed" societies, see Huntington, *Political Order in Changing Societies*, pp. 78-92; Rothchild, *Scarcity, Choice, and Public Policy*, pp. 74-75; and Nelson Kasfir, *The Shrinking Political Arena* (Berkeley: University of California Press, 1976).

84. *West Africa*, April 24, 1978, p. 775.

85. See Rothchild, "Military Regime Performance," pp. 462-466; and Maxwell Owusu, "Politics Without Parties," *African Studies Review* 22, no. 1 (April 1979): 89-108; and Marvin G. Weinbaum, "Afghanistan: Nonparty

Parliamentary Democracy," *Journal of Developing Areas* 7, no. 1 (October 1972): 60-64.

86. The movement of Japanese-Americans to detention camps during World War II would represent a temporary form of displacement. Cynthia Enloe also extends displacement to genocide, the "physical elimination of a group considered so 'marginal' to the state's needs that its loss is deemed inconsequential." "Internal Colonialism," p. 149.

87. Although Hanoi originally intended to expel only the Chinese upper middle class, less fortunate Chinese who identified with their departing kinsmen on the basis of economic and ethnic ties joined the exodus from Vietnam. See *New York Times*, January 14, 1980, p. A8.

88. CDU/CSU Party, *White Paper on the Human Rights Situation in Germany and of the Germans in Eastern Europe* (Bonn: 1970), pp. 47, 55, 64-65.

89. Similarly, Guinea's Sékou Touré resisted any linkage between Western private investment and outside pressure on human rights in his country. See *West Africa*, December 17, 1978, p. 2472.

90. On doubts concerning the full implementation of these agreements, see Walter Schwarz, *The Tamils of Sri Lanka*, Report no. 25 (London: Minority Rights Group, 1975), p. 8.

91. Donald Rothchild, "Majimbo Schemes in Kenya and Uganda," Jeffrey Butler and A. A. Castagno, eds., *Boston University Papers on Africa: Transition in African Politics* (New York: Praeger, 1967), pp. 291-318.

92. These efforts at external buffering are discussed in Donald Rothchild, "U.S. Policy Styles in Africa: From Minimal Engagement to 'Liberal Internationalism,'" in Oye, *Eagle Entangled*, pp. 314-316.

93. Michael Clough, "From Rhodesia to Zimbabwe," Michael Clough, ed., *Changing Realities in Southern Africa* (Berkeley: Institute of International Studies, 1982), pp. 49-50; Jeffrey Davidow, *A Peace in Southern Africa* (Boulder, Colo.: Westview Press, 1984), pp. 44, 46; and Robert S. Jaster, *A Regional Security for Africa's Front-Line States: Experience and Prospects* (London: International Institute for Strategic Studies, Adelphi Paper 180, 1983), p. 12.

94. Rothchild, *Racial Bargaining*, Chapter 4; Y. P. Ghai and J. P. W. B. McAuslan, *Public Law and Political Change in Kenya* (Nairobi: Oxford University Press, 1970), pp. 413-456; and S. A. de Smith, "Fundamental Rights in Commonwealth Constitutions," *Journal of the Parliaments of the Commonwealth* 43, no. 1 (January 1962): 10-19.

95. For a forthright statement to this effect, see The United Republic of Tanzania, *Report of the Presidential Commission on the Establishment of a Democratic One Party State* (Dar es Salaam: Government Printer, 1965), pp. 30-33.

96. Federal Republic of Nigeria, *The Constitution of the Federal Republic of Nigeria 1979* (Lagos: Federal Government Printer, 1978). On group rights, see Vernon Van Dyke, "Human Rights as the Rights of Groups," pp. 730-40; and Karl von Vorys, "Group Rights and Instruments of Public Policy in the Development of Viable, Democratic Systems" (Paper presented at the International Studies Association, Washington, D.C., February 19, 1975), p. 20.

97. Donald Rothchild, "Middle Africa: Hegemonial Exchange and Resource Allocation," in Groth, *Comparative Resource Allocation*, pp. 172-175.

98. See Charles H. Kennedy, "Policies on Redistributional Preference in Pakistan," (Chapter 3) and Gordon P. Means, "Ethnic Preference Policies in Malaysia" (Chapter 4) in this volume.

99. Calculated from *West Africa*, May 10, 1982, p. 1262.

100. See Daniel G. Matthews, "Nigeria 1984:   An Interim Report," no. 24, *CSIS African Notes* (February 29, 1984):   3.

101. *New African*, no. 218 (November 1985): 24; and *Africa Research Bulletin* 22, no. 9 (October 15, 1985):   7786-7787.

102. In India, police opened fire on 30,000 people rioting in Gujarat against government redistributive policies that set aside a number of civil service jobs and university positions for the disadvantaged castes and classes, *New York Times*, April 29, 1985, p. 6.

103. Frequently, one is inclined to link the short-term benefits of hegemony with long-term costs, but as the case of Somalia's military takeover has shown, a hegemonial approach has enabled decisionmakers to establish a language policy that widened the potential decision elite to include broader participation by those from the southern region and rural areas generally.   See David D. Laitin, *Politics, Language, and Thought: The Somali Experience* (Chicago: University of Chicago Press, 1977), p. 132.

104. Aaron Wildavsky, *Speaking Truth to Power* (Boston: Little, Brown, 1979), p. 389.

3

Policies of Redistributional Preference in Pakistan

CHARLES H. KENNEDY

Pakistan has suffered, before and since its emergence as an independent nation-state, from disabilities associated with regional differences and the resultant nationalist demands that these differences generate. The creation of Pakistan itself was fueled by the spectre of prospective second-class citizenship for Muslims in a Hindu-dominated independent India. From Partition until the dismemberment of the state in 1971, Pakistan served as the ideological battleground for antithetical visions of Punjabi and Bengali nationalisms. Indeed, the consequences of such conflicting visions—the 1971 civil war and the emergence of Bangladesh—have marked what may prove to be the only instance in the twentieth century of a successful violent secessionist movement. Ominously, since the mid-1970s the spectre of regionalism and possible future secessionist sentiment has been voiced by disaffected, if ambitious, Pathan, Baluch, and Sindhi leaders.

Pakistan's decisionmakers have addressed such demands through a variety of policies running the gamut of hegemonic and hegemonic exchange strategies.[1] Arguably (at least according to actual or would-be secessionists), Pakistan has consistently pursued policies of "subjection" since Partition, first in the quest for West Pakistani and later Punjabi dominance. Indisputably, Pakistan has also attempted assimilative strategies at several points—Muhammed Ali Jinnah's Urdu language policy; the One Unit Scheme of 1959 which called for the administrative unification of West Pakistan; and, currently, President Zia-ul Haq's Nizam-i-Islam (Islamic Order). Indeed, the Islamic response to ethnic diversity is inherently assimilationist, with its stress on the unity of the *ummah* (community of believers) and on egalitarianism. President Zia took such assimilative tendencies a step further by pursuing a strategy of avoidance, duly buttressed by Islamic precedence, to justify the banning of political parties (many regionally based), in the Federal

Council election of March 1985. His argument was that partisan divisions are not countenanced by Islam.[2]

More extensive and comprehensive, however, have been Pakistan's redistributional responses to ethnoregionalist demands. Since 1949 Pakistan has instituted complex regional and special interest quotas for recruitment to federal, provincial, and semigovernmental posts. Similar quotas with myriad variations have also been applied to the admission policies of educational institutions. Currently, within Pakistan, recruitment to most public sector jobs and admission slots to educational institutions are subject to ethnoregional quotas. Indeed, Pakistan's policies have approached the logical extreme of a redistributional strategy. But despite such policies, which are ostensibly designed to reduce ethnoregional conflict, Pakistan has remained persistently beset by ethnoregional conflict. Ironically, some of this conflict is attributable to the redistribution policies themselves.

This chapter analyzes Pakistan's redistributional policies and is divided into four sections. The first presents the case for the adoption of such policies in Pakistan, that is, the policy logic of redistributional programs; the second provides a brief history of the development of policies of ethnoregional preference in Pakistan; the third examines the operation of the system; and the final section offers general conclusions derivative of Pakistan's experience.

The Policy Logic of Pakistan's Redistribution Policies

The origin of Pakistan's policies of ethnic preference can be traced to the pre-Partition sentiments and strategies of the Muslim League. Perhaps the most compelling argument for the creation of Pakistan, one stressed with increasing fervor by Muhammed Ali Jinnah following the Lahore Resolution of 1939, was that Muslims in an undivided India would remain subservient to the Hindu majority. To substantiate this hypothesis it was only necessary to point out the wide discrepancies in Muslim and non-Muslim representation in the civil service, the military, educational institutions, and the business elite. Muslims, the argument ran, underrepresented in each could not bridge the gap until they had a state of their own. The eventual form such an interpretation took was the demand for a separate state based on the amalgamation of majority Muslim communities. Therefore, the demand for a state was linked inextricably with the demand for increasing regional representation of Muslim majority areas.

After Partition the focus shifted to similarly defined gaps between East and West Pakistan. Bengalis (East Pakistan) were underrepresented in the civilian bureaucracy, the professions, business, the military, and politics.[3] The politicization of these gaps eventually led to the dismemberment of the

Pakistani state in 1971. Before this occurred, however (as will be detailed below), regional quotas were introduced in the federal bureaucracy and in educational institutions that were designed to ameliorate such perceived gaps. Since 1971 the justification for the continuation of such regional quotas has been predicated on three characteristics of post-Bangladesh Pakistan: multiethnicity; developmental gaps between regions of the state; and the persistence of unbalanced institutional and political development.

Multiethnicity

Since the secession of Bangladesh from Pakistan in 1971, truncated Pakistan has contained four major ethnic groups. In numbers the largest of these are the Punjabis, followed in respective populations by the Sindhis, the Pathans, and the Baluch.[4] Each of these groups is defined by an admixture of linguistic and geopolitical attributes. For instance, Punjabis are centered in the province of the Punjab and their ostensible mother language is Punjabi, Sindhis are domiciled in the Sind and speak Sindhi, Pathans live in the Northwest Frontier Province (NWFP) and speak Pushto, and Baluch live in Baluchistan and speak Baluchi or Brohi.

However, there is significant slippage in such definitions of ethnic identity. Pakistan's ethnic compostion has been deeply affected by external and internal migration. Most obvious are the so-called *muhajirs* (literally, pilgrims), Indian Muslims who opted for Pakistan at the time of Partition and who settled primarily in the urban areas of Pakistan, particularly Karachi.[5] Further, since Partition there has been a largely ignored though significant "trickling" of in-migration, primarily from India and Bangladesh. The 1981 census estimates that this trickle has accounted for 4 million immigrants to Pakistan since 1948.[6] Not included in the census data are the variously estimated 2.5-4 million temporary migrants/refugees from Afghanistan. Most such individuals speak Pushto and are ethnically related to the Pathans. Most live in border communties or camps in the NWFP, but there have been recent attempts to officially disperse some of these residents to the Punjab and Sind, and considerable unofficial resettlement of individual Afghans in the major cities of Pakistan has already taken place.

In addition to such in-migration, there has been considerable interprovincial and intraprovincial migration as well. Two patterns deserve note. One has been the migration from rural to urban areas, spurred by brighter employment opportunities in the cities. The urban population of Pakistan grew by 7.25 million from 1972 to 1981.[7] A second phenomenon, also largely fueled by employment prospects, has been the interprovincial shifting of population from the Punjab and the Federally Administered Tribal Areas (FATA) to Baluchistan and Sind.[8] One consequence of these population shifts has been the ethnic diversification of Pakistan's major urban areas—Karachi, Lahore, and Rawalpindi/Islamabad. Another has been the threat to the indigenous population of the smaller provinces, particularly Baluchistan, of outside domination. For instance, Quetta, the capital of Baluchistan, has more Pathan residents that indigenous Baluch.[9]

There is also slippage in regard to linguistic determinants of ethnicity. Pakistan has a national language—Urdu—and perhaps 90 percent of the population can speak or at least understand it.[10] Conversely, less than 5 percent of the population can speak or understand English, yet it has remained the predominant medium of higher education, the courts, and the government since Partition. Though there have been numerous attempts to enhance the significance of Urdu in the national life of Pakistan, and parallel attempts to limit the importance of English, such assimilative strategies have been blunted from two directions. On the one hand, it is argued that increasing the importance of Urdu will detract from the importance of provincial languages, particularly Sindhi and Pushto. On the other hand, President Zia's recent attempts to enhance the importance of Urdu by replacing English as the language of examination at the matriculation level by 1989 and by making Urdu instruction compulsory have been met with firm resistance from educators, the middle class parents of affected students, and provincial autonomists. In brief, their respective arguments are that (1) no adequate Urdu language classroom materials exist; (2) discarding English will limit the international prospects of Pakistani graduates; and (3) such a policy will favor native speakers of Urdu and closely related Punjabi at the expense of other linguistic communities.[11]

Underlying the debate regarding the enhancement of Urdu in Pakistan is the fact that Urdu, though the link language of the state, is the primary language of only a small minority of the population. The 1981 census found that Urdu is "usually spoken" by only 7.6 percent of the households in Pakistan (mostly *muhajirs* or children of *muhajirs* and primarily in Karachi or Islamabad), while Punjabi is spoken in 48.2 percent of the homes, Pushto in 13.1 percent, Sindhi in 11.8 percent, Siraiki in 9.8 percent, Baluchi in 3 percent, Hindko in 2.4 percent, and Brohi in 1.2 percent.[12] A further complicating factor is that such linguistic diversity is not related exclusively to provincial domicile. For instance, only 79 percent of those domiciled in the Punjab speak Punjabi in their homes; correspondingly, 68 percent of those domiciled in the NWFP speak Pushto; 57 percent of the Baluchistan population speak Baluchi or Brohi; and only 52 percent of people living in the Sind speak Sindhi.[13]

Developmental Gaps

However loose the definition of ethnic groups in Pakistan, indisputable gaps exist in the respective levels of development of the four provinces. Generally speaking the province of the Punjab and the region of urban Sind are the most highly developed, while other provinces are relatively less developed.[14] Indicators of such gaps include differentials in per capita income,[15] life expectancy,[16] levels of industrialization,[17] urbanization,[18] literacy,[19] and electrification.[20] Such gaps are widely perceived and politicized in Pakistan and have resulted in a fear of an actual or potential Punjabi or, to a lesser extent, urban Sindhi (*muhajir*) domination. Indeed, the most traumatic event in the history of Pakistan, its dismemberment, was occasioned by perceptions on both sides of a widening inequality between East and West Pakistan. Arguably, Pakistan currently faces several prospective Bangladeshes. Most serious is the demand for greater provincial autonomy in Baluchistan. But there are also significant autonomist sentiments in the Sind, and episodic, though recently dormant, demands for an independent Pathan state—Pakhtunistan.[21]

Institutional and Political Imbalance

A third factor underlying the adoption of redistributional policies has been the inability of Pakistan to achieve balanced levels of institutional development. Pakistan inherited a political system from Britain that was crafted to suit the needs of a colonial power whose overriding concern was to rule a subject people. As a consequence, a primary tool for effecting this control—the administrative system inherited by the new state—demonstrated highly complex patterns of organization, well-established forms of socialization of its members, and a remarkable degree of institutional autonomy. Countervailing institutions, particularly those responsible for ensuring governmental responsiveness to the demands of the public—legislatures, interest groups, local governments—existed only in attenuated forms.

This developmental gap has persisted since Partition. For example, Pakistan has been unable to establish an orderly succession of political leaders. Indeed, the outcomes of the four national elections held in Pakistan—1965, 1970, 1977, 1985—were each challenged by the losers as "rigged."[22] Similarly, Pakistan, ostensibly a republic, has been subject to extensive periods of martial law and military rule. During such periods elected national assemblies,[23] albeit only marginally consequential during periods of civilian rule, have been disbanded, and political activity has been prohibited or placed under severe restraints. Also, despite numerous attempts at reform, local governments are still dominated by civilian bureaucrats deputed from the federal government for service in the provinces. Functionally, such "district adminstration" has performed the roles typically entrusted in other systems to elected officials—revenue collection, revenue distribution, rule adjudication, and the execution and formulation of local policy.[24]

Given this context, meaningful input into the policymaking process can only be ensured by securing representation in the civilian bureaucracy. Therefore, to represent the interests of ethnic groups within Pakistan, or to redress the consequences of inequalities between such groups, requires the direct incumbency of "nationals" in the civilian bureaucracy. This factor makes redistributional policies critical to federal policymaking in Pakistan. It can be argued that denial of civilian bureaucratic office in Pakistan is functionally equivalent to the denial of political representation. Also, as we will see in more detail below, such policies provide needed mechanisms for distributing benefits to special interests.

These three factors—ethnic diversity, unequal regional/provinical development, and unbalanced institutional growth—explain the nature of Pakistan's policies of ethnic preference. Accordingly, Pakistan's policies of preference have been based on three principles: (1) the remedial or compensatory principle; (2) the proportional principle;[25] and (3) the principle of patronage. The first provided legitimacy for the introduction of the quota system in Pakistan. Before 1971 the quota was designed to ameliorate inequalities between East and West Pakistan and after 1971 to mitigate inequality between "more developed" and "less developed" regions. The quota was justified as a necessary expedient designed to close the gap between levels of development while promoting national integration. The second principle, that of proportional representation, has been invoked both as a goal and a strategy for effecting the compensatory principle. That is, there is a loose fit between ethnic groups and provincial domicile; therefore, proportional representation favors backward regions or groups. More directly, the proportional representation principle is invoked as a mechanism to ensure equality of representation in governmental institutions. Finally, patronage serves to lubricate the wheels of government by providing a mechanism to benefit one's friends and, by implication, to punish one's enemies. Of course, such patronage provokes the formation of vested interests whose existence in turn partially explains the persistence and growth of the policies of preference.

The Development of Ethnoregional Policies of Preference

Public Sector Quotas

Due to a number of factors, the most salient of which was the disparity of service representation between East and West Pakistan immediately subsequent to Partition, a federal quota that applied to candidates seeking competitive entry to officer level ranks in the federal bureaucracy was introduced in 1949.[26] The provisions of this policy stipulated that 20 percent of the vacancies in the Central Superior Services were to be filled by "merit" as a consequence of the Central Superior Services (CSS) Exam. The remaining 80 percent of the vacancies were to be filled by the application of the following formula: East Pakistan, 40 percent; Punjab and Bahawalpur, 23 percent; Karachi, 2 percent; and Sind, Khairpur, Northwest Frontier Province and Frontier States and Tribal Areas, Baluchistan, Azad Kashmir, and Kashmir refugees, 15 percent.[27] As originally formulated the quota had application to approximately one hundred vacancies per year. Its thrust was to "prudently" increase the representation of Bengalis who were woefully underrepresented at the time of Partition, by, in effect, creating separate competitive pools in East and West Pakistan.

Advocates of the quota considered it a temporary remedial expedient, which would be phased out five to ten years after its introduction.[28] However, the quota grew and prospered in the fertile soil of regional animosities between East and West Pakistan. By 1956 the quota policy, which had started as an adminstrative directive within the Establishment Division, had grown to the status of a statutory exception to the nondiscrimination clause in the first constitution.[29] This status was reiterated in the 1962 constitution.[30] The quota also became a frequent topic of debate in the National Assembly. Perhaps more importantly, however, its range also underwent steady expansion. By the early 1950s the quota was applied to vacancies filled by the Federal Public Service Commission (FPSC), through interview, and eventually to departmental and attached departmental recruitment to posts in the central government. Indeed, by 1971 the quota had application to approximately two thousand entry level positions in the federal government each year.[31]

Despite the phenomenal growth of the quota designed to keep East and West Pakistan together, centrifugal tendencies became too great, and the resultant civil war left Pakistan dismembered. With the secession of Bangladesh went the most potent original rationale for the quota system. Since 1971, however, instead of disintegrating, the quota system has become increasingly vibrant. Immediately following the war (1972-1973) the quota was temporarily transformed into a confusing array of six "zones" and four "provinces,"[32] and in August 1973 the quota emerged in its present form.

The current formula reads 10 percent merit; 50 percent Punjab (including Islamabad); 7.6 percent urban Sind (Karachi, Hyderabad, and Sukkur); 11.4 percent rural Sind (areas in Sind other than those above); 11.5 percent NWFP; 3.5 percent Baluchistan; 4 percent Northern Areas and Centrally Administered Tribal Areas; and 2 percent Azad Kashmir.[33]

Why this particular formula was chosen is open to conjecture. It is true that the percentages roughly accord with the respective populations of the regions[34] and that the modified system follows the relative weightings of the 1949 formulation. However, no public sources indicate that such criteria were used in formulating the regional quotas. More importantly, the more general questions of whether in the aftermath of the 1971 war the quota should have been continued, and if continued what form it should take, seem to have had no formal public consideration and were not addressed directly by any of the numerous administrative commissions of the late 1960s and early 1970s.

In any event, following the war Zulfikar Ali Bhutto's economic policies served as a catalyst for the continued expansion of the quota system. Between 1972 and 1975 Bhutto nationalized numerous industries (banks, insurance, heavy machinery, natural resource extraction, rice, cotton, textiles, cement, automobiles, and so forth). As a consequence, such industries, which were formerly in the private sector, became subject to the terms and conditions of federal employment. That is, recruitment to autonomous and semiautonomous corporations (188 such institutions existed in 1981) became subject to the quota.[35]

However, the quota expansion was not restricted solely to federal initiative. During the early 1970s the provinces established their own quotas for provincial recruitment. In the Punjab recruitment to provincial posts became subject to three intraprovincial reservations—Zone 1, developed districts; Zone 2, undeveloped districts; and merit on an all-Punjab basis.[36] Since the reorganization of the Punjab in 1982, such distinctions have remained.[37] In the Sind provincial recruitment has followed the federal demarcation of rural and urban.[38] In the NWFP provincial recruitment has been divided into five zones, two that are relatively "less developed," and three that are relatively "more developed."[39] The scope of the provincial quotas is analogous to that of the federal quota. That is, recruitment to competitive posts in the Provincial Civil Service, direct recruitment to posts advertised by the provincial public service commissions, recruitment of provincial departments, and recruitment to provincially administered public enterprises are all subject to the relevant quotas.

Educational Institution Quotas

The development of admission quotas to educational institutions has paralleled the evolution of public sector quotas. Though it has not been possible to determine the precise origin of quota policies in educational institutions, several such quotas were in operation by the early 1950s. The main rationale for such early policies was to ensure the admission to professional schools of candidates domiciled in provinces or regions in which no such institutions existed. For instance, one early quota, the 1956 Prospectus for Dow Medical College, Karachi, delineated twelve separate regional quotas, or "reservations" for candidates domiciled in areas in which no medical school facilities existed.[40] As the number of professional schools increased in Pakistan, admission policies became "tagged" to certain regions. The 1964 West Pakistan Medical Colleges Prospectus outlined a complex system of tagged and nontagged reservations. For instance, one college that fell under the ambit of this prospectus, King Edward Medical College, Lahore, admitted 150 students in 1964—114 from the tagged region (89 general merit and 25 reserved for rural tagged region) of Rawalpindi and Lahore divisions, and Lyallpur and Sargodha districts; 13 from general merit all-West Pakistan; and 23 from fourteen separate categories (five of which were made applicable to King Edward Medical College) of potential reservations for nontagged candidates.[41]

Since the abolition of One Unit in 1969 (the disestablishment of West Pakistan into four provinces), the authority for the establishment of educational institution admission quotas has devolved to provincial boards of admission. Though the constitution of such boards varies from institution to institution the dominant pattern is for the board to consist of the vice chancellor or principal of the relevant university, the governor or governor's representative(s), and several relevant provincial secretaries. These boards compose an annual prospectus of admission, which is sometimes published in newspapers and provincial gazettes. Though such prospectuses vary between institutions and within institutions across time, there are three basic patterns of intraprovincial quotas. The first treats the province as a whole for merit, then sets regional quotas for each individual district/division within the province. For instance, admission to Bolan Medical College (1977) called for the selection of 33 candidates on an all-Baluchistan basis of merit and divided the remainder of the vacancies, 100, among the sixteen districts of the province.[42] The second pattern treats the province as a whole for merit, as in the first pattern, then provides reservations for an exceptional handful of "backward" regions/districts. For instance, admission to Gomal University's (NWFP, 1982) MBA and MSc programs reserved seats for only two relatively underdeveloped regions: Dera Ishmail Khan division, and the Tribal/Frontier region of Peshawar, Hazara, and Malakand divisions.[43] The third pattern, less common than the preceding patterns, treats each institution as a "neighborhood school" and restricts admission to surrounding subprovincial regions. For instance, in 1982 admission to Sind Medical Colleges was determined as follows: admission to Dow Medical College was restricted to those candidates domiciled in Karachi districts; Liaqat Medical College was restricted to those domiciled in Hyderabad, Thatta, Badin, Tharparkar, Nawabshah, and Sanghar Districts; and admission to Chandka Medical College was restricted to candidates from Larkana, Sukkur, Shikapur, Khairpur, Jacobabad, and Dadu districts.[44]

Most institutions allow interprovincial admission only on the basis of ad hoc reciprocity between consenting admission boards, except for candidates from regions without relevant academic institutions. In the latter category fall candidates from Azad Kashmir, FATA, and Baluchistan. Accordingly, most institutions provide modest reservations for candidates from one or more of these regions. At the behest of the federal government more formal interprovincial agreements have been established for Baluch nationals. In 1982, 116 seats in various medical colleges, 88 seats in engineering universities, 15 seats in the College of Home Economics in Karachi, 7 seats in the National College of Arts, 50 seats in cadet colleges, 7 seats in the College of Dentistry, and 8 seats in various MBA programs were reserved for Baluch students in institutions outside their home province.[45] The individual merits of such Baluch candidates is determined by a separate Baluch selection committee, which has established its own set of intraprovincial quotas against the vacancies.[46] Admission to the only federal university in Pakistan, the Qaid-i-Azam University, is subject to the application of the federal quota.

Unlike public sector quotas, which have been protected from litigation, the application of educational quotas has generated a considerable legal literature. Recent court opinion has stemmed from the Supreme Court's decision in Muhammed Iqbal Khan Niazi v. Vice Chancellor, University of Punjab[47] in which the court ruled that the prospectus of a college was akin to a bylaw and therefore could be challenged by the courts and could be struck down in whole or in part due to unreasonableness. Citing this finding superior courts in Pakistan have ruled that age is not a reasonable basis of discrimination in admission policies;[48] that denial of admission on the basis of technicalities is unreasonable and hence invalid;[49] and that to be valid the terms of the prospectus of admission must be complied with exactly.[50]

Gender Quotas

Much less significant than regional quotas in Pakistan are gender quotas. Indeed, direct recruitment to the federal and provincial services has never been subject to a gender quota, and since 1973 there have been no gender restrictions on assignment to occupational cadres either.[51] Furthermore, the application of gender quotas to other public sector posts is relatively infrequent and informal. Occasionally, advertised posts in individual ministries and autonomous corporations are made gender specific, but there is no comprehensive policy that governs such assignment. Indeed, it appears that such quotas are established on an ad hoc basis by the relevant ministry or department. Despite such informality, however, the percentage of women in the federal bureaucracy, though still modest, has increased dramatically from 1.8 percent of the total in 1973 to 3.1 percent in 1980.[52]

Gender quotas are more prevalent and important in admission policies to educational institutions, particularly in regard to medical colleges. The usual pattern employed is to subdivide relevant intraprovincial quotas into male and female slots and to conduct separate competitions within each. Such quotas have been challenged in the courts both by aggrieved unsuccessful male candidates on the grounds of reverse discrimination and by aggrieved female candidates who would have fared better in open competition.[53] All such suits have been dismissed on the grounds that there is no ban against gender preference in the constitution.[54]

Special Interest Quotas

Interacting with and complicating the already complex systems of regional and gender quotas in Pakistan are what for want of a better term may be called special interest quotas. This is a residual category including all quotas that are not based on region or gender. In the public sector the most important special interest quotas are the reservations for military officers. Since 1979 10 percent of the vacancies in the competitive entry examinations conducted at the federal and provincial levels have been reserved for former military officers.[55] Ten percent of the vacancies in the prestigious All-Pakistan Unified Grades (the elite cadre of the federal bureaucracy) are also set aside for military officers. Other examples of special interest quotas in the public sector include age relaxations (extensions of age limits for application) for governmental servants and military personnel in various recruitment forums and episodically applied age relaxations by the FPSC for recruitment from specified minority communities.[56]

However, such public sector initiatives pale in comparison to myriad special interest quotas applied to admission policies of educational institutions. To name but a few, there are quotas that reserve seats for *children* of medical doctors, attorneys, central government servants, provincial government servants, military officers, engineers, university employees, and recipients of military decorations;[57] there are also quotas for "sportsmen" (usually field hockey or cricket players), widows, destitutes, foreigners, and non-Muslim minorities. In many institutions there are governor's seats reserved for appointees by the governor. Seats are also reserved for federal government employees, provincial government employees, holders of various special degrees and diplomas, and employees of business concerns. Additionally, there are numerous provisions for age relaxations for various groups and an across-the-board provision for the addition of twenty exam points to any candidate who had completed training in the National Cadet Corps or Women's Guards.[58]

As is the situation regarding other provisions of educational quotas there is a vibrant case law surrounding special interest quotas for educational institutions. However, the courts have vacillated on this issue. On the one hand, the courts have ruled that age relaxations in admission policies for governmental servants are invalid[59] and that reservation of posts for governmental servants are unjustifiable,[60] but other cases have upheld the persistence of both practices. The courts have also upheld the validity of governor's seats and have ruled that reservations in medical colleges for sportsmen and doctor's children are valid because "it is to be borne in mind that marks and marks alone cannot be the sole criterion for determining the suitability of a person for admission to medical colleges."[61] One consequence of such vacillation is that, barring violation of their own prospectuses, admission boards of educational institutions are allowed to establish whatever special interest quotas they deem fit with little fear regarding prospective legal reversals.

This section has demonstrated two characteristics of Pakistan's policies of preference. First and most obviously, Pakistan's policies of preference are extraordinarily, if not hopelessly, complex. Second, they have an extremely wide range of applicability. Currently, recruitment to virtually every position in the federal and provincial governments and admission to all major institutions of higher education in the state are subject to one or more quotas. Neither development was intentional. What started out as a relatively simple and limited program designed to ameliorate the unhappy effects of Bengali underrepresentation in the secretariat and the negative consequences of geographical concentration of educational institutions has in three decades been transformed into a highly complex, if not out of control, program of entitlement for virtually every governmental vacancy and training slot.

The Operation of the System

We now turn to three sets of questions associated with the operation of the quota system: (1) How is the quota system applied to the selection process of recruits at the various levels of its operation? How precisely and enthusiastically is it implemented? How does the system work? How is an individual's domicile determined? (2) Is the bureaucracy of Pakistan regionally representative? Do such levels of representation differ in regard to rank, type, or governmental service? (3) How does the quota system interact with the bureaucratic system of Pakistan? What are the fixed costs of the system?

How Does the Quota System Work?

Procedures. At the federal level the quota is applied to the selection process in three distinct patterns. The first pattern applies to competitive entry through the Central Superior Services Examination administered by the FPSC. The quota is applied to both entry level competition and to the competition for entry into occupational cadres. After the number of vacancies is determined for a given year by the Establishment Division, an open competition is held in which candidates from all domiciles participate. Ten percent of such vacancies are filled by candidates who scored highest on the exam regardless of domicile (the merit quota). The remainder of the vacancies are filled by the respective merit-rank within domiciles. For example, if, in a hypothetical year, there are one hundred vacancies—ten will be filled on the basis of overall merit, fifty will be drawn from the remaining most meritorious Punjabis, eight from the most meritorious rural Sindhis, and so forth, as per the federal quota. Since 1979, given our hypothetical sample, ten additional appointments would also be made from the pool of military candidates. The suitability of such military candidates for appointment is determined by a military personnel board—military candidates do not take the CSS Exam. Vacancies in occupational cadres are simply allocated on the basis of the quota, the preferences of individual candidates, and exam scores. They are also subject as above to the 10 percent military quota. This pattern applies to the recruitment and assignment of approximately two hundred fifty vacancies each year.

The second pattern is applicable to the selection of candidates who enter on the basis of interview, either administered by the FPSC or directly by the ministry or department concerned. Here posts are advertised or listed against regional vacancies. For example, if the Ministry of Defense needs to recruit communication engineers, the ministry sets domicile requirements (ostensibly based on regional balances within the ministry) for the relevant vacancies. In an illustrative case the ministry had to fill fourteen vacancies: seven appointments were to come from the Punjab, four from the NWFP, and three from rural Sind. Accordingly, the FPSC interviewed candidates only from such domiciles and made appointments on the basis of such interviews.[62] This pattern applies to the recruitment of approximately three thousand candidates each year.

The third pattern is primarily applicable to the recruitment of individuals to autonomous corporations and public enterprises. This pattern requires the submission of "domicile certificates" by the candidates to the relevant personnel boards, but the domicile limits are typically not binding on the actual hiring practices of such boards. However, considerations of regional balance often play a significant role in hiring decisions, and pressure to comply with the terms of the quota is sometimes exerted by concerned federal and provincial ministries.

The recruitment to competitive-entry provincial posts is subject to provincial quotas analogous to the first pattern; recruitment to other provincial posts follows the second pattern; and recruitment to provincially administered public enterprises reflects the third pattern. Selection to educational institutions (predominantly under provincial control) is determined by the independent decisions of college and university personnel boards/selection committees in light of their relevant institutional quotas.

The Determination of Domicile. The determination of an individual candidate's place of residence, usually and confusingly referred to as a "domicile," is critical to the functioning of Pakistan's regional quota systems. Given the stakes of such determinations as well as the inherent litigiousness of Pakistani culture, it is not surprising that such determination is replete with labyrinthine complexities. Indeed, even the lexicon that refers to the all-important proof of residence requires careful interpretation. For instance, there are two general species of proof of residence in Pakistan—the federal domicile certificate and the provincial residency certificate. Unfortunately, both are usually referred to interchangeably as domicile certificates. Properly speaking, the federal domicile certificate only indicates an individual's nationality. The origin of the certificate is rooted in the requirements of the Pakistan Citizenship Act of 1951. As part of the latter's procedure for proving Pakistani citizenship, applicants were required to complete the infamous Form P, which among other things called for a declaration of a "place of domicile" including place, tehsil (subdistrict region), district, and province of domicile.[63]

This declaration of domicile has drawbacks as a procedure for establishing residency for the purposes of the regional quotas. First, under the Pakistan Citizenship Act of 1951 no proof of district residency has to be given the district magistrate (DM), the relevant authority. Second, the DM cannot revoke the domicile certificate on the grounds of a false declaration of residency; the certificate can only be revoked for the commission of traitorous acts against the state of Pakistan or for the fraudulent claim of Pakistani citizenship.[64]

To close such gaping loopholes and to protect their respective sons of the soil, the provinces have established their own methods for determining

be demonstrated that such domination would be particularly severe in the case of selection to the prestigious All-Pakistan Unified Grades.[76]

Therefore, it appears from all available evidence that the operation of the quota has made the bureaucratic system of Pakistan more representative. However, there are two major caveats to this finding. First, as Table 3.3 demonstrates, district-level representation in the bureaucracy is anything but equitable.[77] Indeed, five districts, each centers of education and culture, predominate: Lahore, Karachi, Rawalpindi, Islamabad, and Quetta. In each, district representation is at least three times the mean district representation (controlling for population) prevailing in the state as a whole. Further, less developed districts of Pakistan have remained woefully underrepresented, particularly in the NWFP, Sind, and Baluchistan, despite modest gains since 1973. One conclusion to be drawn from these figures is that the urban educated, relatively westernized elite of the society is favored in selection to the federal bureaucracy. Another is that inequalities of intraprovincial representation are greater than interprovincial inequalities. Finally, the quota system was not designed and consequently has done little to bridge the developed/backward gap within the state.[78]

The second caveat is derivative of the first. Namely, the operation of Pakistan's quota has proven an imperfect tool to dispense compensatory justice. Because the criterion for favored status (domicile) is largely ascribed and not based on need or achievement, it follows *et ceteris paribus* that the quota favors the relatively well-off candidate from both backward and developed regions. It does not serve to select less favored individuals to the bureaucracy but rather relatively favored individuals domiciled in relatively less favored regions. Therefore, it can be argued that the quota system, rather than weakening class distinctions in the state, actually serves to reinforce such distinctions.

What are the Fixed Costs of the System?

Regardless of the quota system's relative degree of success in promoting regional equality, the introduction of quotas has had several unhappy consequences in Pakistan. The first and most obvious is the systematic frustration of the merit principle in selection to public sector posts and educational institutions. In regard to posts subject to competition (direct recruitment bureaucracy and educational admissions), some candidates are selected who would not be eligible in the absence of the quota, and conversely, others are denied positions for which they would have been eligible solely on merit. In regard to posts subject to interview, prospective candidates with requisite qualifications for particular posts are systematically excluded because of regional or special interest considerations. In both

Table 3.3   Officers[a] of Federal Bureaucracy by District of Domicile
per 100,000 Population

Region	1973	1980	1983
Pakistan	9.2	12.7	13.3
Punjab	8.5	12.3	13.3
Islamabad	23.8	53.4	64.2
Rawalpindi	30.5	43.9	41.4
Campbellpur/Attock	3.1	9.2	9.4
Jhelum,	8.2	16.1	17.5
Gujrat	6.4	10.7	11.7
Mianwali	1.8	5.2	4.8
Sargodha	5.9	8.6	9.0
Lyallpur/Faisalabad	6.6	10.6	10.7
Jhang	4.3	6.3	7.1
Sialkot	9.7	13.9	15.4
Gujranwala	7.0	9.3	9.9
Sheikupura	2.4	4.7	6.6
Lahore	44.2	51.3	51.4
Kasur	---	4.2	4.1
Dera Ghazi Khan	1.9	3.2	3.2
Muzaffargarh	1.7	2.5	1.7
Multan	4.1	5.2	6.1
Sahiwal	3.3	5.1	4.4
Vehari	---	2.6	1.9
Bahawalpur	2.9	5.4	5.5
Bahawalnagar	1.7	2.6	2.5
Rahim Yar Khan	2.1	2.9	3.1
Rural Sind	2.0	5.0	5.4
Jacobabad	0.6	2.0	2.4
Larkana	3.0	5.2	6.9
Nawabshah	2.1	5.0	5.2
Khairpur	3.6	7.4	8.8
Dadu	2.6	6.1	6.2
Badin	---	2.1	1.8
Sanghar	1.6	5.4	5.4
Tharparkar	2.5	5.5	4.9
Thatta	3.0	3.0	4.5
Shikarpur	---	8.6	9.0
Baluchistan	3.8	7.5	7.3
Quetta	14.8	50.5	52.6
Pishin		5.9	3.9
Loralai	1.6	3.1	3.4
Zhob	1.2	5.0	2.5
Chagai	1.5	6.7	5.0
Sibi	3.9	7.8	12.5
Nasirabad	---	2.5	1.5
Kachi	1.8	2.9	8.4

(cont'd)

Table 3.3 (cont'd)

Region	1973	1980	1983
Pakistan	9.2	12.7	13.3
Baluchistan			
Kalat	0.7	2.7	3.1
Khuzdar	---	1.3	1.1
Kharan	1.3	2.3	1.4
Lasbela	0	2.7	1.0
Makran/	1.0		
Turbat		1.3	1.0
Gawadar		0.9	3.4
Panjgur		1.2	1.4
NWFP	5.0	10.9	11.9
Chitral	0.6	4.3	5.8
Dir	0.6	1.4	2.5
Swat	0.5	2.9	2.7
Malakand	4.8	9.3	6.8
Hazara/	4.3		
Kohistan		0.9	0.3
Manshera		9.1	11.3
Abbotabad		15.0	17.0
Mardan	4.8	10.3	12.1
Peshawar	9.6	17.8	18.8
Kohat	3.8	11.7	12.6
Bannu	4.8	12.4	13.7
Dera Ishmail Khan	9.1	18.3	19.7
Urban Sind	33.5	28.8	25.6
Karachi	49.9	40.0	33.6
Hyderabad	8.7	10.9	12.2
Sukkur	8.2	8.3	10.9
Northern Areas/FATA[b]	2.8	7.7	14.0
Azad Kashmir[b]	2.2	3.4	5.3

Sources: Government of Pakistan, Population Census Organization, Housing Population Census of Pakistan, 1980-1 (Islamabad: 1982); GOP, Report on the Sixth Triennial Census of Federal Government Servants as of 1st January 1980 (Islamabad: MPCPP, 1981); GOP, Report of the Fourth Triennial Census ...1973 (Islamabad: MPCPP, 1976); and GOP, Federal Government Civil Servants Census Report, January 1983 (Islamabad: MPCPP, 1984).

[a]For 1973, gazetted officers; for 1980 and 1983, officers of grade 16 and above.

[b]Based on estimate of population.

instances the quota selects candidates who, according to whatever criterion of merit is employed, are not the "best" available for appointment. Arguably, such a selection policy makes the bureaucracy less efficient and educational institutions and those trained in them less professionally competent.

Second, the procedures for implementing the quota often result in significant delays in filling vacant posts. For example, if a post falls vacant in a federal department subject to FPSC rules, the notification of the vacancy is passed on to the FPSC both for advertisement and for the assignment of the quota. Then the post is listed, candidates with the requisite qualifications and domicile are interviewed, and ideally an individual is recommended for appointment. If all runs smoothly, this process takes approximately six months. However, if, as is often the case, it proves difficult to find an individual possessing both the requisite qualifications *and* domicile, the process can be delayed considerably. It is not unusual for a case of this type to drag on for two or three years, with the post left vacant or filled on an ad hoc basis by the relevant department. It is also not uncommon for vacancies to go unfilled because no candidates with the requisite qualifications and domicile apply for the given job. In recent years this latter phenomenon has occurred with increasing frequency, particularly in regard to technical vacancies.[79] Also, since 1977 the FPSC has had trouble filling vacancies through the competitive examination process. Indeed, in 1982 the FPSC was forced to conduct an extraordinary competitive examination limited to candidates from urban Sind, rural Sind, the Northern Areas, and Azad Kashmir to address the shortfall.[80]

Delays caused by attempts at compliance with domicile regulations are also frequent in admissions to educational institutions. It is not uncommon for individual candidates to miss an entire academic year because of their inability to produce requisite certificates of domicile. An extreme but not atypical example of such delay culminated in a Supreme Court judgment. One Shahnaz Maqbool was denied entry to the 1974 class of Liaqat Medical College on the grounds that her domicile form was not properly signed by the relevant district magistrate and therefore her application for admission was incomplete. After pursuing her case in several administrative and legal forums she was finally admitted on an order from the Supreme Court five years later to the class of 1979![81]

Third, the complexities of the quota may discourage prospective candidates from standing for the competitive examination and/or from seeking other government employment. The opportunity costs of participating in the recruitment process to the Central Superior Services are great. A candidate must first prepare and stand for the examination, then wait for the results before knowing whether he or she has gained entry to a preferred occupational group.[82] Such costs are compounded by the uncertainty of the operation of the quota. From the perspective of an individual candidate there are two avenues to assure assignment to one's preferred occupational group: score in the top 10 percent of the successful recruits (i.e., within the merit range); or score relatively high in comparison with one's domicile cohorts. However, it is impossible to adequately assess the probabilities of either of these outcomes given the limited amount of information available to candidates. Until group assignment takes place candidates do not know how they stand in relation to other candidates. Similarly, as mentioned above, recruitment by interview is a slow and uncertain process. Given such considerations would-be candidates are encouraged in effect to seek alternative careers.

Fourth, the quota system as it operates in Pakistan encourages the perception of widescale corruption in the bureaucracy and in the universities. Obviously, the implementation of the quota has opened up new and potentially lucrative avenues of corruption, but its prevalence is exaggerated at least in regard to domicile fraud. However, there remains a widely held belief (which contains more than a kernal of truth) that special interest slots, particularly in educational institutions, are open only to the influential and/or to the highest bidder. Such perceptions do little for the morale or status of such institutions, nor for that matter do they serve the cause of national integration.

Finally, the quota system, though demonstrably increasing regional representation in the bureaucracy, has also served to reinforce invidious distinctions between regions. The system's reliance on a small merit reservation, its use of widely publicized, regional-based distinctions of performance in scoring examinations, and its variability in determining relevant qualifications or levels of skill lead many to believe that job-seekers from the more favored regions bear the brunt of the government's attempts to equalize access to the bureaucracy or to the professions. Indeed, hardly a day passes when one of the major Pakistani dailies does not run an editorial by a disaffected individual, usually a Punjabi, calling for greater reliance on merit in some phase of federal personnel policy and implicitly claiming reverse discrimination. Conversely, individuals domiciled in less favored regions must reconcile themselves to the fact that they are perceived to be less qualified than their counterparts from the Punjab or Karachi. Such perceptions are given added credence due to the quota's implicit paternalism, and they reinforce the already formidable ethnic, cultural, racial, and linguistic cleavages between regions. Indeed, the very existence of the quota provides statutory verification of the belief that some regions/peoples are superior/inferior to others.

Conclusion

It may be dangerous to attempt to draw general conclusions from the admittedly unique particulars of Pakistan's experience with policies of preference.[83] However, I maintain that four tendencies relevant to the Pakistani experience are likely to be found in any state adopting policies of preference. The intensity of such tendencies is a function of the contextual pattern of ethnicity in the relevant society and the enthusiasm of policy implementation. Clearly, Pakistan's experience is extreme both in regard to the strength of ethnoregionalist sentiment and in regard to the enthusiasm of implementation and the wide range of policies designed to combat such regionalism.

First, *policies of preference tend to spread.* The quota system in Pakistan had relatively humble origins, with application to barely one hundred vacancies per year. But once established, the logic of its spread became irresistible. Namely, if the quota was necessary to redress inequality of representation through the competitive examination process for bureaucratic posts, was it not also necessary for it to be applied to the arguably more arbitrary process of selection of candidates through interview? If the quota was necessary to redress inequalities of qualifications in federal governmental departments, wasn't it also necessary for provincial recruitment? Finally, if the quota was necessary to redress distinctions in qualifications, was it not also necessary to get at the font of such inequalities — the educational institutions themselves?

Second, *policies of preference are hard to terminate.* The framers of Pakistan's quota system expected that the need for the system's operation would end five to ten years after its commencement. Further, since the quota's introduction, virtually every administrative report, numerous service associations, and innumerable editorials have called for the quota's dismantlement.   But even modest proposals calling for marginal modifications in the terms of the quota's operation have been ignored by successive governments because the quota has become a political bombshell.[84] Any modification of the terms of the quota would most likely be interpreted as favoring some groups at the expense of others and would be attributed to the ulterior motives of clever politicians.   Given this consideration, prudent policymakers in Pakistan have given the quota a wide berth.

Third, *policies of preference create vested interests.* Pakistan's quota policies distribute benefits, both to those domiciled in less favored regions and those eligible for special interest considerations. It is obviously in the interest of those who benefit to maintain such benefits. Accordingly, the most ardent supporters of the quotas are groups representing the smaller provinces; those most opposed to the quotas are the civilian young from the

Punjab and Karachi. In such an environment it is easier to extend the number of quotas than to dismantle the existing programs. In the former case little opposition to implementation is encountered.

The final tendency may be the most important. No matter how thoroughly implemented, *policies of preference have fixed costs.* The more obvious costs include the effects of abandoning the merit principle on adminstrative efficiency and professionalism and the attendant procedural entanglements associated with implementing such policies. Pakistan has suffered enormously from both types of costs. However much one imagines a set of policies that minimizes such costs, the cost of the inevitable trade-off between equality of outcome between groups and policies of preference remains.

Paradoxically, Pakistan's redistribution policies have been effective in increasing ethnoregional proportionality, but they have done little to restrict, or in some cases have served to enhance, the level of ethnoregional conflict in the state. An unintended by-product of the effectiveness of Pakistan's redistributional policies has been the exacerbation of perceptions of inequities between ethnoregional groups. After all, the effectiveness of policies of preference is measured, finally, by the level of ethnoregional conflict in the society. Pakistan has already suffered one successful seccessionist movement and is currently faced with the prospect of several others—a record of performance unforeseen by the proponents of such policies.

Perhaps redistributional policies are less effective in dampening ethnic conflict in societies in which such conflict is potentially severe; or, alternatively, such policies are more effective in societies in which there is already an established history of accommodation along ethnoregional lines. Indeed, the adoption of redistributional policies before such a bedrock of accommodation exists may actually enhance rather than diminish ethnoregional conflict. Pakistan's redistributional policies at least have made ethnic allegiance more salient in the political process, thereby enhancing class distinctions that already existed at the time of Partition. Unfortunately, once the redistributional strategy was in place, it became, and still is, increasingly difficult to reverse the course of its policy logic.

Notes

This is a much expanded and revised version of "Policies of Preference in Pakistan," *Asian Survey* 24, no. 6 (June 1984): 688-703.

1.   Terminology used to describe policies of preference in this chapter accord with Donald Rothchild's usage in Chapter 2 of this volume.
2.   The most cogent expression of this argument is found in Government of Pakistan (hereinafter referred to as GOP), Cabinet Division, *Ansari*

Commission's Report on Form of Government 24th Shawal 1403 (Islamabad: Printing Corporation of Pakistan Press, 1984), pp. 21-44.

3. One prevalent interpretation of the causes of the 1971 war posits that grievances generated by such inequalities exacerbated the racial and linguistic gaps between the two groups and made the civil war inevitable. See, for instance, Rounaq Jahan, *Pakistan: Failure in National Integration* (New York: Columbia University Press, 1972).

4. Approximate provincial populations in 1984 were Punjab, 52.4 million; Sind, 20.8 million; NWFP, 14.5 million, (including Federally Administered Tribal Areas, excluding Afghan refugees); and Baluchistan, 4.7 million. Comparable figures for ethnic communities do not exist. Populations were calculated by the author using 1981 census data and assuming 3 percent annual growth in each province since that date.

5. Such individuals enjoyed a disproportionate amount of influence in the professions, the civil bureaucracy, and the business community of Pakistan, particularly during the early years of the state. However, as this group ages its influence has and will continue to decline. See Theodore P. Wright, Jr., "Indian Muslim Refugees in the Politics of Pakistan," *Journal of Commonwealth and Comparative Politics* 12, no. 2 (July 1974): 189-201.

6. GOP, Population Census Organization, Statistics Division, *Main Findings of the 1981 Population Census* (Islamabad: MPCPP, 1983), p. 15.

7. Calculated from ibid., p. 5.

8. Ibid, p. 15.

9. Selig Harrison, *In Afghanistan's Shadow: Baluch Nationalism and Soviet Temptation* (Washington, D.C.: Carnegie Endowment, 1980).

10. See Agha Iftikhar Husain, "Introduction of Urdu in Administration," Agha Iftikhar Husain, ed., *Studies in Public Administration of Pakistan* (Islamabad: Pakistan Administrative Research Center, 1979).

11. Arguments gathered from a reading of *Muslim, Dawn,* and the *Pakistan Times,* January-June 1984.

12. GOP, Population Census Organization, *Main Findings of the 1981 Population Census* (Islamabad: 1983), p. 13.

13. Given such complexity, an assimilative linguistic policy is perhaps doomed to failure. It is interesting to note that ballot papers in the December 19, 1984, referendum were written in Urdu, English, and Sindhi. Responses, however, were recorded only in Urdu.

14. For the purposes of the federal quota Sind is divided into urban areas —Karachi's three districts and Hyderabad and Sukkur districts—and rural areas —the remaining ten districts of the province.

15. Shahid Javed Burki, "A Note on Perspectives on Economic Development and Regional Inequalities in Pakistan" (Paper presented to the 32nd Annual Association of Asian Studies (AAS) Meeting) calculates that in 1977 the mean per capita income in the two richer provinces (Punjab and Sind) was 28 percent higher than that of the poorer provinces, p. 4.

16. In 1977 the mean life expectancy in rural Baluchistan was forty-two years and rural NWFP, 44 years. The mean life expectancy in the Punjab and Sind was sixty years. Ibid., p. 7.

17. In 1977 there were 3000 "registered factories" with more than 20 employees in the Punjab and 2889 in Sind, while in the NWFP there were only 262 such factories and in Baluchistan 9. GOP, Statistics Division, *Enquiry on Labour Welfare, 1977* (Karachi: GOPP, 1981), pp. 1-15. Similarly, in 1977,

of all "establishments with 20 or more employees excluding defense establishments," 7,859 were found in the Punjab, 2,673 in the Sind, 1,046 in NWFP, and 290 in Baluchistan. GOP, *Report on Annual Establishment Inquiry, 1976-7* (Karachi: GOPP, 1981), p. 1.

18. GOP, Population Census Organization, *Housing and Population Censuses of Pakistan* (Islamabad: 1983), p.1.

19. GOP, Population Census Organization, *Main Findings of the 1981 Population Census* (Islamabad: 1983), p. 11.

20. GOP, Population Census Organization, *Housing Census of Pakistan, 1980,* (Islamabad: 1982), p. 17.

21. Useful overviews of the nationalities question are found in Lawrence Ziring, *Pakistan: Enigma of Political Development* (Boulder, Colo.: Westview Press, 1980); Khalid bin-Sayeed, *Politics in Pakistan* (New York: Praeger, 1981); Anwar Syed, *Pakistan: Islam Politics and National Solidarity* (New York: Praeger, 1983); and in Selig Harrison, *In Afghanistan's Shadow*.

22. Actually, the "winner," General Ayub Khan, was already in power in 1965. The 1970 election resulted in an overall plurality for Sheik Mujibur Rehman; the eventual prime minister, Zulfikar Ali Bhutto, received a plurality only in West Pakistan. The aftermath of the 1977 election resulted in charges by the Pakistan National Alliance of widespread rigging and fraud on the part of the Pakistan People's party. Partially as a consequence of these charges, Bhutto was overthrown by a military coup that installed General Zia-ul Haq in July 1977. The 1985 elections were held on a partyless basis and have been challenged by opposition parties as unrepresentative.

23. The Majlis-i-Shura (Federal Council) established in 1982 is an advisory body that was wholly appointed by the president, General Zia-ul Haq. Elections for the council were held in March 1985.

24. Major local government programs in order of original implementation include Panchayats, Village Panchayats, Basic Democracies, Integrated Rural Development, and the People's Works Program. Since 1979 the Local Government Program has been in effect. Elections to local bodies were held in 1979 and 1983.

25. "Proportionality recognizes the group basis of politics in communally divided societies and attempts to achieve rough equity among groups rather than among individuals." Milton J. Esman, "The Management of Communal Conflict," *Public Policy* 21, no. 1 (Winter 1973): 62.

26. The first quota system for which written documentation exists was implemented in 1950 with application to the entering recruits of that year. GOP, *Second Report of the Pakistan Public Service Commission for the Period 1st January to 31st December 1949* (Karachi: Manager of Publications, 1950), p. 7. However, according to members of the 1948 recruits (those who entered service in 1949) the quota was in effect during their selection as well. The terms of the 1949 quota, slightly different from the 1950 quota, were 15 percent merit; 43 percent East Pakistan; and 42 percent West Pakistan. West Pakistan was further subdivided into Punjab, 23 percent; NWFP, Sind, Baluchistan, and Northern Areas and Tribal Territories, 17 percent; and Karachi, 2 percent. Source: interviews.

27. Ralph Braibanti, "The Higher Bureaucracy of Pakistan," Ralph Braibanti, et al., *Asian Bureaucratic Systems Emergent from the British Imperial Tradition* (Durham, N.C.: Duke University Press, 1966), p. 265.

28. Interviews with principals.

29. Article 17.

30. Article 240.

31. Three hundred sixty-seven candidates entered through competition (CSS Examination), 912 entered through Central Public Service Commission direct recruitment (by interview), and approximately 800 were admitted through departmental and attached departmental recruitment.

32. In January 1982 the quota read Zone 1 = Quetta, Kalat, and Lasbela; Zone 2 = Hyderabad and Khairpur divisions; Zone 3 = Lahore division and the districts of Rawalpindi, Gujrat, Sargodha, Lyallpur, Multan, and Sahiwal; Zone 4 = Bahawalpur division and the districts of Muzaffargarh, Dera Ghazi Khan, Campbellpur, Jhelum, Mianwali, and Jhang; Zone 5 = Agencies, states and tribal areas, including Added and Special Areas Adjoining Settled Areas; Zone 6 = Peshawar and Dera Ishmail Khan divisions (excluding Zone 5). Recruitment also was continued separately for the NWFP (Zones 5 and 6), Sind (Zone 2), Punjab and Bahawalpur (Zones 3 and 4), and Karachi. Percentile bases for such recruitment during 1972-1973 were never finalized.

33. GOP, Establishment Division, memo no. F 8/9/72 TRV, August 31, 1973.

34. In 1973 approximate populations were Punjab, 55.5 percent; urban Sind, 6.8 percent; rural Sind, 13.8 percent; Baluchistan, 3 percent; NWFP, 12.3 percent; Northern Areas and Tribal Territories, 3.7 percent; and Azad Kashmir, 4.4 percent.

35. GOP, *International Symposium on Economic Performance of Public Enterprises* (Lahore: Pakistan Administrative Staff College, 1981).

36. Zone 1 (developed) is the Lahore division and the districts of Rawalpindi, Gujrat, Sargodha, Lyallpur, Multan, and Sahiwal; Zone 2 (less developed) is the Bahawalpur division and the districts of Muzaffargarh, Dera Ghazi Khan, Campbellpur, Jhelum, Mianwali, and Jhang.

37. After reorganization the Punjabi quota reads Zone 2 is the Bahawalpur division, Dera Ghazi Khan, Jhang, Mianwali, Bhakkar, Attock, and Jhelum. All other areas of the Punjab make up Zone 1. *Pakistan Times,* November 4, 1983.

38. See note 14.

39. Individuals from the "less developed regions" are allowed age relaxations. Also part of the NWFP quota is a 10 percent provincial reservation for military personnel domiciled in the province.

40. Syed Abdul Wadood v. Pakistan, *All-Pakistan Legal Decisions, PLD* 1957 Kar 740.

41. Naseem Mahmood v. Principal, King Edward Medical College, *PLD* 1965 Lah 272.

42. Nasreen Fatima Awan v. Principal, Bolan Medical College, *PLD* 1978 Quetta 17.

43. *Pakistan Times,* November 25, 1981.

44. *Dawn,* February 2, 1982.

45. Interview, Services, and General Administration Department, Baluchistan.

46. Mir Ajmal Khan v. Selection Committee and 2 others, *PLD* 1984 Quetta 61.

47. *PLD* 1979 SC 1.

48. Rehmatullah v. University of Punjab, *PLD* 1982 Lah 411; University of Punjab v. Rehmatullah, *PLD* 1982 Lah 729.

49. Shahnaz Maqbool v. Province of Sind, *PLD* 1979 SC 32; Shahida Khatoom v. Government of Sind and 2 others, *PLD* 1982 Kar 454.

50. Muhammed Anwar v. Government of NWFP, *PLD* 1980 Pesh 83; Ali Muhammed v. Admission Committee, University of Engineering and Technology, *PLD* 1982 Pesh 106; Shoaib Dastgir v. Government of Punjab, *PLD* 1979 Lah 559.

51. Before 1973 women were not allowed to be members of the Civil Service of Pakistan or the Police Service of Pakistan. All such gender restrictions were lifted with the promulgation of Bhutto's administrative reforms.

52. Calculated from GOP, *Report on the Sixth Triennial Census of Federal Government Servants as on 1st January 1980* (Islamabad: MPCPP, 1981); and GOP, *Report on the Fourth Triennial Census of Federal Government Servants as on 1st January 1973* (Islamabad: MPCPP, 1976), p. 9.

53. Respectively, Ehsanul Haq v. Federation of Pakistan, *PLD* 1976 Lah 501; and Hamara Satwat Yusuf v. Government of Punjab, *PLD* 1971 Lah 641.

54. Ehsanul Haq v. Federation of Pakistan, *PLD* 1976 Lah 501. Gender quotas are likely to become increasingly significant in the near future because of the contemplated effects on women's educational institutions of the Islamization process in Pakistan.

55. Regularized in the Federal Public Service Commission Act, February 1980.

56. The standard employed by the FPSC since 1981 is a "three year relaxation to candidates belonging to scheduled castes, Buddhist community, recognized tribes of the tribal areas, Azad Kashmir, Northern Areas/Districts of Gilgit, Ghizar, Skardu, and Diamir." Classified advertisement, *Muslim* 1: 1981.

57. For instance, children of naval personnel who received the Sitara-i-Harb (Star of War) are reserved seats in the Sind Medical Colleges. See Miss Nasira Jabeen v. Pakistan, *PLD* 1980 Kar 128.

58. National Guards Act 1973 (Act LXI of 1973). The litany of special interest quotas is derived from prospectus notices found in Pakistani newspapers, 1982-1984, and from relevant court cases found in *PLD* 1957-1984.

59. Rehmatullah v. University of Punjab, *PLD* 1982 Lah 411.

60. Syed Abdul Wadood v. Pakistan, *PLD* 1957 Kar 740.

61. Naseem Mahmood v. Principal, King Edward Medical College, *PLD* 1965 Lah 272.

62. Example drawn from GOP, FPSC, *Annual Report for the Year 1976* (Karachi: MPCPP, 1978).

63. Muhammed Yar Khan v. Deputy Commissioner cum Political Agent 1980, *SCMR* 456.

64. Abdul Hafiz Khan v. Deputy Commissioner, Khuzdar, *PLD* 1983 Quetta 20.

65. Sind Permanent Residence Certificate Rules, 1971, found in *PLD* 1972 Sind Statutes 14-19.

66. Section 15 of the Sind Permanent Resident Certificate Rules reads: "The applicant claims a certificate of permanent residence because: i) he was born in Sind and at the time of this birth his father was domiciled in Sind; ii) he was born in Sind after the death of his father, who at the time of his death, was domiciled in Sind; iii) he was born in Sind of illegitimate birth, and his mother, at the time of his birth, was domiciled in Sind; iv) his parents are

domiciled in Sind, and have resided in Sind for a period not less than three years; v) his parents are not domiciled in Sind, but he is domiciled in Sind and has resided or been educated in Sind for a period not less than three years; vi) his father or mother is in the service of the Government of Sind and have put in not less than one year's service as such." *Gazette of Sind*, Extraordinary, 9 September 1971.

67. Sind PRC Rules, Section 8(1).

68. Zahar Ahmed v. Province of Baluchistan, *PLD* 1979 Quetta 57.

69. For example, Miss Riffat Parveen v. Selection Committee, Bolan Medical College, *PLD* 1980 Quetta 10 ruled that length of stay in a province was only one and not the exclusive factor in determining residency. Mir Ajmal Khan v. Selection Committee and 2 others, *PLD* 1984 Quetta 61 ruled that a special selection committee's determination of evidence could not be challenged by the high court.

70. Samina Nighat v. PRC Appellate Tribunal and 3 others, *PLD* 1983 Kar 324.

71. For instance, DMs cannot revoke a domicile certificate unless they can show cause and give the impugned holder a chance to be heard. Saeed Amir v. Principal, Khyber Medical College, *PLD* 1982 Pesh 51; Miss Nishat Saeed v. Chairman, Nomination Board, Azad Jammu, and Kashmir, *PLD* 1980 SC (AJK) 1; Munir Ahmed v. Government of Baluchistan, *PLD* 1981 SC 335. The courts also have overruled the findings of the Sind PRC Appellate Tribunal when the latter institution violated the terms of its constitutive act. Aziz Ahmed v. PRC Appellate Commission, Karachi, *PLD* 1980 Kar 568; and Tariq Majeed v. DM Jacobabad and Commissioner Sukkur, *PLD* 1983 Kar 202.

72. Unfortunately, it proved impossible to obtain adequate data regarding the regional composition of provincial services or of educational institutions, but considerable information exists regarding the composition of the federal bureaucracy. This section relies exclusively on the latter data.

73. Table 3.1 is compiled from GOP, *Federal Government Civil Servants Census Report, January 1983* (Islamabad: MPCPP, 1984); and GOP, *Report of the Fourth Triennial Census of Federal Government Servants as on 1st January 1973* (Islamabad: MPCPP, 1976).

74. Table 3.2 is compiled from for "secretariat," GOP, Cabinet Division, Statistics Cell, *Data on the Distribution of Federal Civil Servants by Grade, Etc., as on 1-11-74* (Islamabad: xerox, 1976); for "attached departments," GOP, Cabinet Division, Statistics Cell, *Report on Distribution of Federal Civil Servants Employed in Attached Departments and Subordinate Offices by Grade, etc.* (Islamabad: mimeo, 1976); and for "autonomous corporations," GOP, Cabinet Division, Statistics Cell, *Provisional Data on Distribution of Employees of Autonomous Organizations and Taken-Over Establishments by Grade, etc.* (Islamabad: mimeo, 1976).

75. Charles H. Kennedy, "Context, Content, and Implementation of Bhutto's Administrative Reforms" (Ph.D. diss., Duke University, 1979), pp. 188-223.

76. Ibid., p. 212.

77. Table 3.3 calculated by author from GOP, Population Census Organization, *Housing Population Census of Pakistan, 1980-81* (Islamabad: 1982); GOP, *Report on the Sixth Triennial Census of Federal Government Servants as on 1st January 1980* (Islamabad: MPCPP, 1981); GOP, *Report on the Fourth Triennial Census of Federal Government Servants as on 1st January*

1973 (Islamabad: MPCPP, 1976); and GOP, *Federal Government Civil Servants Census Report, January 1973* (Islamabad, 1984).

78. It is possible that provincial and educational quotas have been more responsive to such inequalities than the federal quota.

79. GOP, Federal Public Service Commission, *Annual Reports for the Years 1975, 1976, 1977, 1978, 1979, 1980, 1981, 1982, 1983* (Karachi/Islamabad: various dates).

80. There were 73 vacancies in all—urban Sind, 21; rural Sind, 36; Baluchistan, 5; Northern Areas, 9; and Azad Kashmir, 2. For the special exam, age limits were lifted from 25 to 35 years, and third division candidates, normally barred from participation in the CSS Exam, were allowed to compete.

81. Shahnaz Maqbool v. Province of Sind, *PLD* 1979 SC 32.

82. From 1974 until 1979, assignment to occupational groups was delayed an additional nine months due to the requirement, since discontinued, of a Final Passing Out Exam from the Academy for Administrative Training before assignment.

83. Cf. Myron Weiner, Mary Katzenstein and K. V. Narayana Rao, *India's Preferential Policies* (Chicago: University of Chicago Press, 1982).

84. For example, the Pay and Services Commission of 1978 examined the question of terminating the quota and recommended a modification calling for 20 percent merit, instead of the current 10 percent merit reservation. The proposal has not been accepted by the government nor has the report been released. Indeed, in March 1984 President Zia announced a ten year extension of the federal quota until 1994.

4

Ethnic Preference Policies in Malaysia

GORDON P. MEANS

The salience of ethnicity in politics and in public choice theory has become increasingly important in the study of Third World countries. This is not to suggest that other approaches may not also have important contributions to make. However, the increasing political mobilization of ethnic groups based on emotive symbols of exclusive cultural, religious, and ethnic identities has resulted in many countries becoming enmeshed in a bitter struggle for power and for the control of public policies by cultural-ethnic collectivities who tend increasingly to view politics as a life and death contest for domination or survival. Tolerance and accommodational solutions to problems become more difficult to achieve and implement when there is heightened ethnic mobilization. The conflict posed by ethnic mobilization forces dominant political elites to devise and experiment with various public policy strategies, both to harness and to control ethnic conflicts, which in many cases are the product of failed policies of an earlier era and of ineffective political institutions.

The nature of public choice options and strategies in ethnic conflict management is analyzed in depth by Donald Rothchild. While much of his analysis could be applied to a non-African setting, its applicability becomes central only after ethnic mobilization has reached a high level of intensity. In the case of Malaysia, ethnic diversity existed well before the colonial era, and with the advent of colonial rule public policy took account of ethnic diversity. There were clearly defined "ethnic management" policies. Even so, the emergence of "ethnic groups as utility maximizers," to use Rothchild's phrase, did not occur until popular democratic institutions were introduced and the country had attained its independence in the postwar era. For this reason, it is important to trace the evolution of ethnic preference policies in order to examine their implicit strategies and to explore how these policies eventually contributed to the preconditions implied in Rothchild's analytical schema.

During the colonial era most colonial powers attempted to establish an overarching system of European law while making some form of accommodation for indigenous cultural and legal norms. When the colony also had great cultural and ethnic diversity, the usual strategy of rule was to compartmentalize the legal system according to major religiocultural communities; thus, in some matters the legal system became highly ascriptive and particularistic according to the categories recognized by colonial authorities as the relevant cultural boundary markers in the colonized society. This is the pattern of rule and public policy that J. S. Furnivall characterized as a "plural society" in his seminal comparative study of British and Dutch colonial policy and practice.[2]

With the onset of the nationalist movement indigenous elites had to confront the issue of whether ascriptive and particularistic legal norms should be abolished, phased out, continued, or expanded. In the interest of national integration many former colonial states moved toward more universalistic legal principles, gradually or rapidly terminating ascriptively defined privileges and preferences. By contrast, other new states expanded the system of ascriptive compartmentalization of society by formulating new particularistic policies and programs. Malaysia is a prime example of the latter trend, where a system of ethnic preferences and privileges has been steadily expanded from the time of independence to the present day.

This chapter traces the origins and evolution of ethnic preferences in Malaysia and then examines contemporary policies in regard to public service, education, and the economy. Finally, some evaluation of trends, prospects, and problems is made.

Colonial Rule and Malay Special Rights

British rule in colonial Malaya was called an indirect system of rule because it was based on treaties with the Sultans of the Malay states. These treaties were signed between 1874 and 1914 and provided that each Malay ruler would accept a British officer "whose advice must be asked and acted upon on all questions other than those touching on Malay Religion and Custom."[3] Although these treaties made no mention of special rights for Malays, they implied that colonial rule was a form of trusteeship on behalf of the Malay rulers and their traditional subjects. Therefore, as the British began formulating laws for administration, the distinction between Malays, as the subjects of the rulers, and other immigrants to Malaya was made.

The first explicit system of Malay special rights applied to land tenure and was designed initially as a remedial measure to mitigate the impact of the new land laws established in the 1880s. The British had decided to establish a uniform system of land tenure based on the Torrens system as applied in

Australia. Under this system all land was vested in the crown (the Malay rulers for each state), and rights to land were based on leases issued by the crown. Land taxes were collected as "quit rent" on the leases. The system ignored proprietary rights based on custom and tradition and facilitated the economic development and exploitation of the country by developers, planters, and miners. This system of land tenure encouraged investments by Europeans and by the economically aggressive Chinese who were new immigrants to the country. As a consequence, Malays became concerned that land traditionally occupied by them should be exempted from the Torrens land tenure system. Thus, the Selangor Land Code of 1891 established the first definition of Malay land rights, providing "the original customary land holder must be a Mohammedan." Those holding such land were prevented from selling or mortgaging their land to non-Muslims.[4] Despite the recognition of customary rights, few Malays secured formal titles, so that the protection of customary land tenure ultimately depended on further legislation. Between 1913 and 1941 the Malay states passed legislation designating large areas of land as "Malay reservations" where only Malays could own or lease land, and non-Malays were prevented from holding mortgages or seizing land in discharge of debts.[5] While these laws protected Malay peasants from land speculators, they also insulated peasant Malays from the market economy and tended to encapsulate them in their traditional peasant economy and way of life. Whether these Malay land rights were a privilege or a preference is a matter of interpretation.

By treaty and legal fiction the responsibility of the British in the Malay states was to advise and assist the Malay rulers in the governance of their states. Therefore, the government was acknowledged as Malay, even though the top administrators were British officers. In the process of establishing the administrative structure it became apparent that local people were needed to fill lower and routine positions in the public service. The British, responding to the concerns of the Malay rulers about their loss of powers, established in 1905 the Sultan Idris College, which admitted the sons of aristocratic Malays for training in preparation for the public service. A separate Malay Administrative Service (MAS) was also created as a junior service to the Malayan Civil Service. The latter was staffed by Europeans, while the MAS recruited only those who were legally defined as Malays. In practice, the MAS recruited exclusively from the graduates of the Sultan Idris College until 1921, after which there was also some recruitment of Malays from some of the English-medium schools in the country. While local non-Malays were recruited for some public service positions, they entered the technical and professional services rathre than the more politically sensitive administrative positions that were monopolized at the top levels by Europeans and at the middle levels by the Malays.[6] This system of ethnic recruitment later became the basis for quotas and privileged access by Malays to the higher administrative positions as the date of Malayan independence approached.

In the field of education colonial policies also provided a precedent for Malay special rights. Chinese and Indians who had migrated to Malaya were considered aliens and transients. As a consequence, the government did not assume direct responsibility for their education but instead allowed the founding of private schools operated by Christian missions or private school boards, which were aided by some government grants if they met minimal government standards. A haphazard system of English-, Chinese-, and Indian-media schools were established under the direct administration of foreign missions or private school boards. The only direct responsibility the government assumed for education was for the system of Malay primary schools.

Free and compulsory education for Malays began in 1891, but because of limited funding and a shortage of teachers, it was many years before schools were provided for most Malay communities. In comparison to the private schools, Malay government schools were of poor quality; schooling was initially limited to four years and restricted to boys, and little else besides the three Rs and the Koran was taught. Malays who sought to obtain a better education had to enter the English-medium schools, many of which had, for the Maly, the stigma of being operated by Christian missions. Despite their poor quality, the Malay schools were free, whereas other schools, although government aided, required school fees.[7] Although Malays only had access to inferior educational facilities, the system of government-run Malay schools provided a precedent for later arguments that the Malays had acquired "special rights" in matters of education. Such arguments became more salient in the postwar era when politics were focused on the issues of Malayan independence.

In this brief survey of the colonial origins of preference policies, it should be noted that colonial policymakers accepted responsibility for the welfare of the Malay rulers and their subjects, but policymakers did not assume that colonial rule included a mandate for the social transformation and modernization of Malay society. Rather, colonial authorities acted on the premise that Malays should be encouraged to preserve their traditional way of life and that they deserved special policies and protection from the disruptive effects of economic development and competition from the immigrant communities and alien cultures. Malay special rights, in their embryonic form, were designed to preserve Malay traditions and social structures. It was only later, after independence, that Malay special rights were viewed as an appropriate public policy mechanism to effect the economic uplift of the Malays and the transformation of the ethnic compartmentalization of society as a whole.

Ethnic Preference in the Politics of Independence

When World War II ended the political situation in Malaya had been decisively altered. Although the British returned, it was obvious to all that Malaya was on the road to independence. Nationalism was on the rise, and democracy was extolled as the fundamental basis for future political institutions. However, the prospect of democracy combined with Malaya's ethnic diversity raised the fundamental question of the allocation of power. While there was some pious talk about a "noncommunal" approach to politics, the new democratic norms raised the calculus of ethnic numbers to the paramount consideration in politics. In 1947 the racial composition of Malaya (excluding Singapore) was 49.8 percent Malay, 38.4 percent Chinese, 10 percent Indian, and 1.8 percent others.[8] A mixture of nationalism, democracy, and ethnic cleavages is a potentially explosive combination in almost any setting. Malaya was no exception.

In 1946 the British Labour government prepared a constitution that embraced the principle that "all those who have made the country their homeland should have the opportunity of a due share in the country's political and cultural institutions."[9] The proposed constitution permitted every permanent resident in Malaya to qualify for citizenship eventually. No provisions were made for the continuation of special rights nor for a privileged position for the Malays. Because the reaction of the Malays to the Malayan Union proposals has been recorded in numerous works, it need not concern us here. What is of note is that the massive political mobilization of the Malays in response to this issue forced the British to withdraw their constitutional proposals for the Malayan Union and negotiate with those Malay leaders who had aroused such determined Malay resistance to the proposals. The issue was stated succinctly in the agreement negotiated between the British and the leaders of the United Malays National Organization: "As these States are Malay States ruled by Your Highnesses, the subjects of Your Highnesses have no alternative allegiance or other country which they can regard as their homeland, and they occupy a special position and possess rights which must be safeguarded."[10]

The constitution for the Federation of Malaya was drafted after prolonged negotiations with the Malay rulers and leading Malay politicians. It was designed to placate Malay hostility toward the Malayan Union proposals. Even so, the new constitution avoided giving explicit constitutional status to Malay special rights. Instead, such rights or privileges as already existed under prewar colonial policies were permitted to continue as a matter of ordinary law.

With the introduction of elections in 1952, the issue of Malay special rights became the object of much political dispute. For the first elections, the three largest communal parties had joined forces to contest the election and field a single slate of candidates. Together the United Malays National Organization, the Malayan Chinese Association, and the Malayan Indian Congress formed what came to be called the Alliance. This coalition quickly eclipsed all its rivals to dominate the political scene, and in 1955 it captured all but one of the seats in the first federal elections. Although the Alliance was formed as a united front to win elections, in office it was forced to seek agreement among its partners and resolve the difficult communal issues by negotiation among the leaders of the three coalition parties.

Earlier the British had put pressure on the leading political spokesmen for an intercommunal accommodative bargaining system; the British assumed that reasonable nonexploitive and balanced compromises could be reached to check the rising ethnic paranoia stimulated by the rapid political mobilization of ethnic communities.[11] The Alliance bargaining system was not quite what the British had originally envisioned, but it worked in much the same way. Alliance policies were worked out either through informal agreements among its leaders or within the structure of the Alliance National Council. In either case, the negotiations were always secret, and the agreements or compromises were seldom revealed to the public except in the form of subsequent government policy statements. Government policy on Malay special rights was but one of a series of complex compromises on a variety of communally sensitive issues. To understand the politics of special rights, it is necessary to elaborate the nature of the communal bargaining and to suggest the political calculations of the Alliance leaders.

The Malays were recognized as having a fundamental stake in the political system, while the non-Malays were assumed to be concerned primarily with their dominant position in the economy of the country. In effect, the communal compromises involved some trading of economic power for political power in an attempt to equalize the disproportionate distribution of power and wealth. Thus, communal compromises worked out within the Alliance involved policies designed gradually to increase non-Malay participation in the political system at the same time that Malays were to be given a greater stake in the economy. The Alliance leaders never made clear whether their ultimate objective was to eliminate, or merely to reduce, the gross inequities of ethnic distribution of economic and political power.

The demands of non-Malays for increasing political participation were met by the acceptance of the principle of *jus soli*: Everyone born in Malaya after independence would be counted as a citizen. Citizenship also could be obtained by naturalization, which involved meeting residency requirements (five to eight years), taking the oath of allegiance, and exhibiting proficiency in the Malay language.[12] In return, the Malayan Chinese Association and the Malayan Indian Congress adopted educational and linguistic policies that made the teaching of Malay compulsory in all schools and provided for a unified "Malayan" curriculum in all the different language media school systems.[13]

Malay special rights were a peculiar part of the communal compromise because they were designed to improve the economic position of the Malays and to ensure their dominant role in the political system. Malay special rights were thus perceived by many Malays as a key to their political control of the country and to their economic advancement as well. For this reason, the perpetuation and expansion of Malay special rights became a primary demand of many Malay politicians. The non-Malays were told, however, that special rights were necessary only because of the Malays' inferior economic condition. It was implied that when the Malays achieved economic parity with the non-Malays, special rights would be "reconsidered" and presumably be eliminated as "no longer necessary." Thus, through the years two contradictory sets of expectations have been generated among the Malays and the non-Malays as to whether Malay special rights are temporary, remedial and transitional, or permanent and inalienable.

What began in 1952 as a fairly balanced negotiating system gradually developed into what Donald Rothchild calls a hegemonial exchange relationship—the political power of the parties in the bargaining process always was unequal, and even more important, Malay special rights were designed to assure the political supremacy of the Malays in perpetuity.[14] Within the Alliance this meant the United Malays National Organization was assured the dominant role in the Alliance and in the government.

When the constitution for Malayan independence was being drawn up, the issue of Malay special rights was once again reexamined. A constitutional commission composed of foreign experts and headed by Lord Reid was charged with responsibility for drafting a new constitution. The Reid Commission found it impossible to reconcile two principles in its terms of reference: providing for "a common nationality" and "safeguarding the special position of the Malays." The first principle presumed the equality of all citizens while the second implied the creation of separate rights for two classes of citizens. The commission expressed its preference for the principle of equality, but it also acknowledged that the Malays would suffer if special privileges were suddenly withdrawn. To resolve the contradiction, the commission did not give Malay special rights constitutional status; rather, it allowed the system to continue by law, thus permitting termination or diminution by legislative enactment.[15] The commission's most controversial proposal provided that Malay special privileges would be continued "for a substantial period, but that in due course the present preferences should be reduced and should ultimately cease."[16] Accordingly, the commission recommended that the existing Malay privileges be reviewed fifteen years after independence with the objective of preparing for their eventual abolition.

The basic approach of the Reid Commission toward Malay special rights was vehemently rejected by the Alliance government, which mounted a successful campaign to include constitutional guarantees of Malay rights and to delete all provisions for their future reevaluation or eventual reduction. In the constitution that came into operation with Malayan independence in 1957, Malay special rights received special constitutional sanction and protection. Article 153 authorizes a system "to safeguard the special position of the Malays" through a system of quotas applied to the public service, to scholarships, to "training privileges," and to licenses for any trade or business. Article 89 sanctions the system of Malay reservations and permits the state legislatures to add to the land area declared a Malay reservation. The only limitation is that at least an equal area should be made available for general alienation and that the new area added to Malay reservations should include no land already owned by non-Malays.

To ensure that the operation of the democratic process would not erode or terminate Malay special rights, the Malays were given a unique constitutional status. Article 153 begins, "It shall be the responsibility of the *Yang di-Pertuan Agong* [paramount ruler][17] to safeguard the special position of the Malays and the legitimate interests of other communities."[18] Similarly, approval of the Conference of Rulers[19] is required for any change of policy relating to the "speical position of the Malays" and "Malay rights" as defined in Article 153; any amendments to Article 153 require the assent of the Conference of Rulers.[20] As a consequence, these provisions made Malay special rights as defined in Article 153 more difficult to amend than the constitution itself.[21]

The 1969 Riots, *Rukunegara*, and the New Economic Policy

On May 13, 1969, the capital of Malaysia was paralyzed by serious racial rioting in the immediate aftermath of a federal election during which Malay special rights had been an important issue. An account of the riots and various alternative explanations of their cause need not concern us here.[22] I shall merely note that the king declared an emergency, Parliament was suspended, and the National Operations Council assumed the reins of government; discussions were initiated with community leaders who were appointed to the National Consultative Council that acted in an advisory capacity to resolve the political crisis. After almost two years of emergency rule, Parliament was reconvened and asked to approve a series of constitutional amendments and a set of policy proposals that had been published in two white papers: *Rukunegara*[23] and *Towards National Harmony*.[24] The proposals and the amendments to the constitution were passed by Parliament by a vote of 125 to 17 in March 1971.[25] Finally, the economic aspects of the new strategy were enunciated as the New Economic Policy (NEP) and incorporated into the Second Malaysia Plan (1971-1975).

The NEP has remained a cornerstone of all subsequent national economic plans.

Whatever the immediate precipient of the riots might have been, the government assumed that the apparent challenge to Malay political hegemony and Malay rights was the primary issue at stake. Malaysia's prime minister at the time of the riots, Tunku Abdul Rahman, explained: "The last elections resulted in chaos and shook the very foundation of unity . . . because opposition parties criticized Malay rights and brought up other sensitive issues."[26] In formulating its new strategies, the government appeared to be making three main assumptions about the 1969 crisis and its political aftermath. First, political mobilization along ethnic lines regarding sensitive political issues was too intense. Second, there was inadequate public support for the earlier interethnic political bargains that had been incorporated into the constitution and public policies. Third, Malays were especially alienated because they suffered from relative deprivation and had not been achieving economic advancement as rapidly as non-Malays. Proceeding from this analysis, the post-1969 strategy included the following measures: A national ideology was proclaimed, called *Rukunegara*, which sought to enshrine "guiding principles for the nation," including key ethnic issues that had been incorporated into the constitution. The government strategy also sought "to remove sensitive issues from the realm of public discussions so as to allow the smooth functioning of parliamentary democracy."[27] Accordingly, Parliament passed constitutional amendments prohibiting public discussion or criticism of various parts of the constitution deemed to be "sensitive issues," including those relating to the powers and status of the Malay rulers, citizenship, the special position of the Malays, and the use of Malay as the sole national language. In order to end public debate and political mobilization, the sections of the constitution dealing with those "sensitive issues" were "entrenched" — that is, the consent of the Conference of Rulers was required if these sections of the constitution were to be altered by any future amendments. The prohibition against public discussion of these subjects applied to all, including Parliament itself.

Although not immediately apparent at the time, the most far-reaching of the post-1969 strategies were incorporated into the New Economic Policy, which was enunciated in the Second Malaysia Plan.

> The plan incorporates a two-pronged New Economic Policy for development. The first prong is to reduce and eventually eradicate poverty, by raising income levels and increasing employment opportunities for all Malaysians, irrespective of race. The second program aims at accelerating the process of restructuring Malaysian society to correct economic imbalance, so as to reduce and eventually eliminate the identification of race with economic function.[28]

The first objective, the eradication of poverty, was to be pursued by overall policies of economic growth and development that would be beneficial to all Malaysians regardless of race. For the second objective, that of "restructuring Malaysian society," the government proposed an expansion of the system of Malay special rights and preferences with new quotas and government assistance programs to give Malays privileged access to education, the professions, investment opportunities, ownership of capital, and new jobs and management positions arising from expansion in the economy. It was argued that these policies designed to "restructure Malaysian society" were necessary for ethnic peace and social justice. Impressive statistics were presented to show how the Malays lagged behind the non-Malays in various sectors of the economy and in the distribution of wealth, investments, and ownership of capital. The anxiety of non-Malays about these policies was met by an assurance by Prime Minister Abdul Razak that the expansion of Malay privileges would not involve the expropriation of property, the loss of jobs, or the denial of the rights of the non-Malays. He explained that "what is envisioned by the Government is that the newly created opportunities will be distributed in a just and equitable manner."[29]

In practice, the New Economic Policy has been a blend of policies stressing both economic growth and the redistribution of economic opportunities to the Malays. The NEP established the target of 30 percent Malay ownership and participation in all industrial and commercial activities by 1990. With this target as a goal, government policymakers have been hard pressed to devise an ever-expanding set of policies designed to bring Malays into all aspects of the economy in the proportion promised and by the target year of 1990. In practical terms, the implementation of the NEP has meant the extension of ethnic quotas, not only within the government and in public institutions but in the private sector of the economy as well. Most of the quotas are set by administrative decision and are not to be found in legislation. Therefore, the regulations are extremely diversified, and they are subject to constant revision, depending on the evaluation by policymakers of progress toward the goal enunciated in the NEP policy statement of 1971. Because of the massive expansion of the system of ethnic preference quotas, it is possible to trace only the general outlines of the operation of the policies of ethnic preferences as applied in Malaysia today.

Ethnic Preferences in the Public Services

The Malay character of the government is reflected in the recruitment patterns for the civil service. At independence the colonial Malay Administrative Service, with its total Malay membership, was merged into the elite Malayan Civil Service. The latter established a 4:1 recruitment ratio in favor of

Malays. The External Affairs Service, the Judicial and Legal Services, and the Customs Service employed 3:1 Malay recruitment ratios, but no quotas were established for the professional and nonprofessional (technical) services.[30] Because the top administrative and elite services were covered by Malay recruitment quotas, Malays predominated in the top policymaking positions in the public service. Thus, administrative positions formerly filled by British expatriate officers were filled almost exclusively by Malays who were promoted at a rapid rate to fill the gaps created by the "Malaysianization" of the public services. Later the Malayan Civil Service, the External Affairs, Judicial, Legal, and Customs Services were all combined into the unified Malaysian Administrative and Diplomatic Service, which recruits on the basis of a 4:1 Malay ratio. Quotas also apply to the military services, but the ratios are not disclosed for security reasons.

Because the recruitment quotas are applied to the higher level positions, the bias in favor of Malays increases and is most discernible in the higher ranks. For example, in 1968, 36.3 percent of the Division I government officers were Malay, 36.1 percent were Chinese, and 21.5 percent were Indian. In the same year 85.1 percent of the superscale positions in the Malayan Civil Service were Malay, 7.4 percent were Chinese, and 6.4 percent were Indian.[31] However, if the entire public service of the federal government in all divisions including the industrial and manual group are included, the ethnic division in 1969 was about 37 percent Malay and 63 percent non-Malay.[32]

More recent figures on the ethnic composition of the public service are not readily available, but it is very likely that the quota system is transforming the ethnic distribution of positions in the middle levels of the public services as well as the higher levels. In 1973 a respected leader of the opposition, Dr. Tan Chee-khoon, revealed in Parliament that out of 9,000 persons recruited into government service between 1969 and 1973, 98 percent were Malay. Furthermore, if the armed forces were also included, the Malay percentage increased to 99 percent.[33] If these figures are accurate, then it is clear that hiring practices, not formal quotas, have determined most of the shifting configuration of employment in the public sector. As more Malays have acquired education and qualifications for technical or specialized jobs, the natural proclivity of the government, particularly after the NEP, has been to fill the positions with Malays if at all possible.

Both the police and the armed forces have a quota system for hiring. However, for the police, the problem has been to recruit sufficient Chinese, who tend to view police work with disdain. Considering the problems of policing a multiethnic society, the police have succeeded in recruiting a fairly well balanced ethnic mix for its constabulary. As in the other service, Malays predominate in the top positions. In the armed services, the army is heavily Malay while Chinese officers were in the majority in the air force in 1969, apparently because of the technical qualifications required and the opportunity to move from the air force to employment with a civilian airline. The government has made an effort to assure that the ethnic balance in the air force is not too out of line with the other services. I can only speculate that the proportion of Malay air force officers has been rising steadily since the mid-1970s.

Ethnic Preference in Education

Three major developments have occurred in the field of education since the early 1970s. The first was the dismantling of the four separate education streams based on four different languages of instruction and their replacement by a unified education system using Malay as the medium of instruction and examination at all levels of the education system. The second has been the rapid expansion of postsecondary educational institutions. The third has been the extension of the ethnic quota system in a more comprehensive way to postsecondary education. All these developments have affected the ethnic balance in education. Only the briefest survey of developments is possible within the confines of this chapter.

The conversion to Malay as the sole medium of instruction was begun in 1970 at the primary level, and in each succeeding year a higher class was converted until the process was completed by 1982.[34] The process of conversion inevitably involved the lowering of standards, but it also gave the Malays an added advantage, especially in the initial stages of conversion. This was reflected in the Malaysia Certificate of Examinations in 1973, when of the 27,784 non-Malays sitting for the exams, 18,470 failed—14,166 failed solely on the basis of their performance in the Malay examination.[35] That Malay was the medium of examination may also have affected the non-Malay performance in other subjects. With time, this problem has abated, and the performance of non-Malays has steadily improved to match the performance levels of Malays. Nonetheless, the conversion to Malay as the sole medium of instruction provided a tremendous advantage to Malays for access to higher education, quite apart from other ethnic preference policies.

The investment in education has been steadily increasing since independence. For example, in 1960 the total public expenditure on education was M $179 million; by 1982 the figure had increased to M $2,928 million.[36] Even more important was the rapid expansion of postsecondary education. Total university expenditures increased from M $25.8 million in 1969 to M $350.8 million in 1980.[37] Before the crisis of 1969 there was only one university — the University of Malaya. Today there are six universities and a number of postsecondary colleges and technical institutes. In the 1969 to 1980 period university enrollment increased from about 6,900 to 27,100, while the public expenditure per student increased from M $3,700 to M $12,900.[38] Not only were there more facilities for university education and more places for admission, but many more Malays were qualified for admission. Therefore, a large cohort of Malay students, many from rural peasant origins, entered universities, nearly all of whom were supported by generous government stipends. What would have been a natural trend was greatly accelerated by the Malay special rights quota system.

Following the 1969 crisis, the admission quotas for Malays were raised, and for the first time, admission quotas were applied to specific fields of study. Under the "sensitive issues" constitutional amendments of 1971, the *Yang di-Pertuan Agong* [paramount ruler] was given the power to reserve places for Malays at postsecondary institutions "in those selected courses of study where the numbers of Malays are disproportionately small."[39] Thus, Malay quotas were applied not only for admission but also for entrance to specified subjects within universities. The quotas varied from field to field and also between universities. Two universities were founded on the assumption that their student body would be almost excluvsively Malay— Universiti Kebangsaan Malaysia (the National University of Malaysia) and Universiti Islam (the Islamic University). However, under pressure from the non-Malay partners in the government coalition, the number of non-Malays being admitted to the National University is being increased by 2 percent per year until the non-Malay quota reaches 40 percent. The ethnic balance at the University of Malaya, which is the oldest of the universities, has remained closer to the national ethnic balance, but even there, the Malays constitute more than their proportion of the total population. The number of Malays at the University of Malaya rose from 49.7 percent in 1970 to 66.4 percent in 1979, while at the National University the proportion of Malays exceeded 90 percent.[40] Because of the overrepresentation of non-Malays in postsecondary institutions prior to 1969, the balance was somewhat restored by 1970-1971 and became much more skewed toward the Malays after 1975.

The system of government bursaries and scholarships for higher education has a much greater pro-Malay bias than the quota system for university admissions. Practically all Malays attend university with a government bursary, which is adequate to support the full costs of attending a university. Very few bursaries are awarded to non-Malays, although an increasing number have been reserved for non-Malay natives of the Borneo states of Sabah and Sarawak. In addition, there are a large number of government scholarships available for advanced university study abroad. Although figures are not available, probably more than 90 percent of these scholarships are awarded to Malays. Thus, the large numbers of Malaysians studying abroad can be divided into two groups: those on government scholarships, most of whom are Malays; and those who are self-supporting, most of whom are non-Malays and have sought foreign university education because of their inability to be admitted to universities in Malaysia. Prior to the raising of foreign fees in the United Kingdom, there were about seventeen thousand Malaysians studying there, and the total studying in North America has probably approached fifty thousand.

Although the ethnic preference system is supposed to apply only to admissions and scholarships, it also affects the system of academic evaluation. Because non-Malays have a more restricted access to education, their performance level has generally been substantially above the norm for the Malays. Although grading is supposed to be without reference to ethnicity, all grades must be submitted to an evaluation review committee having heavy Malay representation. Individual faculty members report various instances when grades were unilaterally raised, apparently for purposes of "ethnic balance."

Hiring policies at universities are also seriously influenced by ethnic preference policies. The lack of qualified Malays for university faculty meant that non-Malays were grossly overrepresented in the faculty appointments made prior to 1975. However, many non-Malays were given contractually limited appointments, and promotion was frequently delayed. When qualified Malays became candidates for appointment, they were eagerly appointed and given rapid promotion. Thus, there are instances when a Malay, returning from study abroad, is appointed to a permanent position and made department head, with no previous teaching experience and perhaps even without a Ph.D. in hand. Such practices not only generate interethnic animosity, but they also contribute to the rather low staff morale that seems to afflict Malaysian universities.

Economic Preferences

In 1971 the New Economic Policy set as the government's target "that within a period of 20 years, Malays and other indigenous people will manage and own at least 30% of the total commercial and industrial activities in all categories and scales of operation."[41] In practical terms this strategy has been applied to income, employment, participation in the professions, management and entrepreneurial activities, and the ownership of share capital (see Table 4.1). Prior to 1969 the Malay preference system applied almost exclusively to the operation or distribution of government services. With the NEP, however, the entire economy was targeted, including the private sector. Therefore, the NEP called for the government to extend a preference and quota system to all sectors of the economy.

Quotas for the employment of Malays were established for commercial and industrial enterprises. Also, such enterprises were required to establish plans for the training and promotion of Malays to the more skilled and the higher managerial positions. In the case of foreign corporations,

Table 4.1.   Malaysia: Ethnic Distribution, Income Estimates, and Share Capital Ownership

	Population (percent)	Mean per household income (est. M$/month)		Ownership of Share capital (%)	
		1957/8	1970	1970	1975
Malays & Muslim natives	45.9	139	177	2.4	9.2
Non-Muslim natives	6.6	---	---		
Chinese	35.7	300	399	36.7	46.7
Indians	9.6	237	310		
Others	2.2	---	---		

Sources: Donald Snodgrass, *Inequality and Economic Development in Malaysia* (Kuala Lumpur: Oxford University Press, 1980), p. 83; K. S. Jomo & R. J. G. Wells, eds., *The Fourth Malaysia Plan, Economic Perspectives* (Kuala Lumpur: Malaysian Economic Association, 1983), p. 56.

specifications for Malay quotas, training, and promotion were tied to the terms of agreement under which these corporations operated and did business within the country. The renewal of government business and commercial licenses as well as the tax and tariff concessions available to new industries also provided the occasion for periodic review and revision of the quotas and agreements regarding Malay preferences. For local businesses, special regulations were issued, and the awarding of government contracts, construction permits, and the sale or lease of commercial or industrial land were tied to compliance with the quota system for employment, training, and promotion of Malays. There was no uniform quota for all industries, but the nature of the industry was taken into account along with the potential availability of Malays to fill particular positions in each enterprise. Very small local enterprises were exempt from most of the Malay preference quotas. For most of the larger industries, however, Malay employment was initially set at about 40 percent, but this figure was raised for those industries that were sited in the industrial estates located near larger concentrations of Malay population.[42]

One of the NEP's most difficult objectives has been to bring Malay ownership and control of industry to the 30 percent level by 1990. It was estimated that in 1969 Malays owned only 1.5 percent of capital assets in limited companies.[43] To achieve the target would require a 25 percent annual increase from the beginning of the NEP in 1971. If Malays had little to invest to begin with, their participation could not rely on mere market inducements and exhortation. Instead, the government decided to act as a trustee for the Malays, using massive government investments in quasi-public corporations operated and managed by Malays. These Malay corporations are known as Bumiputra (indigenous) trust agencies, and their investments in the economy are now counted as Malay ownership share capital. Although the money comes as loans from government appropriations, the investments are supposedly held in trust until Malays can buy shares and acquire control through private investment. In 1980 the total Malay-Bumiputra share of ownership of corporate shares was estimated to be 12.4 percent, but of that total only 4.3 percent was attributed to individuals while 8.1 percent was held by Bumiputra trust agencies.[44]

Frequently, when foreign corporations invest in Malaysia or engage in joint stock agreements with Malaysian government corporations, the terms of the agreement specify that stock should be offered for sale locally, with a certain quota reserved for sale to Malays. This has resulted in a two price system; thus, the lack of Malay private investment capital has assured Malays of a lower price in the share market.

The government has attempted to encourage private Malay investment in the economy through various attractive investment schemes. The government has established special banks to provide financial services to the

Malay community. These include Bank Rakyat and Bank Bumiputra, which operate according to Islamic rules in avoiding "interest," but nonetheless do provide returns on investments as "profits." In 1981 the Amanah Saham Nasional (ASN) was launched to promote Malay investment and entrpreneurship. The ASN sells shares to individual Bumiputra (Malays and other indigenous peoples) and provides a vehicle for transferring shares of corporations held by government agencies on behalf of Bumiputra. The ASN assures maximum corporate control and voting rights and monitors the sale of Bumiputra shares to non-Bumiputra. Malay equity investment is also facilitated by the Bumiputra Investment Foundation and Permodalan (National Equity Corporation), both of which purchase portfolios of shares in limited companies for subsequent sale to Malay or native investors.[45]

In the field of housing, developers are usually required to sell a certain quota of new houses to Malays. This is ostensibly to assure Malays a share of new housing and also to prevent new housing estates from becoming monoethnic ghettos. In practice, the Malay quota is difficult to sell, so it is common for some houses in newly developed areas to remain vacant for several years, and the Malay quota houses, when sold, are usually below market price as the houses are subsidized indirectly by non-Malay buyers.

To assist the economic advancement of the Malays many new government agencies were created. Some had been formed prior to 1969, but the large expansion of government assistance programs targeted for the Malays came after that date and were part of the overall NEP strategy. Space permits the mention of only a few of these agencies: The Federal Land Development Authority, the Fisheries Development Authority, the Livestock Development Corporation, Bank Bumiputra, Bank Pertanian (Agricultural Bank), the Malaysian Industrial Development Fund, the National Unit Trust Scheme, the National Unity Equity Corporation, Perbadanan Nasional (PERNAS, the State Trading Corporation), the Federal Agricultural Marketing Authority, Majlis Amanah Ra'ayat (the Council of Trust for the Indigenous People), plus thirteen State Economic Development Corporations. The activities of all these agencies are monitored through the prime minister's department and the economic planning unit within that department. The progress toward targets is reviewed with each economic plan and with a midterm review. This review process has provided the opportunity for more detailed and specific elaboration of targets for Malay employment, promotion, and ownership acquisition. Therefore, the system of Malay preferences is under constant review, with the objective of meeting the overall targets set for the year 1990.

Ethnic Preference Categories

As ethnic preferences have increased, so, too, have disputes about ethnic boundaries and new categories of ethnic classification. The first Malay land rights were afforded to "Mohammedans." Later, Malay rights belonged to those who were traditional subjects of a Malay ruler in one of the Malay states. At the time of independence the constitution defined a Malay as one who professes the Muslim religion, habitually speaks Malay, conforms to Malay custom, and was born within the country prior to independence, or is the issue of a person born within the country prior to independence. Thus, religion, language, custom, and place of birth are used to define ethnicity. Former chief justice Tan Sri Mohamed Suffian bin Hashim has observed that an ethnic Indian could be counted as a Malay if he met these "nonethnic" requirements.[46]

Because the Malays constitute a bare majority in the country and because the rationale for Malay rights usually was based on the claim that the Malays were indigenous, it became politically expedient to generate new categories, especially after the formation of Malaysia, which included the Borneo states of Sabah and Sarawak. The term Bumiputra (literally, prince of the earth — hence, equivalent to son of the soil) came to be applied to indigenous people.[47] With this term the ethnic category was expanded to include Sarawak and Sabah natives, many of whom are not Muslims. The term Orang Asli (literally, original people or aborigines) is applied to the non-Malay aborigines of the Malay peninsula, most of whom are animists. Converts to Islam are known as Saudara Baru, meaning new friends. The complexities of these overlapping categories complicate the system of ethnic preference. In general, constitutionally defined preferences are available only to Malays and natives of the Borneo states, while many of the quotas and preferences under the NEP are made available to Bumiputra. Some minor concessions and advantages have been given to Saudara Baru. Finally, the Orang Asli who can trace their origins in the country before all others, and who are also the poorest, are counted as Bumiputra for census purposes, but given almost no preferences because they are treated as wards of the Department of Aborigines. The problems of defining ethnic boundaries for the preference system can only increase as Malaysian society becomes more diversified and the ethnic boundary markers become more susceptible to manipulation.

Effects of the Ethnic Preference System

Malay special rights and the New Economic Policy are making dramatic changes in Malay society. Progress is being made toward the goals enunciated by the government. Whether all the targets will be reached by the year 1990 is doubtful, but there has been a more complete transformation of Malaysian society than most observers thought possible. When ethnic comparisons are made, it is clear that there has been much progress toward reducing economic disparities. However, many critics allege that greater interethnic equality has been achieved by creating greater economic and class differences within ethnic groups. Some evidence supports this charge. However, the government is particularly sensitive to this line of criticism, and public policy is being formulated to divert additional resources to assist the poor. The government is especially concerned about the Malay peasantry, whose expectations have been raised but who have not been keeping pace with the overall economic growth of the nation.

Although the ethnic preference system was designed to resolve some of the problems created by ethnicity, it also reinforces ethnicity by defining more and more issues in ethnic terms. The quotas may be the subject of interethnic political bargaining, but they also intensify ethnic identities and ethnic conflicts. On the other hand, the system has also helped to break down ethnic compartmentalization, and schools, the workplace, and the neighborhood have been made much more ethnically balanced. The result has not been integration or loss of ethnic identity but a more pluralized form of interaction in many more aspects of the economy and the society.

To bring the complex pattern of Malaysian policies of preference into clear comparative analytical focus is a difficult task. Donald Rothchild identifies nine conflict regulating strategies in ethnically divided societies.[48] The nine strategies are subjection, isolation, cultural assimilation, avoidance, displacement, buffering, protection, redistribution, and sharing. Although his scheme is innovative and comprehensive, it is rather difficult to apply to the Malaysian case because more government policies appear to pursue a mix of these analytically devised strategies. Indeed, a case could be made that all nine strategies have been utilized in one form or another to "manage" ethnic conflict. Perhaps the greatest emphasis has been put on cultural assimilation, displacement, buffering, protection, and redistribution. In the Malaysian case the mix of these strategies has always been made with an eye to the political support of the Malays, who remain the primary constituency whose support is fundamental to the government. The government takes as its premise that a hegemonial exchange system—to use Rothchild's terminology—must be maintained while some concessions are given to the non-Malay communities. The government assumes that the paramount power and vital interests of the Malay community must not be threatened or compromised if the country is to avoid fratricidal civil conflict.

One strategy not mentioned in the Rothchild scheme is patronage. Perhaps this is because patronage is present in all political systems, and although it may be a matter of utmost concern to power holders, policymakers seldom advertise patronage as a key policy instrument. In the Malaysian context the material benefits available under the ethnic preference system have also created the environment for an expansion of patronage networks. These networks cross ethnic boundaries and, indeed, can provide the means for non-Malays to survive and prosper in what might seem an inhospitable environment. The patronage system is particularly important as government expands into business activities in joint venture schemes and political leaders get involved in commercial and industrial ventures with established entrepreneurs in the private sector. Patronage ties not only build a base of political support, but in Malaysia they also help mute some of the more abrasive aspects of ethnic hostility, especially among ethnic elites.[49] Because the patron-client networks extend across ethnic boundaries, it is through these networks that informal arrangements are made to manage ethnic conflict and ameliorate some of the more problematic aspects of official policy in regard to ethnic preferences.

The New Economic Policy and the rapid expansion of the system of Malay ethnic preference have depended on an expanding economy to avoid confiscatory measures against non-Malays. It was particularly fortuitous that offshore oil production reached significant levels in 1971. Oil has been a major factor sustaining Malaysia's steady economic growth; it provides an increasing amount of revenue for the government. By 1982, 24.7 percent of total federal revenues were derived from oil.[50] These revenues provided the funds for most of the government's development programs. A shrinking economy would have severely strained domestic harmony and probably forced the abandonment of the goals and strategies of the NEP.

One of the severe costs of the ethnic preference system has been the alienation of many non-Malays. They see the system as an intolerable form of discrimination that is given official sanction and that is used to justify further and greater discrimination in social and private relations. This sense of alienation is becoming severe, in part, because it seems so pervasive and insurmoutable. Many non-Malay professionals have emigrated abroad, are actively exploring that as a possible option, or vainly hope to do so in the indefinite future. Although non-Malay emigration may be welcomed by the more politically paranoid in the Malay community, it is a tremendous drain of talented human resources, which most responsible governments would seek to stem.

It should be apparent that ethnic preferences in Malaysia have multiplied and spread to more and more aspects of society and the economy. There is a built-in crisis in the system, which will occur shortly before 1990, the target date for attaining the "restructuring goals." In 1966, Malaysia's present Prime Minister Mahathir stated that Malay special rights would not last forever and called on Malays to be prepared for competition on equal terms with the other communities.[51] Whether in 1986 Dr. Mahathir is still committed to that position is uncertain. From his more recent statements and actions, it would seem he will try to find some formula to ensure the continuation of some form of Malay special rights, perhaps in a slightly different guise. Malays in the ruling United Malays National Organization already have proposed that preference system goals be raised to 50 or 51 percent.[52] On the other hand, many non-Malays assume that the preference system will be phased out once the exaggerated aspects of ethnic inequality have been remedied. Because the issue is deemed to be "sensitive," it cannot be discussed in public. Even so, it remains on the minds of the politically aware and is an issue that cannot be postponed forever. The logic of the system makes these policies very easy to initiate but extremely difficult to dismantle. As more and more people get a stake in the preference system, it will be easier to expand the system than to take privileges away. In the past, Malaysia's leaders under pressure have exhibited magnanimous innovation as well as authoritarian vindictiveness. The challenge of the 1990s will very likely produce a mix of both.

Notes

1. See Chapter 2 in this volume.
2. J. S. Furnivall, *Colonial Policy and Practice: A Comparative Study of Burma and Netherlands East Indies* (Cambridge: Cambridge University Press, 1948).
3. J. deV. Allen et al., eds., *A Collection of Treaties and Other Documents Affecting the States of Malaysia, 1761-1963*, vol. 1 (London: Oceana Publications, 1981), p. 391. Also see C. Nothcote Parkinson, *British Intervention in Malaya, 1867-1877* (Singapore: University of Malaya Press, 1960), pp. 323-324.
4. *Selangor Land Code*, no. 13 of 1891, cited in Philip Loh, "Some Aspects of British Social Policy in the Protected Malay States, 1877-1895" (M.A. thesis, University of Malaya, 1967), p. 40.
5. The International Bank for Reconstruction and Development, *The Economic Development of Malaya* (Baltimore, Md.: John Hopkins Press, 1955), pp. 311-313.
6. See William R. Roff, *The Origins of Malay Nationalism* (New Haven, Conn.: Yale University Press, 1967), p. 102: and Robert O. Tilman, "The Public Services of the Federation of Malaya" (Ph.D. diss., Duke University, 1961), pp. 180-181.
7. For accounts of the development of educational policies, see D. D. Chelliah, *A History of the Educational Policy of the Straits Settlements* (Kuala Lumpur: Government Press, 1947); Fredric Mason, *The Schools of Malaya* (Singapore: Donald Moore, 1954); David J. Radcliffe, "Education and Cultural Change Among the Malays" (Ph.D. diss., University of Wisconsin, 1970); Martin Rudner, "Education, Development and Change in Malaysia," *South East Asian Studies* (Kyoto) 15, no. 1 (June 1977).

8. Gordon P. Means, *Malaysian Politics*, 2nd ed. (London: Hodder Stoughton, 1976), p. 12.

9. *Malayan Union and Singapore* Cmd. 6724 (London: HIs Majesty's Stationery Office, 1946), p. 1.

10. Government of the Malayan Union, *Constitutional Proposals for Malaya, Report of the Working Committee* (Kuala Lumpur: Government Press, 1946), p. 7.   Part of this section is taken from Gordon P. Means, "'Special Rights' as a Strategy for Development," *Comparative Politics* 5, no. 1 (October 1971): 37-40.

11. In 1949 British Commissioner-General Malcolm MacDonald attempted to establish an intercommunal discussion and bargaining committee to resolve communal discord.   It was called the Communities Liaison Committee.   See Means, *Malaysian Politics*, pp. 122-124.

12. *Report of the Federation of Malaya Constitutional Commission, Appendices II, III, and IV* (Kuala Lumpur: Government Press, 1957), pp. 128-133, Articles 14-23.

13. Federation of Malaya (hereinafter referred to as FOM), *Report of the Education Committee, 1956* (Razak Report), no. 21 of 1956; and FOM, *Report of the Education Review Committee, 1960* (Talib Report) (Kuala Lumpur: Government Press, 1960).

14. See "Group Demands" in Chapter 2 of this volume.

15. The commission also proposed to prevent an increase of the total area of land allotted to Malay reservations; it provided for their reduction or dissolution by a two-thirds majority in the appropriate state legislature.   FOM, *Report of the Constitutional Commission, Appendices II, III, and IV*, no. 41 of 1957, pp. 150-151, 183.

16. FOM, *Report of the Federation of Malaya Constitutional Commission* (Kuala Lumpur: Government Press, 1957), p. 72.

17. The Malay rulers elect one of their number to be paramount ruler for a five-year term; he serves as sovereign for the federation as a whole.

18. Although the constitution defines specific Malay special rights, it provides no guidance as to the legitimate interests of other communities.   In practice the latter phrase has acquired no meaning because the rulers have never recognized any specific "legitimate interests of other communities."   See *Malaysia Federal Constitution*, Reprint no. 4 of 1970, Art. 153, pp. 156-159.

19. This body is composed of all Malay rulers and the governors of states without Malay rulers.   On some matters only the Malay rulers act for the conference, while on other matters the full membership is entitled to participate.   See Tan Sri Mohamed Suffian bin Hashim, *An Introduction to the Constitution of Malaysia* (Kuala Lumpur: Jabatan Chetak Kerajaan, 1972), pp. 37-44; and *Malayan Constitutional Documents*, 2nd ed., Vol. I (Kuala Lumpur: Government Printer, 1962), pp. 48-49.

20. In the exercise of their responsibility for Malay special rights, the rulers are bound by the advice of their ministers.

21. Federal provisions for Malay rights are supplemented by additional provisions in state constitutions.   All nine Malay states give the ruler the power "to safeguard the special position of the Malays and to ensure the reservation for Malays of such proportion as he may deem reasonable of positions in the public service of the State and of scholarships, exhibitions and other similar educational or training privileges or special facilities given or accorded by the State Government and, when any permit or license for the

operation of trade or business is required by State Law." All nine Malay states require that the *mentri besar* (chief minister) of the state must be a Malay and a Muslim, although six of the nine allow an exception to this rule if no Malay Muslim can be found who is able to command the support of the Legislative Council. Six states also require that the state secretary (chief administrative officer) be a Malay Muslim. Similarly, most states require that the members of state councils associated with the monarchy be Malay Muslims. These include Council of Succession, Council of the Royal Court, Dewan di-Raja (Rulers Council), Council of Regency, and a number of other bodies unique to certain states. In non-Malay states it has become customary for the post of governor or chief minister to be held by a Malay, even where Malays constitute less than one-tenth of the population. For an examination of the legal aspects of Malay special rights and the operation of citizenship laws, see Huang Ying Jung, *Double Citizenship in Malaysia* (Singapore: Nanyang University, Institute of Southeast Asia, 1970).

22. See John Slimming, *Malaysia: Death of a Democracy* (London: John Murray, 1969); Tunku Abdul Rahman, *May 13: Before and After* (Kuala Lumpur: Utusan Melayu Press, 1969); Leon Comber, *13 May 1969, A Historical Survey of Sino-Malay Relations* (Kuala Lumpur: Heinemann Asia, 1983); and Goh Cheng Teik, *The May Thirteenth Incident and Democracy in Malaysia* (Kuala Lumpur: Oxford University Press, 1971).

23. Government of Malaysia (hereinafter referred to as GOM), *Rukunegara* (Kuala Lumpur: Jabatan Chetak Kerajaan, 1970).

24. GOM, *Towards National Harmony* (Kuala Lumpur: Jabatan Chetak Kerajaan, 1971).

25. *Malaysian Digest*, March 15, 1971, p. 1.

26. *Straits Times*, January 12, 1970, p. 1.

27. GOM, *Towards National Harmony*, p. 2.

28. GOM, *Second Malaysia Plan, 1971-1975* (Kuala Lumpur: Government Printing Office, 1971), p. 1.

29. *Malaysian Digest*, July 15, 1971, p. 1.

30. Robert O. Tilman, "The Public Services of the Federation of Malaya" (Ph.D. diss., Duke University, 1961), pp. 96-97, 110; and David S. Gibbons and Zakaria Haji Ahmad, "Malaysia: The Politics of Selection for the Higher Civil Service" (Manuscript, University of Singapore, 1971), p. 3.

31. Gibbons, ibid., pp. 1-9.

32. Suffian, *An Introduction to the Constitution*, pp. 255-256.

33. "Speech by Dr. Tan Chee Khoon on Debate on King's Speech on 18.4.73" (Reprint of Dewan Ra'ayat speech, Kuala Lumpur: Syarikat Chip Seng Trading Sdn. Bhd., n.d.), pp. 3-4.

34. Kementerian Pelajaran, Malaysia, *Laporan Mengenai Pelaksanaan Shor2 Jawatankuasa Penyemak Dasar Pelajaran, 1960* [Report on the Implementation of the Recommendations of the Education Review Committee, 1960] (Kuala Lumpur: Government Printer, 1971), pp. 48-51.

35. *Straits Times*, April 4, 1973, p. 1.

36. Rudner, "Education, Development and Change," p. 39; and Ministry of Finance, Malaysia, *Economic Report, 1982/83* (Kuala Lumpur: National Printing Department, 1982), p. 61.

37. Yip Yat Hoong, "The Cost of University Education in Malaysia" (Manuscript, Institute of Advanced Studies, University of Malaya, 1982), p. 6.

38. Ibid., p. 14.

39. GOM, *Towards National Harmony*, p. 6.

40. Judith Nagata, *The Reflowering of Malaysian Islam: Modern Religious Radicals and Their Roots* (Vancouver: University of British Columbia Press, 1984), p. 56.

41. GOM, *Second Malaysia Plan, 1971-1975* (Kuala Lumpur: Government Press, 1971), pp. 41-42.

42. *Straits Times*, March 28, 1972, p. 26.

43. *Straits Times*, July 20, 1971, p. 21.

44. Jomo Kwame Sundaram, "Prospects for the New Economic Policy in Light of the Fourth Malaysia Plan," K. S. Jomo and R. J. G. Wells, eds., *The Fourth Malaysia Plan, Economic Perspectives* (Kuala Lumpur: Malaysian Economic Association, 1983), p. 56.

45. Sieh-Lee Mei Ling, "The Scheme for Bumiputra Investment in Malaysia: Some Implications," ibid., pp. 92-97.

46. Suffian, *An Introduction to the Constitution*, pp. 247.

47. Sharon Siddique and Leon Suryadinata, "Bumiputra and Pribumi: Economic Nationalism (Indiginism) in Malaysia and Indonesia," (Manuscript, Institute of Southeast Asian Studies, Singapore, n.d.), p. 2.

48. See "Group Demands" in Chapter 2 of this volume.

49. For an account of patronage related to Malaysian government agencies, see Bruce Gale, *Politics and Public Enterprise in Malaysia* (Kuala Lumpur: Eastern Universities Press, 1981).

50. Ministry of Finance, *Malaysia Economic Report, 1982/83* (Kuala Lumpur: National Printing Department, 1981), pp. 5-7. Also see Gordon P. Means, "Energy Resource Department and Management in Malaysia," *Contemporary Southeast Asia 5*, no. 3 (December 1983): 330-351.

51. *Straits Budget*, March 23, 1966, p. 19.

52. Siddique, "Bumiputra and Pribumi," p. 25.

5

Ethnic Aspects of Privatization in Malaysia

R. S. MILNE

In March 1983 Prime Minister Datuk Seri Mahathir Mohamad announced a policy of privatization for Malaysia.[1] Such a policy made good sense in purely economic terms: The public sector had become swollen and inefficient, and the cost of supporting it was becoming increasingly burdensome during the recession of the early 1980s. Privatization also accorded with the prime minister's emphasis on discipline and hard work, his dislike of subsidies and doles, and his admiration for Japanese business efficiency. Mahathir's admiration was exemplified in his already declared Look East policy, which was also linked to a "Malaysia Inc." policy.[2]

However, as readers of this book might properly suspect, there was more to the privatization policy than Mahathir's personal likes and dislikes. The policy had ethnic implications that can be analyzed along the lines of Donald Rothchild's notion of hegemonial exchange.[3] More precisely, privatization constituted a logical extension, albeit with a twist, of the New Economic Policy (NEP) launched in the early 1970s, which was meant to help the Malays economically.[4]

This chapter, building on Gordon Means's discussion of Malaysian ethnic preference policy, outlines the privatization proposals, what has been done to implement them, and the main economic and technical problems encountered. An account of the ethnic considerations and allocations involved follows. The chapter concludes with a consideration of the implications of privatization for ethnic and class interpretations.

The Privatization Proposals and their Implementation

The first pertinent question in our analysis of privatization is not why is privatization occurring but, rather, why did the public sector grow to be so big that a pressing need was felt to reduce it? Malaysia is not a "socialist" country, although it has some welfare state aspects such as a comprehensive medical care scheme. Yet, in addition to the government's provision of standard infrastructural services, such as water, electricity, education and transportation, the public and quasi-public sector grew rapidly from 1970 onward. The New Economic Policy intended, *inter alia*, to improve the economic position of the Bumiputra (Malays and other indigenous peoples) and sought to do so by builidng up large government bodies such as PERNAS (Perbadan Nasional—the State Trading Corporation), UDA (the Urban Development Authority), MARA (Majlis Amanah Ra'ayat—the Council of Trust for the Indigenous People), and at state level, State Economic Development Corporations (SEDCs).[5] The idea behind the NEP was that the business capabilities of Malays could be improved only by training and/or aiding them with advice and money funneled through such organizations. Similarly, if Malay ownership of capital was to be increased, individual savings would be too small to be significant; saving would have to be done "on behalf of" the Bumiputra through large-scale governmental bodies. Consequently, public and quasi-public bodies grew; the government set up new organizations and also took over existing, largely foreign-owned, concerns through market transactions. Subsidiaries multiplied, and government control was weakened. Public employees and public expenditure increased. In 1983 the public service employed nearly one-quarter of the total work force, but the cost of public service salaries and pensions amounted to two-thirds of the government's total operating expenditure.[6]

Even before the privatization policy was launched, action to reduce the size of the public sector had been stimulated by the inefficiency of many SEDC ventures, which had been started without adequate planning or control in all kinds of areas, including agriculture, wholesale and retail trading, hotels, mining, finance and real estate, housing, and industrial sites. In 1982 the government, appalled by the poor performance of many SEDCs, closed some down, ordered a reassessment of the activities of others, and restricted SEDCs from operating in certain fields, for example, in the construction industry.[7] The Ministry of Public Enterprises, to which the SEDCs and some other government bodies were responsible, had already closed some SEDCs down on its own initiative. When a 1982 investigative report by the ministry was published, it was revealed that 103 SEDC companies had made profits totalling M $346.8 million, while 125 had accrued losses adding up to M $360.6 million.[8] The remaining 86 companies did not submit reports, a good indication of the low degree of government control over the SEDCs that existed in the first place. In 1983 about fifty of these ventures were closed down, and the privatization policy heralded an even tougher policy toward ventures run by the SEDCs and similar bodies. Now, in order for a venture to be started by an SEDC, it has to be shown that no private firm is capable of operating in the sector. Undoubtedly, the poor performance of SEDCs produced a receptive atmosphere for the privatization idea.

It is perhaps ironical that the originator of the actual privatization policy, Dr. Mahathir, was the first prime minister to have administered a government enterprise, with conspicuous success.[9] Reactions against the growing size and inefficiencies of the public sector were now reinforced and became elevated to the status of a policy. Faced with the economic recession of the early 1980s and after an early attempt at using countercyclical measures, the government curtailed its spending. Less money was available to support public enterprises. Simultaneously, growing expectations of help from the government tended to produce what the prime minister regarded as a "subsidy mentality," and these expectations had to be checked. The solution put forward was privatization: the transfer of certain government services and industries to the private sector.

The government conceded that under privatization consumers might have to pay more for better services.[10] But it also contended that consumers would have had to do this anyway unless subsidies had been raised still further. Also, the government argued that because private enterprise was more efficient, there actually would be less of a price rise than if the services had remained under government direction. The aim of privatization, then, was to get the private sector to "spearhead" development after extensive government involvement in running the economy had led to heavy losses that could no longer be supported.

Irrespective of the main forms that privatization would assume, two main obstacles to privatization were immediately apparent: adverse trade union reactions and insufficient private capital to pay for the operation. The unions were right to see privatization as a threat. Studies in other countries showed that privatization had led to a reduction in the number of public service jobs.[11] After all, this was the aim of the policy; the public service was too large for what it accomplished, too rarely subject to competition, and too lacking in appropriate incentives and penalties. Government assurances that privatization would not lead to a loss of pensions or allowances were not intended to sanction the continuation of inefficiency. The most vociferous opposition naturally came from CUEPACS (Congress of Unions of Employees in the Public and Civil Services), which had a membership drawn largely from threatened industries such as telecommunications and the railways. A spokesman put the union's cards face up on the table when he objected to privatization not only because it threatened job security but also because the union would be crippled and workers would be exposed to an "alien business environment," which would be "volatile and competitive."[12]

The amount of capital needed to buy out some of the larger government concerns was massive; one estimate for telecommunications was between M $4 billion and M $5 billion. The problem of obtaining capital could be alleviated if the government retained a portion of its existing holdings (partial privatization) and/or split the operations to be privatized into two or more segments. In either case the amount of capital needed by a particular private firm or combination of firms for a buy out would be reduced. Examples of the first of these two options will probably be Port Kelang, where the government is likely to retain some of the operations,[13] and the proposed additional railway system in which the government probably will have a 10 or 15 percent share.[14] In the latter case, this is a looser use of privatization, as the railway is new, not previously public. It was also proposed at one time that the aerobus system for Kuala Lumpur would have a public component (city hall). However, afterwards, the entire scheme was changed.

The second option is that large government monopolies, if privatized, could be broken up and assigned among several private firms.[15] This procedure has been recommended for telecommunications, electricity, and some other public utilities. For Port Kelang it has been suggested that, after such a split, some of the segments remain initially in government hands, while others are dispersed among more than one private firm.

Yet another variation consists in so-called turnkey projects. In these a firm that has constructed, say, roads, is allowed to recoup its outlays by receiving toll revenues for a specified number of years, after which the government takes over.[16]

The existence of obstacles to privatization has not prevented the idea from being taken up enthusiastically, sometimes overenthusiastically, by various people or groups who wish to follow the fashion or the prime minister's lead. For example, in a seminar, "Mr. Tan Khoon Swan . . . identified a myriad of investment opportunities from gold-mining to potato-growing that would be released with privatization. When he finished, one participant said, 'Hearing Mr. Tan speak, I fear my mother's backyard too may be privatized.'"[17] The government, however, has proceeded with caution in implementing this policy. To use the government's own terms, it has been "pragmatic" and "selective," and government committees have been used to look into particular cases before action is taken. Additionally, as in all important policy decisions, the final word (and usually the first mention) comes from the prime minister.

The origins of the new privatization policy are not deeply rooted in any philosophy or ideology. The influence of similar policies in Britain or the United States or of such thinkers as Milton Friedman was slight, according to politicians who have discussed the topic in conversation. Privatization in Malaysia was largely a local response to local problems.

So far the major instances of actual privatization have included telecommunications,[18] a third television channel (TV3), and some of the government's container operations formerly carried on by Kontena Nasional. The new railway network, the Malaysian Airlines System (MAS), the Malaysian International Shipping Company (MISC), and some of Port Kelang's activities are definitely earmarked for privatization. Less important examples of privatization include some MARA operations, state housing in Penang, the ferry service between Sabah and the federal territory of Labuan, and the part-time employment of private anesthetists in government hospitals. Other possibilities in various stages of discussion or implementation are maintenance of some highways (combined with the collection of tolls), some ports, airports, water, electricity, postal services, the social security system, health services, and further educational services.[19]

Candidates for privatization are not limited to activities undertaken by government after 1969 as part of the NEP. Other older government functions, such as transportation and public utilities, are being looked at with an eye to privatization.[20] The premise that privatization promotes greater efficiency underlies the arguments in its favor. This premise has been stated by the prime minister, who, from a theoretical angle, has pointed to the beneficial influence of self-interest in the private sector, and, from an empirical perspective, to evidence that enterprises that were previously private cease to earn profits after nationalization.[21] Tun Tan Siew Sin has observed that, even in Japan, with its widespread reputation for efficiency, "enterprises in which the Government had a hand do not do as well as those which were left entirely to the private sector."[22] The Malaysian public ownership dilemma seems to reflect the experience of other countries. There has been conspicuous slackness in government offices, which Dr. Mahathir's campaign for discipline and hard work has sought to combat, but has not eradicated.[23] Civil service regulations encourage unnecessary overtime, for which extra payment is made, and in some cases prohibit the award of bonuses for hard work and devotion to duty.

A specific example of public versus private enterprise efficiency concerns Kontena Nasional, which after some organizational changes remains governmental, but which now faces competition from two private, regionally demarcated firms. One of these, which pays by results based, for example, on the number of trips made by trucks per day, makes more comparable trips than Kontena Nasional does, even with overtime payments. The government organization also has purchased similar trucks at a substantially higher cost than has this competitor. A comparison indicates that the private operation is the more efficient.[24]

There may be excetpions to the generally valid argument that privatization will improve the quality of service. When car parks were privatized in Petaling Jaya there was an initial public outcry about inefficiency and overcharging.[25] In many cases the problem is that the change is not from public monopoly to private competition but from public monopoly to private monopoly. The happy case, as with the private television organization TV3, may be a rarity. In that instance the new private competitor, within geographical limits and with some government restraint on content, provided a service that many viewers found more attractive than the existing ones. At the same time the minister of information said that efforts would be made to improve what was offered on the two government channels in order to compete with the newcomer.[26]

The ideal situtation is one where, after privatization, competition exists or can be promoted by the government.[27] The government has accepted responsibility for seeing to it that minimum disadvantages accompany privatization—for instance, undue price rises or gaps in service—but government regulation, whatever shape it assumes, is a poor substitute for competition.[28]

Ethnic Considerations

Ethnic considerations also must have been prominent in the mind of the prime minister when he announced the policy of privatization. In a country where, for example, the apparently noncontentious issue of importing oranges can assume ethnic overtones, privatization cannot avoid close scrutiny from the point of view of ethnic arithmetic.[29]

For a decade or more after the New Economic Policy was launched, privatization would have meant handing over government functions to non-Malay workers and businesses. A major aim of the NEP would have been negated, and the outcry of the Malays would have rivalled that directed at Malayan Union in 1946.[30] But by 1983 the time was ripe for privatizations. This is not to say that in 1983 the increased numbers of Malay managers constituted a sufficient reason for privatization; but there was no longer a large deficit in the supply of Malay managers and entrepreneurs. It was believed by the government that the shortage had been sufficiently made good for Malays as well as non-Malays to reap benefits from privatization. For this reason privatization could actually strengthen the NEP instead of inevitably wrecking it.[31]

In point of fact, privatization now provides opportunities for Malay businessmen, who, in conjunction with Chinese and foreign partners, can take over and manage enterprises previously run by the government (a role examined in the next section). At a rather lower level some public servants are being given the chance to move into the private sector, after undergoing training, at higher rates of pay.[32] Other public servants, of course, may enter that sector in a less planned way as a consequence of privatization of the government organizations in which they serve. Consequently, although many trade unionists in the public sector are apprehensive because privatization might lead to a loss of jobs or to less favorable working conditions, some higher level civil servants see it as providing attractive opportunities for mobility, more challenging tasks, and improved economic rewards.[33] In telecommunications ". . . the guys who are being more innovative, more efficient, are people who used to be with the public sector. Look at different parts of the private sector and, more often than not, the people who stand out used to be with the public sector."[34] On the other hand, of course, there is no reason why some civil servants who are, in effect, "drafted" into the private sector should immediately cast off their public sector "vices" and assume private sector "virtues."

Large numbers of Malay managers (about one thousand per year) are still needed, but, curiously, some versions of the privatization process do not call for any additional managers.[35] The process does not always take the form of a straightforward transfer of functions from a government agency to a private organization or group of private organizations. There is not always a change of management as well as a change of ownership. A principal vehicle for changes confined to ownership is the PNB (Permodalan Nasional Berhad—National Equity Corporation) and its subsidiary, the ASN (Amanah Saham Nasional Berhad).[36] The PNB is, in effect, a "conglomerate of well-established companies that Malays have a stake in."[37] These organizations are intended to act as channels through which the savings of Malays can be used to achieve Malay ownership of particularly desirable assets. The aim in this instance is to further the NEP objective of greater Malay ownership rather than NEP employment and management goals. The difference between the transfer of both ownership and management, as compared with ownership alone, is illustrated by the recent disposal of various SEDC ventures. In 1982 twenty-eight of these were sold to Bumiputra companies or individuals, while another eleven were transferred to the PNB. There have also been substantial transfers of shares from PERNAS to PNB that have allowed individual Malays to participate in ownership via the latter body or its main subsidiary, the ASN.[38]

Here, also, the timing was propitious. The existence of a large and coordinated body such as the PNB (along with the ASN), which had been set up only a few years before, was necessary in order to consolidate this particular aspect of privatization. Malay ownership would continue to be promoted by the efforts of large institutions, but through shareholding, not, as in the past, as a result of vague actions "on behalf of" the Malays.[39] According to Datuk Musa Hitam, the deputy prime minister, the PNB, along with the newly privatized companies' management and staff, is offered the first choice of shares in government companies that are being privatized. After that, up to a maximum of 25 percent of the total shares are allocated to various Bumiputra bodies.[40]

Currently, some Malays also benefit from a version of privatization by which a state government allocates land to a private firm at a certain price, and in return the firm uses part of the land to construct subsidized low-cost housing for Malays. The firm recoups its losses on this service by selling more expensive housing at market prices on the remainder of the land.[41] Thus, some poorer Malays are subsidized. Similar "package" offers have been suggested in order to induce firms to take over commercially unattractive projects by offering profitable ones as part of the deal.[42] Whether or not these will help Malays will depend on the circumstances.

Malays may also "benefit," in the sense of avoiding losses, if the government, despite some privatization measures, continues to provide services judged to be socially necessary that private enterprise is unwilling to take over.[43] An obvious example is some MARA programs to aid Bumiputra, programs the government intends to continue, even though MARA's total budget is being cut.[44]

Finally, although the question of privatization of land has been mentioned, this is a highly sensitive subject because of the Malays' deep attachment to the land. The National Agricultural Policy provides for cuts in agricultural subsidies and for the promotion of rural development through the concentration of holdings and the infusion of private capital.[45] But the implications of these politically delicate proposals for privatization are not yet clear.

Nevertheless, in spite of the obvious advantages that Malays will derive from privatization, the prime minister has given the assurance that the policy is not "being formulated for the benefit of any group or political party."[46] This statement certainly applies to ethnic groups; the government explicitly favors partnerships between Bumiputra and non-Bumiputra in order to take over public sector functions.[47] It would seem that the interests of non-Bumiputra have been considered, just as they have been until now in the implementation of the NEP (one of the government objectives for 1990 is that non-Malay, and in particular Chinese, capital, should have a 40 percent share in corporate ownership). Apart from anything else, for government policy to succeed, Chinese capital is needed, as is foreign capital. However, more progress has been made under the NEP in producing Malay managers (at least numerically) than in building up Malay capital assets.[48] Similarly, and with equal realism, the government welcomes foreign firms because they provide not just capital but also technological expertise (for example, in privatization of telecommunications or railways). On the other hand, the claims of nationalism dictate that the foreign firms' share of corporate ownership should be limited.

However, it is difficult for Chinese businessmen to participate effectively in privatization because the amounts of capital required are too large for most of them to raise. Apart from a few organizations such as the huge Multi-Purpose Holdings (created by the Malaysian Chinese Association), there are still few sizeable, as opposed to family, Chinese firms in existence.[49] Furthermore, like other possible "takers" for existing government operations, Chinese firms are rightly profit-conscious and skeptical of the financial viability of some candidates for privatization, such as the Malaysian Airlines System (MAS). Chinese businessmen also fear that in case of failure, the government might not bail them out financially, whereas, because of political considerations, it would be forced to bail out Malay firms.[50]

These fears may be exaggerated. The experience of other countries suggests that it is hard for governments to refrain from intervening to rescue important employment-generating firms from disaster. It would also be invidious for a government to hold out help only to Malay, and not also to Chinese, components of such a firm.

Some of the capital for the privatization schemes that have so far been formulated is being provided by non-Bumiputra. But among the various combinations of firms that are to take over, Bumiputra predominate over non-Bumiputra or foreigners. A main objective of the New Economic Policy, to increase Malay ownership and Malay management, still applies.

Additionally, privatization did not imply that non-Malay managers would now become superfluous, or even less necessary. The same source that estimated that one thousand new Malay managers a year would be required also stated that a similar number of non-Malay managers would be needed annually for the economy.[51]

Implication for Ethnic and Class Interpretations

The operation of privatization illustrates the existence of Malay hegemony but also the willingness of the ruling ethnic group to cooperate with and make allocations to other ethnic groups. Similar willingness to accommodate has been evident in the implementation of the NEP. The policy was indeed formulated by Malays, and it envisaged, for example, a higher rate of growth in Malay than in Chinese ownership. However, the original 1990 target—30 percent Malay, 30 percent non-Malay (mainly Chinese) and 40 percent foreign ownership—was changed to 30 percent, 40 percent, and 30 percent respectively, after representations by the Malaysian Chinese Association leadership. Similarly, Chinese and foreign complaints about the working of the Industrial Coordination Act of 1975 led to concessions, especially after Dr. Mahathir took over the Ministry of Trade and Industry in 1977.

These examples fall into Rothchild's category of hegemonial exchange, which rests on the existence of rules, both formal and informal, although the Malaysian system is not precisely one-party, as in his definition.[52] The pressures from the main Malay opposition party, PAS (Parti Islam Se-Malaysia) or Malaysian Islamic Party, now strengthened by fundamentalist Islamic support, are too great for such a description to apply.[53]

Some aspects of Rothchild's schema are not found in the Malaysian case. Both the original NEP and the new privatization policy are intended to benefit Malays more than Chinese. But is this necessarily an "inequitable" resource allocation, given the previous economic disparity between the two groups?[54]

Also, the Rothchild analysis does not distinguish clearly between demands that are negotiable, demands that may occasionally, but not usually, be negotiable, and demands that are certainly not negotiable.[55] The second group includes demands for the cession of Malay land rights, or demands that recruitment to the armed forces or the police be ethnically proportional. The third group includes demands that would place a check on absolute power (for example a mutual veto). By definition, any concession that gave up the power to decide on how the "rules" should be applied would endanger hegemony. So, when speaking of a system, as opposed to individual transactions within a system, in Malaysia or some other countries, the exchange element in a hegemonial exchange system must be ultimately subordinate to the hegemonial.[56]

Bargaining, in the sphere in which it is permissible, must provide possibilities for non-Malays, especially the Chinese, to believe that they have some control over matters that particularly affect them, so they do not feel they have been driven to the wall. The state of the Malaysian economy is obviously important because, if healthy, it allows Malay demands to be defused within the context of an "expanding pie." It was fortunate that in the recession of the early 1980s although the rate of economic growth fell in Malaysia, it still maintained a minimum of about 4 percent per year. However, the "pie's" ability to accommodate increasing appetites could be jeopardized in two respects. The government has launched a drive to increase population growth, which could exert greater demands unless accompanied by a corresponding growth in production.[57] Also, some Malays have urged a continuation and escalation of the targets for Malay ownership and employment opportunities after the existing date for the end of the New Economic Policy (1990).[58] The adoption by the government of such a strategy could lead to a squeeze on non-Malays.

Rothchild's focus is appropriately on ethnicity, but he also refers briefly to some class considerations. This aspect of privatization in Malaysia also deserves attention.

The *Mid-Term Review* of the Fourth Malaysia Plan draws attention to the importance of dispersing ownerships among Malays as privatization takes place.[59] But ownership through shareholding is not the only point at issue. The most spectacular short-term rewards will not go to buyers of shares; the main beneficiaries are almost certain to be those who are able to take over, control, or even manipulate enterprises that were formerly run by the government. The prime minister has declared that the day of the small-scale family business is over,[60] and this is certainly true for the majority of the enterprises now being transferred to the public sector because they are large scale. To be sure, the amount of Malay capital available has increased somewhat, but the funds needed to buy out public enterprises are vast in comparison. The chief benefits for small-scale or medium-scale Malay businesses would be of the "trickle-down" variety in the form of, say, subcontracting.

Consequently, it is hard to resist the conclusion that large, influential Malay business groups stand the best chance of benefiting from privatization. On a political level, there could even be "pressure from certain influential groups in UMNO (United Malays National Organization) to hasten the process of privatization in their own self-interest."[61] In selecting the firms to take over, the problem is that, given the requirement of size, the choice may be so restricted that a system of open tendering may be judged unworkable or superfluous. It is known to government which firms are interested, and the number is usually small.[62] Allegedly, the contracts for laying telephone lines, awarded to four Bumiputra contractors in October 1983, were negotiated "on a restricted basis" and not tendered out, although the minister concerned was satisfied that the price was fair.[63]

Given the small circle of capable Malay entrepreneurs and financiers, it is not surprising that the Fleet Group, which obtained the contract for TV3, is headed by Encick Diam Zainuddin, a confidant of the prime minister who in July 1984 was appointed minister of finance.

At the other end of the economic scale, although privatization is likely to improve the quality of services, it is also likely to increase their price.[64] In the telecommunications example mentioned previously, when contracts were awarded to private firms the cost of the contracted work was higher, although the lines were laid more quickly, thus providing a higher standard of service. For an efficiency calculation, therefore, the higher standard of service would have to be balanced against the higher cost. Government thinking has apparently been based on the premise that in general consumers are demanding a higher quality of service and are prepared to pay for it.[65] The corollary, however, is that those who were previously satisfied with existing standards of service will perhaps now be worse off if standards and prices are raised. They may set little store by the "upgrading" of services. These people may form the majority of consumers in some cases and will almost certainly constitute a majority of *poorer* consumers.[66] Because the majority of the poor are Malays, it is quite likely that Malays in particular may suffer as a result of privatization for this reason.[67]

The overriding role of ethnicity in Malaysia is so plain to see that it has been hard for even determined proponents of the class-struggle thesis to ignore it in their presentations. It is hypothesized that whereas the fundamental contradiction in Malaysia, an essentially capitalist society, is between capital and labor (fundamental in the sense of being determinative in the last instance), it is not necessary that these contradictions assume a primary position or express themselves in class forms at all times—i.e., they can take the forms of ethnic or religious conflicts. It is argued that the *primary* contradiction in Malaysian society at this point is not between capital and labor but between fragments of the dominant class, each of which has its own distinct ethnic or national identity. As a result, ethnic conflicts have become the *prevalent* form of contradiction in Malaysian society.[68]

Such an analysis, if followed up, would invite speculation about the relations between Malay capitalists and Chinese and foreign capitalists respectively. With an eye on the Look East policy, one might also ask, what kind of foreign capitalists, Japanese or Western?[69] To proceed further in this direction would be to go beyond the scope of Rothchild's thesis and the theme of this book. Nevertheless, one consequence of the NEP that is being reinforced by privatization is the rise of a sizeable and powerful Malay business group (or capitalist class).[70] It would perhaps be incorrect to claim that such a group has seriously infringed as yet on state autonomy for two reasons. One is that, even conceding that state autonomy is subject to considerable ethnic pressures, the powerful UMNO General Assembly voices too great a range of Malay viewpoints for Malay pressures unequivocally to assume a class form. Another, of course, is that government policy on important issues is very largely determined by the prime minister, who is indeed convinced of many of the virtues of capitalism, but whose views are far from being stereotypical or predictable. However, businessmen are now reckoned to have greater representation in the UMNO General Assembly than any other group—about 40 percent. Also, for the first time, the money spent at the 1978 elections for the assembly (estimates are as high as M $30 million) came mainly from Malay, not Chinese, sources.[71] It is also noteworthy that Encick Daim is the fist example of a really rich Malay businessman who has been appointed to the cabinet; previous Malay ministers acquired political power before economic power.

Perhaps more than in most African countries, the degree of economic development in Malaysia has led to the emergence of an indigenous capitalist economic group, which is largely the creation of government.[72] This group is increasingly a source of influence on government as well as a contributor to the complexity of the country's "ethnic politics."

In conclusion, what seems to be unusual about Malaysia is that it provides a "two-act" case study of changes in economic policy intended to help a particular ethnic group. The Malays and other Bumiputra benefited from the NEP and the mechanisms set up to implement it and are also benefiting now from the reverse process of privatization. In broad terms, the main points of Rothchild's argument still apply to Malaysia. Malay hegemony continues, economically as well as politically, as embodied in the New Economic Policy. However, numerous public enterprises are being replaced by private enterprises in which, generally, Malays exercise control but in which non-Malay firms are also included. The essential point is that privatization would not have been attempted as a means to increased efficiency unless mechanisms had been available that would at the same time have successfully preserved Malay hegemony.

This chapter is not explicitly comparative, but as a stimulant to discussion, reference may be made to the failure of privatization proposals to be implemented in Thailand. From 1975 to 1977 and again from 1980 to 1981, Boonchu Rajanasthien, a banker, was the highest-ranking member of the Thai government responsible for economic policy. During each term of office he advocated privatization of some government undertakings, but his advocacy produced little response.

Apart from ethnicity, there were several reasons why this was so: There were fewer government enterprises than in Malaysia and consequently less financial pressure on government resources to support them. Thai governments were formed by temporary coalitions and were therefore less resolute in implementation than their Malaysian counterparts. Many enterprises were unattractive to private enterprise because they suffered losses. However, ethnic aspects were prominent, maybe decisive. Many high-ranking Thai military officials were on the boards of these enterprises, and their say in national policymaking was immeasurably more authoritative than that of their equivalents in Malaysia where the military is politically weak. Above all, perhaps because of the absence of an indigenous Thai business class (even a recently manufactured one as in Malaysia), the private interests that would certainly have benefited under privatization were Chinese, a group of which Boonchu was himself a conspicuous member.[73]

Notes

1. For a statement of its meaning, see Mahathir Mohamed [sic], "New Government Policies," Jomo, ed., *The Sun Also Sets: Lessons in Looking East* (Petaling Jaya: INSAN, 1983), pp. 277-278.
2. South Korea and Japan also were taken as models. See ibid., pp. 279-335; Diane K. Mauzy and R. S. Milne, "The Matathir Administration in

Malaysia: Discipline Through Islam," *Pacific Affairs* 56, no. 4 (Winter 1983-1984): 627-630.

3. See Chapter 2 of this volume.

4. See Chapter 4 of this volume. See also R. S. Milne, "The Politics of Malaysia's New Economic Policy," *Pacific Affairs* 49, no. 2 (Summer 1976): 235-262.

5. See Chapter 4 of this volume. Often in Chapter 4 the term, Malays, is used instead of Bumiputra because Malays constitute a high proportion of Bumiputra and were the greatest beneficiaries from privatization. Chinese also are referred to specifically, rather than as part of the wider group, non-Malays.

6. *New Sunday Times*, March 11, 1984 (Datuk Musa Hitam). Federal outlays as a percentage of Gross National Product are double those in South Korea and nearly two-and-a-half times those of Thailand.

7. *New Straits Times*, July 16, November 17, and November 20, 1982.

8. *New Straits Times*, March 4, 1984. Also see *Kementerian Perusahaan Awam: Laporan Tahunan 1982* (Kuala Lumpur: Percetakan Watan, 1983).

9. FIMA   (Food Industries, Malaysia), 1973-1975, interview with Dr. Mahathir, *New Straits Times*, April 12, 1982.

10. *Mid-Term Review of the Fourth Malaysia Plan 1981-1985* (Kuala Lumpur: National Printing Department, 1983), pp. 200-201; *Malaysian Digest*, July 31, 1983 (Dr. Mahathir); and *New Straits Times* , August 26, 1983 (Dato Abdullah Ahmad Badawi).

11. Ibid., November 23, 1983 (quoting a report of the International Labor Organization).

12. Ibid., November 6, 1983.

13. Ibid., July 2, 1983, interview with Dato Michael Chen, chairman of the Port Kelang Authority, June 29, 1984.

14. *New Straits Times*, June 9, 1983 (Dr. Mahathir).

15. R. Thillainathan, "Privatization—Opening Up Existing Possibilities" (Edited version of a paper given at the Malaysian Economic Association on Privatization and the Malaysia Incorporated Concept, August 25, 1983).

16. Another example is the laying of telephone lines by private enterprise. See *New Straits Times*, May 9, 1984.

17. *New Sunday Times*, November 6, 1983.

18. *New Straits Times*, May 9, 1984.

19. For a theoretical treatment, see Thillainathan, "Privatization."

20. Mavis Puthucheary, "Synopsis of Paper on Privatization," mimeograph (n.d.).

21. *Malaysian Digest*, July 31, 1983.

22. Tun Tan Siew Sin, "Promoting a Climate for Closer Cooperation and Understanding—Malaysia Inc., Privatization and National Productivity" (Speech at a seminar on Malaysia Inc., Privatization and National Productivity, Kuala Lumpur, October 10, 1983), p. 11; and interview with Tun Tan Siew Sin, July 11, 1984. On the problems of Japan's government-owned railways, see *Globe and Mail*, September 1, 1984.

23. Mauzy, "The Mahathir Administration," pp. 623-624.

24. Interview with Datin Padukah Rafidah Aziz, minister for public enterprises, July 10, 1984.

25. Supriya Singh, "Privatization Takes Off," *New Straits Times* , May 29, 1984.

26. *New Straits Times*, August 1, 1983.

27. *New Straits Times*, August 29, 1983.

28. *Malaysia*, November 1983.

29. R. S. Milne and Diane K. Mauzy, *Politics and Government in Malaysia*, 2nd ed., rev. (Singapore: Times Books International/Vancouver: University of British Columbia Press, 1983), p. 378.

30. See Chapter 4 in this volume.

31. *New Straits Times*, May 26, 1984 (Dr. Mahathir's speech at the UMNO General Assembly).

32. *Malaysia*, July 1983 (Dr. Mahathir).

33. See the description above.

34. Singh, "Privatization Takes Off."

35. One estimate is that approximately one thousand Bumiputra managers need to be trained each year (*New Straits Times*, March 13, 1984).

36. See Chapter 4 in this volume. At the end of 1982 the PNB had acquired investments totalling M $32 billion at cost. By 1984 its subsidiary, the ASN, had 1.4 million unitholders with investments of M $985.1 billion, said to be the largest unit trust in the world (Datuk Malek Merican, *New Straits Times*, June 4, 1984). For a later analysis, see *Far Eastern Economic Review*, May 23, 1985, pp. 72-74.

37. Datuk Musa Hitam, quoted in *Malaysian Digest*, June 30, 1983.

38. *New Straits Times*, March 4, 1984.

39. *Malaysian Digest*, October 12, 1983.

40. Of this, twenty-five would be allocated to the *Tabung Haji* (Pilgrims' Fund), Armed Forces Fund, and Bumiputra foundations at state and federal levels. Police, armed forces, farmers, and other Bumiputra cooperatives would be allocated forty (*Malaysian Digest*, May 3, 1984).

41. See Chapter 4 in this volume, and *New Straits Times*, July 14, 1984.

42. *New Straits Times*, October 11, 1983 (Tan Sri Ibrahim Mohamed, chairman of Promet).

43. *New Straits Times*, October 20, 1983 (Datuk Abdullah Ahmad Badawi).

44. *New Straits Times*, August 23, 1983.

45. *Far Eastern Economic Review*, May 24, 1984, pp. 75-77.

46. *Malaysia*, November 1983.

47. Ibid.

48. Only 18.7 and thus unlikely to reach the target of 30 (*Mid-Term Review*, p. 101).

49. On the essentially familial nature of Chinese business, see *The Star*, August 23, 1984.

50. Puthucheary, "Synopsis of Paper on Privatization," pp. 5, 7.

51. See fn. 35.

52. See "Group Demands" in Chapter 2 of this volume.

53. R. S. Milne and Diane K. Mauzy, "Malaysia: Same Leaders: More New Policies," *Current History* 83, no. 497 (January 1984); and *New Sunday Times*, August 12 and 26, 1984.

54. See "State Policies for Managing Conflict" in Chapter 2 of this volume.

55. See "Group Demands" in Chapter 2 of this volume.

56. R. S. Milne, *Politics in Ethnically Bipolar States: Malaysia, Guyana, Fiji* (Vancouver: University of British Columbia Press, 1981), Chapter 8.

57. R. S. Milne and Diane K. Mauzy, *Malaysia: Tradition, Modernity and Islam* (Boulder, Colo.: Westview Press, 1985), Chapter 4.

58. See Chapter 4 in this volume; *New Sunday Times*, June 1, 1980; and *New Straits Times*, December 15, 1983 (Datuk Musa Hitam on the need to make good any shortfalls in the NEP targets after 1990).

59. *Mid-Term Review*, p. 15.

60. *New Straits Times*, June 9, 1983.

61. Puthucheary, "Synopsis of Paper on Privatization," p. 4.

62. Personal interview with Datin Padukah Rafidah, July 1984.

63. *New Straits Times*, May 9, 1984.

64. See the discussion above.

65. *Malaysian Digest*, July 31, 1983 (Dr. Mahathir).

66. See Chandra Muzaffar, "Privatization—Caution!" *Aliran Monthly* 4, no. 5 (May 1984): 9-10.

67. See Chapter 4 in this volume. For conflicting data on poverty in general, see *Mid-Term Review*, pp. 75-77; and *New Straits Times*, December 18, 1983 (figures from the Social and Economic Research Unit of the Prime Minister's Department, quoted by Anwar Ibrahim).

68. Lim Mah Hui and William Canak, "The Political Economy of State Policies in Malaysia," *Journal of Contemporary Asia* 11, no. 2 (1981): 209.

69. I am indebted for some thoughts on this to Professor David Gibbons of Universiti Sains Malaysia (Penang).

70. Chandra Muzaffar, "The UMNO Verdict," *Aliran Monthly* 4, no. 7 (1984): 1-3.

71. Milne, "Malaysia: Same Leaders."

72. R. S. Milne, "Interpretations of the State in the ASEAN Countries" (Paper delivered at the Canadian Council for Southeast Asian Studies meeting, Toronto, November 1983).

73. Issara Suwanibol, "The Politics of Public Enterprise in the Third World: The ASEAN Case" (Ph.D. diss., Australian National University, 1979), pp. 306, 310. On the financial relations of the Thai military and bureaucrats with Chinese businessmen, see J. L. S. Girling, *Thailand: Society and Politics* (Ithaca, N.Y. and London: Cornell University Press, 1981), pp. 72-73.

6

Policies of Ethnic Preference in Sri Lanka

ROBERT OBERST

Ethnic violence and conflict are common features of ethnically divided societies. The occurrence of open intercommunal violence constitutes *prima facie* evidence of the failure of public policies aimed at resolving, or at least managing, interethnic rivalries. This chapter examines communal conflict and public policy in the South Asian democracy of Sri Lanka. It examines the types and consequences of such policies that have been implemented in two phases of postindependence, and it discusses why policies regulating interethnic relations have failed to produce harmony.

The Sri Lankan experience of communal conflict raises several important questions concerning the policy analysis of interethnic relations. Traditionally, Sri Lanka has been one of the most competitive democracies in the world.[1] The government dominated by the Sinhalese majority has allowed the largest minority group, the Tamils, access to the decisionmaking processes of government. This hegemonial exchange state system (to adopt Rothchild's terminology in Chapter 2), however, has increasingly come to resemble a hegemonial state system. It is this transformation—the change from an open system stressing reciprocal exchange obligations between the leaders of the ethnic groups to a system marked by strengthened central control exercised by one ethnic group with limited consideration of the other group's demands—that is central to the following analysis.

As Rothchild has noted, a hegemonial exchange state system must operate on the basis of a set of mutually acceptable rules in order to be effective during a long period of time (see Chapter 2). The elites of both of the major ethnic groups of Sri Lanka have accepted and utilized the rules. However, the effect of exchange policies since independence has been to provide a place in the decisionmaking process for the elites of the minority communities and thus satisfy their demands for political influence while at the same time largely ignoring the nonelites among the ethnic minority groups. It is in this contradiction that the exchange system between the Sinhalese and Tamils has broken down and resulted in the current situation where both sides are increasing the level of violence.

Sri Lanka is an ethnically diverse state. Significant ethnic divisions exist in the areas of religion and language. There are four large ethnic groups on the island (see Table 6.1). The largest group is the Sinhalese, who are believed to be early migrants from North India. They consider themselves the earliest "civilized" inhabitants of the island. Next in size are the two Tamil groups. The Sri Lanka Tamils are the descendants of settlers who came as invaders from South India and may have been the earliest settlers on the island. The Indian Tamils are the descendants of South Indians brought by the British to Sri Lanka as plantation laborers in the late nineteenth and early twentieth centuries. As is noted later, most members of this group were denied Sri Lankan citizenship shortly after independence. The Sri Lanka Tamils and Indian Tamils consider themselves culturally distinct.[2] This distinction has been fostered by their geographic separation. The Indian Tamils are found in the estate areas of the central hill country, and the Sri Lanka Tamils are located in the north and east of the island. The fourth group, the Moors, consists of descendants of early Arab traders and, in some cases, Muslim migrants from India.[3]

There are four religions practiced by the Sri Lankans (see Table 6.2). Buddhism has the largest following and is considered the religion of the Sinhalese majority although some Sinhalese converted to Christianity after the coming of the Europeans. Hinduism is the dominant religion among both the Indian Tamils and Ceylon Tamils. Christianity is practiced by groups of both Tamils and Sinhalese, and Islam is the religion of the Moors. Thus, with the exception of the Christians, the religious groups correspond to the ethnic groups, and ethnic identities are often expressed in religious terms. However, the main division between the ethnic communities is based on the Sinhalese and Tamil languages.

Three major languages are spoken on the island (see Table 6.3). The largest linguistic group is composed of the speakers of Sinhalese, which is the language of the Sinhalese ethnic group. The second major group comprises Tamil speakers, including both the Indian and Ceylon Tamils and most Moors. English is spoken by most of the westernized elite, but generally it is not the mother tongue of any ethnic group except for the numerically insignificant Burghers (see note 3).

The linguistic, ethnic, and religious distinctions in Sri Lankan society tend to reinforce each other. The Sinhalese are predominantly Buddhist and speak Sinhalese. The Tamils, who are predominantly Hindu, speak Tamil. Most Moors are Muslims and speak Tamil.

Table 6.1 Ethnic Population of Sri Lanka

Ethnic Group	Percent of Population
Sinhalese	74.0
Ceylon Tamils	12.6
Indian Tamils	5.6
Ceylon Muslims	7.1
Burghers	.3
Malays	.3

Source: Government of Sri Lanka, Statistical Abstract of the Democratic Socialist Republic of Sri Lanka--1982 (Colombo: Department of Census and Statistics, 1982), p. 32.

Table 6.2 Religious Composition of the Sri Lankan Population

Religion	Percent of Population
Buddhism	69.3
Hinduism	15.5
Islam	7.6
Christianity	7.5
Others	.1

Source: Government of Sri Lanka, Statisticial Abstract of the Democratic Socialist Republic of Sri Lanka--1982 (Colombo: Department of Census and Statistics, 1982), p. 34.

Table 6.3 Languages Spoken by Persons Three Years of Age and Above, 1953

Language	Percent of Population
Sinhala only	58.9
Tamil only	21.6
English only	.2
Sinhala and Tamil	9.9
Sinhala and English	4.2
Tamil and English	2.0
Sinhala, Tamil, and English	3.2

Source: Robert Kearney, "Language and the Rise of Tamil Separatism in Sri Lanka," Asian Survey 17 (May 1978):523.

The Sri Lankan party system reflects the ethnic division of the society. The Tamil community has consistently chosen to support their own political parties rather than the dominant parties of the party system (the United National party, or UNP, and the Sri Lanka Freedom party, or SLFP, both of which have been dominated by members of the Sinhalese community). Thus, for many years two parties contested for the allegiance of the Sri Lanka Tamils—the Tamil Congress and the Federal party. In the 1970s significant elements of these two parties united and formed the Tamil United Liberation Front (TULF).

Table 6.4   Ethnic Composistion of Selected Government Services, 1870–1946

Year	Total number	percent	Sinhalese number	percent	Tamil number	percent	Burgher number	percent
1870	30	100.0	9	30.0	0	0.0	21	70.0
1907	93	100.0	23	24.7	13	14.0	57	61.3
1925	255	100.1	106	41.6	68	26.7	81	31.8
1935	381	100.0	189	49.6	104	27.3	88	23.1
1946	582	100.0	335	57.6	177	30.4	70	12.0
Percent of Population (1946)				69.4		22.7		0.6

Note: The selected government services are the civil service, the public works department, judicial services, and the medical services.
Sources: Adapted from S. J. Tambiah, "Ethnic Representation of Ceylon's Higher Administrative Services 1870-1946," University of Ceylon Review 13, nos. 2-3 (April-July 1955):113-134, as cited in Charles Abeysekera, "Ethnic Representation in the Higher State Services," in Social Scientists Association, ed., Ethnicity and Social Change in Sri Lanka (Colombo: Social Scientists Association, 1984):181.

Communal conflict in Sri Lanka has generally focused on the position of the Sinhalese culture and its traditions in the society. Because the Sinhalese are the majority ethnic community on the island, it is to be expected that they would be at the center of any conflict about ethnicity. The central grievance of the Sinhalese is that they suffered under the colonial rule of Great Britain. At the time of the European arrival the Sinhalese were the dominant political force on the island. It was a Sinhalese kingdom, the Kandyan Kingdom, that held out against the British until the nineteenth century. However, after the British established their authority over the island, the language of government became English, and Christianity became the religion of the colony's Ceylonese elite. This situation tended to favor the Tamils from the Jaffna peninsula in the north. The British sought English speakers for the colonial bureaucracy, and the Tamils benefited because a large number of Christian missionary schools had been established on the Jaffna peninsula that offered the Jaffna Tamils an opportunity for an education in English. As a result, the Tamils received a disproportionate number of the government jobs available in the colonial administration (see Table 6.4).

Therefore, one consequence of the colonial government's hiring practices was a strong sense of discrimination felt by the Sinhalese. Many Sinhalese believed that the British had shown preference to the Tamils. This tended to reinforce Sinhalese fears of assimilation by the Tamil culture, which extends beyond the north of the island into Southern India. The much smaller Sinhalese culture and language are dwarfed in size when compared with the Tamil culture.

Since independence two distinct stages can be seen in the development of ethnic policies in Sri Lanka. The inital stage lasted for the first twenty-five years after independence. It was marked by Sinhalese attempts to claim what they saw as their rightful place in the society. Simultaneously, attempts were made by the Sinhalese to restrict the influence of Sri Lanka's minority communities. By the mid-1970s this policy had succeeded in restoring the Sinhalese to a position of dominance, and it ensured that they would maintain that position. The second and subsequent stage has been marked by policies that enforce minority ethnic group compliance with the Sinhalese-dominated state. Many of the policies enacted during this stage have been influenced by violence between the ethnic communities and have been the direct result of guerrilla warfare by Tamil youths in the north and government responses to that warfare.

The motivating force behind the ethnic policies of these two stages has been the belief held by many Sinhalese that they are, and were (in the colonial era), victims of discrimination. To correct this bias and protect the Sinhalese culture and religion, policies of preference favoring the Sinhalese have been introduced.

The Policies of Sinhalese Restoration, 1947-1977

The period of Sinhalese restoration was marked by three different elements that correspond roughly to three of Rothchild's conflict-regulating strategies. These elements were (1) policies to include the minority group elites in the decisionmaking process of government, a noncoercive strategy of sharing; (2) policies to restrict ethnic minorities or to limit their position in the society, a more coercive strategy involving both displacement and cultural assimilation; and (3) policies intended to directly restore the Sinhalese culture to its rightful place in the society, a strategy of cultural assimilation.

The Inclusion of Minority Elites in Government

Sharing was the least coercive strategy of this period. As a British-styled democracy, Sri Lanka tried to set up political arrangements that would provide representation to all ethnic communities in the society. Most of the political parties in the first few years after independence stressed their national character. One part of this strategy was an attempt to draw significant segments of the ethnic minorities into a broad-based government coalition. The first postcolonial government was established with the support of the Tamil Congress. At that time, the Tamil Congress was the leading political organization of the Sri Lanka Tamils and had elected seven members of the ninety-five-member parliament. Among its fourteen ministers, the government's cabinet included two Tamil independents and one member of the Tamil Congress, G. G. Ponnambalam, who was one of the most politically influential Tamils of his time.[4] However, his support of the government and their policies (to be discussed later) helped lead to a split in the Tamil Congress and the creation of a second Tamil political party, the Federal party, under the leadership of S. J. V. Chelvanayagam. The rise of the Federal party marked the beginning of a decline in the sharing strategy as government policies began to alienate the Tamil community. The sharing strategy ended for all intents and purposes in 1953 when G. G. Ponnambalam resigned from the cabinet of Sir John Kotelawala. The first Parliament saw the Tamils in the cabinet in charge of three ministries with relatively significant cabinet influence and patronage power (see Table 6.5). In the second Parliament cabinet the Tamils lost the Ministry of Trade. Tamil participation in the cabinets since the second Parliament has been in mininstries of relatively limited cabinet power. Thus, the general pattern of this period was a decline in Tamil cabinet power after the initial experiment with power-sharing in the first two cabinets.

In the mid-1950s the Tamil leadership lost much of its influence in government when the coalition of S. W. R. D. Bandaranaike came to power. Bandaranaike was able to defeat the dominant United National party in the 1956 elections because of his support from rural Sinhalese voters. His coalition of leftist parties made a strong appeal to Sinhalese nationalism and promised to restore the Sinhalese to a dominant position in society. One of the coalition's promises was to make Sinhala the national language as well as the language of government.

Although the Tamils were left out of the decisionmaking process during Bandaranaike's government, they were not ignored. The Tamil Language Act of 1958, to be discussed later, is a direct result of Bandaranaike's concern for Tamil interests and the conflict developing between the Sinhalese and Tamil communities. After S.W.R.D. Bandaranaike's assassination and the collapse of his coalition, the Tamil leadership found that the government of Sirimavo

Table 6.5 Tamil Representation in the Cabinets of Sri Lanka

Parliament	Years	Party	Prime Minister	Cab. Size	Tamil Min.	Ministries Held
First	1948-52	UNP	D.S. Senanayake	14	2	Posts & Telegraph, Trade, Indust., Fish.
Second	1952	UNP	Dudley Senanayake	14	2	Posts & Infomation, Industries, Fisheries
	1952-53	UNP	J. Kotelawala	14	3	Posts & Broad., Hous., Ind., Soc. Ser., Fish.
	1953-56	UNP	J. Kotelawala	15	2	Posts & Broad., Hous., Ind., Soc. Ser., Fish.
	1956	UNP	J. Kotelawala	15	1	Indust., Fisheries, Housing, Social Services
Third	1956-59	SLFP	S.W.R.D. Bandaranaike	15	0	
	1959-60	SLFP	W. Dahanayake	22	0	
Fourth	1960	UNP	Dudley Senanayake	8	0	
Fifth	1960-65	SLFP	S. Bandaranaike	11	0	
Sixth	1965-68	UNP	Dudley Senanayake	17	1	Local Government
	1968-70	UNP	Dudley Senanayake	19	0	
Seventh	1970-77	SLFP	S. Bandaranaike	19	1	Posts and Telecommunications
Eighth	1977-78	UNP	J.R. Jayawardene	24	1	Justice
	1978-79	UNP	R. Premadasa	28	2	Justice, Rural Industrial Development
	1979-85	UNP	R. Premadasa	29	3	Home Aff., Regional Devel., Rural Ind. Devel.

Bandaranaike, S.W.R.D. Bandaranaike's widow, was no more sympathetic to their concerns. The Tamil elites again participated in a UNP government in 1965. Once again they found that the leadership was unsympathetic to their demands and left the coalition in 1968.

The history of Tamil pariticipation in Sri Lankan politics during this period was one of limited Tamil influence. The Tamils were not able to stop policies created to benefit the Sinhalese community. However, they found that they did have the power and influence to exact some concessions, although these concessions did not change the thrust of government policies. Clear examples of this can be seen in the education and language policies of this era. The concessions made to the Tamils prompted them to continue participating in the government throughout the period. It was only after it became apparent that the government was not going to be more sympathetic to the Tamil demands, and a new generation of leaders began to appear, that the Tamil leadership changed its demands. The leadership became dissatisfied with the government, and the young began to resort to violence.

Restriction of Ethnic Minorities

The policies that restricted ethnic minorities are best exemplified by two policies enacted in the first twenty years of independence. These were the denial of Indian Tamil citizenship, a strategy of displacement, and the restricting of Christian schools, a strategy of cultural assimilation.

Indian Tamil Citizenship. The first policies dealing with the ethnic minority communities in Sri Lanka were enacted shortly after independence. They were an indication of what was to be expected in the years to come. The first target was the politically weakest community on the island, the Indian Tamils. A series of legislative actions denied the Indian Tamils citizenship and the right to vote. These policies were supported by the Sri Lanka Tamil leadership represented by G. G. Ponnambalam and the Tamil Congress. It is believed that Ponnambalam's fear of communism caused him to support the denial of citizenship and the right to vote to a community that had a history of supporting leftist movements—the Indian Tamils.[5]

The Citizenship Act of 1948 "created two categories of citizenship (1) by descent and (2) by registration."[6] To qualify for citizenship by descent, one had to be able to prove that his or her father, or his or her paternal grandfather and great grandfather had been born in Sri Lanka. Citizenship by registration was granted to people who had rendered distinguished service to the nation "and/or had been naturalised as British subjects in Sri Lanka."[7] A maximum of twenty-five people could be given citizenship by registration each year. Even though most of the Indian Tamils had been born in Sri

Lanka, they were considered by the government to be Indian citizens and thus aliens. The new country's leadership saw them as a product of British colonialism, and therefore, independent Sri Lanka sought to settle the problem by restoring the Indian Tamils to their "rightful" status. The act removed their citizenship while a year later the Indian and Pakistani Residents Act of 1949 established certain criteria that allowed Indian Tamils and Moors to apply for Sri Lankan citizenship. Indians and Pakistanis could apply for citizenship if they had a Sri Lankan income, if their wives and children resided with them in Sri Lanka, if they renounced any other citizenship, and if they had been resident in Sri Lanka for ten years prior to January 1, 1946, if single, and seven years if married.[8] The Ceylon Parliamentary Elections Amendment Act of 1949 further restricted the rights of Indian Tamils. It barred noncitizens from having their names entered in the register of elections. This effectively disenfranchised the Indian Tamils who had elected six members to the first Parliament of independent Sri Lanka.

These acts began a long series of compromises and policies that intended to resolve the ambiguous status of the Indian Tamils. The Indian and Pakistani governments were reluctant to accept these people as citizens, and the Sri Lankan government was faced with a significant number of stateless individuals. In addition, the government was very slow in processing the applications of Indian Tamils for citizenship. The deadline date for applications was August 5, 1951, but all of the applications were not processed until 1962.[9] Of the more than 825,000 Indian Tamils applying for citizenship, only slightly more than 16 percent were granted citizenship.[10]

A series of negotiations began between the prime ministers of Sri Lanka and India to resolve the status of the Indian Tamils. The Indian government initially refused to accept as citizens those Indian Tamils who had been denied Sri Lankan citizenship. In 1964 Prime Minister Sirimavo Bandaranaike and Prime Minister Lal Bahadur Shastri of India came to an agreement on the repatriation of the Indian Tamils (Indo-Ceylon Agreement of October 1964).[11] The act called for the repatriation of 525,000 of the estimated 975,000 Indian Tamils and Sri Lankan citizenship for 300,000. The status of the remaining 150,000 Indian Tamils was to be decided at a later date.[12] Ultimately, the two governments decided to split the remaining Indian Tamils: 75,000 were to go to India and 75,000 were to remain in Sri Lanka. However, the implementation of the agreement has been hindered by slowness in the granting of Sri Lankan citizenship and Indian repatriation as well as by charges that many of the Indian Tamils to be repatriated have overstayed their visit and refused to leave. The government of President J. R. Jayawardene, which came to power in 1977, agreed in 1984 to grant citizenship to the remaining 100,000 stateless Indian Tamils in Sri Lanka.

Christian Schools. The issue of Christian schools began to simmer as soon as independence was achieved. However, it was not forcefully dealt with until the early 1960s. At issue was the question of the type of education available to Sinhalese youths. The best schools on the island had been the Christian-run schools, and their alumni received better employment after graduation.[13] Buddhists wanted their children to attend the best schools available but did not want them to be subjected to Christian proselytizing. The Christians had succeeded in achieving political and economic influence beyond what would have been expected according to their percentage in the population. In 1960 and 1961 the SLFP government of Sirimavo Bandaranaike adopted a strategy of assimilation by nationalizing the Christian schools. The clergy, at first, resisted this attempt but ultimately gave in to the nationalization. The takeover of the prestigious Christian schools was seen as a means to improve the quality of Buddhist education. At the very least it weakened the influence of the Christians in Sri Lankan society. The UNP government that came to power in 1965 did not make any effort to retract the nationalization. In fact, the government carried the policy one step further by replacing the Christian sabbath, Sunday, with the Buddhist holy day, the *poya* day, as a public holiday.

The end result of both these policies was the weakening of the position of the Indian Tamils, which in a sense undermined the Tamil community as a whole, and the weakening of the dominant position of Christianity. Although both policies were intended to restore the Sinhalese to their "rightful" place, this was accomplished by weakening the Tamils and not by directly strengthening the Sinhalese as the next set of policies intended to do.

Policies of Restoring the Sinhalese Culture

The Language Issue. There has been no other issue in Sri Lanka since independence that has created as much controversy and conflict as the issue of language. At the heart of the Sinhalese restoration has been the question of the Sinhala language and its place in society.[14] When the British gained control over Sri Lanka, the language of colonial government became English. The British staffed the colonial bureaucracy with English speakers. However, with the advent of mass education, most Sri Lankans were educated in Tamil or Sinhala and were unable to qualify for prestigious government jobs. This led to a demand for Swabasha, or the people's own language.

At the time of independence the country's leadership was committed to replacing English with Tamil and Sinhala. However, it was not until 1956 and the election of S.W.R.D. Bandaranaike's SLFP that the issue was finally decided by the government. The issue was seen at that time as a Sinhala-Tamil question rather than an English-Swabasha issue. The first enactment of the SLFP government in 1956 was the Official Language Act, which declared that Sinhala was the one official language of Sri Lanka.[15] The act was to be implemented immediately, if possible, and no later than 1960 in areas where it was impractical to implement at once. In essence, the language policy was a strategy of cultural assimilation that sought to make Sri Lanka a one-language state.

The immediate consequence of the language act was the alienation of the country's Tamil speakers. The relations between the Tamil and Sinhalese communities soon deteriorated, and riots broke out in 1958. Bandaranaike responded by supporting the Tamil Language (Special Provisions) Act of 1958. This act provided for the use of Tamil in higher education as well as in public service entrance exams as long as those recruited by the exam developed proficiency in Sinhala in order to continue in service or receive promotions.[16] The act was not implemented until the UNP came to power in 1965 with the support of the Federal party, the Tamil Congress, and the Ceylon Worker's Congress.[17] The Tamil Language (Special Provisions) Regulations, 1966, added to the 1958 act the right to use Tamil in certain government transactions in the northern and eastern provinces and for official correspondence between people literate in Tamil. Once again the language legislation led to violence. A riot resulted after the SLFP-led opposition called for a demonstration against the act.[18]

After the SLFP came to power in the United Front coalition government in 1970, the issue once more arose when the United Front promulgated a new constitution in 1972. From the Tamil perspective, Chapter 3 of the constitution improved on what had been in effect up until that time by granting Tamil an official status in some government transactions.[19] However, Chapter 3 did not enshrine the 1958 Tamil Language Act and left Tamil as a subordinate language. Thus, the new constitution did not alleviate Tamil discontent about the language issue.

In 1977 the UNP was swept into power with a five-sixths majority, and its government changed the constitution in 1978. Under the new constitution (Chapter 4), Tamil is given the status of a national language while Sinhala remains the offical language. The significance of the national language status was not spelled out in the constitution, and the constitutional provisions did not remove Tamil criticism of the government language policy.[20]

Buddhism and the State. Another issue of cultural assimilation—the role Buddhism should play in Sri Lankan society—was coupled with the language issue. The arrival of the Sinhalese in Sri Lanka is believed to coincide with the death of the Buddha.[21] Buddhism holds a very special place in the identity of the Sinhalese. It is not surprising that the religion has been enshrined in the constitution. The constitution of 1978 states in Article 9 that "the Republic of Sri Lanka shall give to Buddhism the foremost place and accordingly it shall be the duty of the state to protect and foster the Buddha *Sasana*" (*Sasana* is the totality of Buddhist teachings). Thus, Buddhism is accorded a special place above the other religions practiced in Sri Lanka. The governments since 1956 have actively promoted Buddhism although guaranteeing the rights of the other religions.

Educational Policies. Education is another area in which policies were implemented to assist the Sinhalese community. The Sri Lankan educational system is one of the best in South Asia. Education has been given very high priority by the government and the people. One consequence of this stress on education has been very stiff competition for admission to the universities of Sri Lanka. The university admission system is modelled on the British educational system with a series of examinations for admission to the universities. Prior to 1970 the exams were conducted in English, Tamil, and Sinhala with those receiving the highest scores gaining admission to the university. Youths from the Jaffna peninsula consistently scored higher on the examinations. This was especially the case in the science exams. As a result of their higher test scores the number of Tamil youths entering the university exceeded their percentage in the university-age population. Many Sinhalese felt that the examiners in the Tamil medium deliberately inflated the scores of the Tamil youths in order to admit more Tamils to the university.

In 1970 the United Front government enacted the first of a series of policies of preference to protect the Sinhalese students by limiting the number of university placements available to Tamil youths. Initially a system of "standardization" was created. Details of the scheme were not disclosed, but it did limit the number of Tamil students admitted to the university by requiring higher entrance exam scores for those taking the examination in the Tamil medium.[22] This was changed in 1973 to a system of "area quotas" in which the number of university openings was limited for each language group.[23] The immediate result of these policies was a reduction in the number of Tamil youths allowed into the universities. In addition, Tamils had to score higher on their examinations in order to qualify for admittance to the university system.[24] The UNP government that came to power in 1977 tried to resolve this controversy by changing the system of standardization through a quota system. The quota system provided for 30 percent of all admittances on merit (raw scores), 55 percent on the basis of the population in administrative districts,[25] and 15 percent for backward districts.[26] This system was not popular and has undergone several revisions. Once again, the policies intended to protect the Sinhalese majority from what was seen as discrimination in favor of other ethnic groups.

The policies described in this section all were meant to help restore the Sinhalese community to its "rightful" place of dominance in the society. By the mid-1970s this largely had been done. There were few areas where the Sinhalese needed to establish new policies. The Sinhalese now had to protect their new gains from Tamil charges that the policies were biased against the Tamil community. The Tamils' demands increasingly reflected their frustration with postindependence policies. The Tamils believed that government policies did not reflect the needs and interests of their community. The Sinhalese found themselves in a defensive position and responded to the Tamil demands by trying to offer concessions to the Tamils without giving up any of the gains achieved.

The Enforcement of Parity (1977 Through Early 1980's)

The second major period of ethnic policies in Sri Lanka began in the mid-1970s. It is marked by more coercive policies and strategies of cultural assimilation and subjection. However, although the government has stressed coercive strategies, it has also tried power-sharing again.

In 1977 the United National party came to power with the largest parliamentary majority in the island's history. The party had the power to change the constitution at will and to enact any policies it sought. The Tamil leadership felt that once again, as in the past, a UNP government would be more sympathetic to its demands than the SLFP had been. However, the policies enacted to restore the Sinhalese community to its position of dominance were largely in place, and there was little to do but protect the status quo. Meanwhile, the Tamil leadership was divided between the older generation represented by the TULF and the more militant youths who were no longer willing to wait for change to come.

These two trends collided after the 1977 elections. The UNP government was faced with a choice between making concessions to the Tamils that would alienate the UNP power base among the rural Sinhalese or trying to protect the gains already made for the Sinhalese community. They chose the second path and thus enforced the status quo. A series of policies were introduced that took a harder line against Tamil demands. The Sri Lanka Tamil leadership as represented by the TULF was shut off from influence in the government and finally expelled from the Parliament in October 1983.[27] The government's choice was made easier by the insurrection of Tamil youths in the northern and eastern provinces.

The violence began after the 1970 elections but increased sharply after 1977. A series of riots in 1977, 1981, and 1983, in which the victims were largely Tamils, occasioned a reaction in kind by Tamil youths.

The policies that emerged in the post-1977 era intended to enforce Sinhalese control over the society while allowing the Tamils power-sharing in a Sinhalese-dominated framework. For instance, for the first time since the early 1950s, the government expanded the number of Tamils in the cabinet (see Table 6.5). However, the three ministries (Home Affairs, Regional Development, and Rural Industrial Development) held by Tamils in the 1980s did not have very much cabinet influence, nor did they have patronage power. But they were important for other reasons. The minister of rural industrial development was S. Thondaman, the most influential leader of the Indian Tamils. He had been first elected to Parliament in 1947 as a member of the Ceylon Workers Congress. His entry into the cabinet in 1978 undermined whatever unity there might have been between the Indian and Sri Lanka Tamils. The ministers of home affairs and regional development (K. W. Devanayagam and C. Rajadurai) were Tamils from the eastern province. Devanayagam, a longtime UNP member, and Rajadurai, a crossover to the UNP from the TULF in 1979, helped to foster a separation between the eastern province Tamils and those from the Jaffna peninsula, although tension had existed between these two groups for some time because of their geographic separation and the large disparity in their levels of development. The Jaffna Tamils tended to be much better educated and economically advanced. The strategy of power-sharing with two relatively disadvantaged Tamil groups isolated the Jaffna Tamils.

Coupled with this power-sharing strategy have been a series of much more coercive policies. One of the first actions of the UNP government was to ignore one of its election pledges. The United National party election manifesto promised to call an All-Party Conference to remedy the Tamil grievances.[28] The manifesto also promised to include the results of the conference in the new constitution they promised to promulgate.[29] The constitution was written and passed into law in 1978. The All-Party Conference did not meet until January 1984 after a sharp escalation in the level of violence betweeen the two communities. By this time both the Tamils and the Sinhalese had become completely disenchanted with each other. Important elements of both communities refused to participate in the conference once it was called. The "tiger" organizations called for a TULF boycott of the conference while the SLFP initially decided not to attend the meetings. In any case, the UNP had successfully alienated the Tamil leadership by failing to call the conference before the writing of the new constitution as had been promised in the election manifesto.

A third set of policies during this era that irritated the Tamils was government hiring practices. The Tamil leadership claimed that the new government was doing an even worse job of hiring Tamils in government positions than the earlier SLFP government. Table 6.6 reports hiring in selected fields by ethnic group during the first two years of the government. It indicates a sharp deterioration in the Tamil position in the three occupations under analysis. The Sinhalese constituted 74.0 percent of the total population but received 89.9 percent of the teaching, clerical, and police constable positions available. The Tamils (both Indian and Sri Lankan) constituted 18.2 percent of the population and received 5.8 percent of the jobs available. Even the Moors, who made up 7.1 percent of the population, received fewer jobs than would be expected from their percentage in the total population (they received 4.3 percent of available jobs).

Table 6.6   Ethnic Group and Government Employees Hired in Selected Fields, 7/22/77-10/12/79

	Sinhalese		Tamil		Moor	
	number	percent	number	percent	number	Percent
Teachers	22399	89.3	1518	6.1	1164	4.6
General clerical	3127	94.0	148	4.4	51	1.5
Police constables	343	91.7	17	4.5	13	3.5
Total	25869	89.9	1683	5.8	1228	4.3
Total number of government employees as of July 1, 1980	311089	84.3	42818	11.4	12283	3.3

Sources: Parliamentary Debates (Hansard) vol. 9, no. 5, col. 364; vol. 10, no. 17, col. 1586; and Government of Sri Lanka, Census of Public Sector Employment--1980 (Colombo: Department of Census and Statistics, 1983).

A fourth set of policies involving the Tamils has been those relating to home rule, or federalism. As noted earlier, federalism was one of the early demands of the Federal party leadership. The concept of decentralized development administration had captured the imagination of Sri Lankan leaders as early as the 1950s; S.W.R.D. Bandaranaike had proposed a system of regional councils in 1958. However, it was not until the SLFP instituted the Political Authority scheme in 1974 that the idea was taken seriously. The Political Authority was later changed to the Decentralized Budget under the UNP government in 1977.[30] The plan called for the allocation of a set amount of money for each electorate in the country. The money was to be spent on development projects by the member of parliament (MP) of that district; the MP had the power to plan and administer the project. The program was quite successful although the amount of money involved was not substantial.

In 1981 the government extended the Decentralized Budget plan by creating District Development Councils (DDCs) that were intended to increase the amount of home rule in the local areas.[31] The councils were to gather revenues through taxation and to assume many of the responsibilities of local government. Each council was to be made up of the district MPs and elected representatives not to exceed the number of MPs on the council, but the plan has not been successful. Many of the councils have been unable to generate any revenue and without finances are largely powerless. In addition, the expulsion of the TULF from Parliament also removed them from the DDCs in their districts.

The councils had the potential to resolve some of the Tamil demands by establishing some regional autonomy in the Tamil areas.[32] However, the government did not seem very committed to the policy it expounded. In the summer of 1984 an influential government official connected with the plan remarked that more power and finances could not be given to the councils in the Tamil areas because there was no way of knowing what the Tamils would do with the money and power.[33] Once again, the Sinhalese leadership appeared to be threatened by Tamil intentions.

The violence by the Tamil youths has provided a pretext for the government to take very harsh action against the violent youth organizations as well as Tamils in general. Since 1977 the government has responded to the violence by the Tamil "tiger" organizations with very harsh policies. The "tigers" are guerrilla groups that had taken up arms against the government over the question of Tamil rights. After 1977 the number of acts by the "tigers" increased rapidly. The government responded by passing the Prevention of Terrorism Act in 1979. The major provisions of this act allow any superintendent of police or subinspector to make warrantless arrests and searches. The minister in charge may order the detention of a suspect for up to eighteen months without the minister's decision being subject to judicial review. Also, the relevant minister may place restrictions on a suspect that limit his or her movements, contact with others, and political activity for up to eighteen months.[34] In addition, the act calls for all offenses under the act to be tried by a single judge without a jury; confessions obtained by the authorities without legal safeguards for the accused are admissible as evidence. The International Commission of Jurists has argued that the law's provisions are so broad that they are not even remotely comparable to similar laws in other democracies operating under the rule of law.[35]

Since the enactment of this law the government has taken much harsher actions in the northern regions of the country. The army has on a number of occasions since 1977 gone on rampages against Tamil citizens in retaliation for attacks by the "tigers." Despite claims to the contrary by the Ministry of National Security, there appears to have been very limited if any disciplinary action taken against those involved in these attacks. By permitting these actions, the government has been able to intimidate the Tamil citizenry.

An important feature of this hard line toward the Tamil youths has been the practice of making "sweep arrests" of Tamil young people in areas where an attack has occurred. In most cases the youths are held for several weeks before being released, but "tiger" suspects are held for longer periods of time. An example of this practice is the case of Velvetthurai, a coastal village, in

August 1984. After two sailors were killed by the "tigers," the army moved into the village and arrested 650 youths. Most of them were between the ages of seventeen and twenty-five. They were held for almost a month before all but 8 of them were released. These policies have led at least one government minister, S. Thondaman, an Indian Tamil, to remark that the policy of "arresting innocent people on mere suspicion that they were terrorists and harassing them" has helped to create terrorists.[36]

The government policies have also been directed against the nonviolent leadership of the Tamils, such as the legal TULF. In 1983, after the July and August riots, the government enacted the Sixth Amendment to the constitution. It barred the peaceful advocacy of separatism. Members of the TULF were required to take an oath affirming their opposition to Eelam (an independent Tamil state). They refused to do so and were removed from Parliament and barred from the practice of law. This action effectively removed the one legal voice of the Tamil people and enhanced the position of the more radical "tigers." The TULF leaders lost the use of Parliament as a forum for their cause, and communication between the Tamils and the Sinhalese deteriorated.

Following the TULF's expulsion from Parliament, some members of the UNP began to carry out a propaganda campaign to discredit the TULF leadership even further. The campaign has included public statements by government leaders excoriating the TULF leadership and prominent display of articles critical of the TULF in both government and private newspapers.

In addition to these policies, actions have been taken that have been directed against all Tamils. These have included threats by the government to discontinue all development projects in Tamil areas and a directive from National Security Minister Lalith Athulathmudali that government workers in the northern and eastern portions of the island would be personally responsible for all state property stolen by the "tigers."[37]

The policies enacted since the mid-1970s have sought to limit the possibility that the Tamils could challenge the gains made by the Sinhalese during the 1950s and 1960s. The employment policy, the failure to call the All-Party Conference, the expulsion of the elected representatives of the TULF from Parliament, and the harsh policies directed against noncombatants in the violence in the Tamil areas have all contributed to the maintenance of the current relationships between the Tamils and the Sinhalese.

Conclusion

The previous discussion has described two major periods of government policies toward ethnic minorities in Sri Lanka. The first period was one of Sinhalese restoration; the second saw the maintenance of the Sinhalese position in Sri Lankan society. Policies in the first stage were intended to reestablish the Sinhalese to a position of dominance in the society commensurate with their position as the majority ethnic group and to restrict some of the minority ethnic groups. Second-stage policies sought to maintain the newly dominant Sinhalese position.

During the first period the Tamil community exercised a fair amount of influence and power in the government. The political system was open and resembled Rothchild's hegemonial exchange system. In the second period the open political system declined with the expulsion from Parliament of the only Tamil party representatives.

What follows is an attempt to explain the deterioration in the hegemonial exchange system in Sri Lanka. As Rothchild has noted, the response of the state to minority ethnic group demands will have an impact on the nature of the relations between the ethnic groups. In Sri Lanka the democratic structure is majoritarian in nature. Without specific safeguards to protect the political influence of the ethnic minorities, the country has pursued majoritarian policies that have reflected the demands of the Sinhalese majority at the expense of the country's minorities.

Rothchild has noted that hegemonial exchange state systems allow more conflict and interaction between ethnic groups because of the placement of representatives of the society's groups in the cabinet and other positions of authority. In Sri Lanka the early attempts to place Tamils in positions of authority soon broke down as the Tamil electorate continued to support only their own parties in the elections and not those of the Sinhalese dominated majority—the UNP and SLFP. Thus, the country was ruled for the first thirty years of independence with a limited amount of Tamil influence in government. One author closely associated with the ruling UNP has argued that the Federal party had a very dismal record of achievement during this period,[39] but it can also be argued that the party's failure was a consequence of the majoritarian system. In any case, the result of policies enacted during these first thirty years has been the failure of the government to process and respond to Tamil demands. This failure, of course, is one of the causes of Tamil separatism and violence. In response to this conflict the government has put the rebellion down with very harsh methods and refused to give into Tamil demands.

The end result of these events has been a move by the government to eliminate militarily any armed opposition by the Tamil people. Violence has resulted as the Tamils have fought back. Large numbers of Tamils have sought asylum in other countries as the system of law and order has broken down in the Tamil regions. The police, the army, and the "tigers" are responsible for this breakdown.

Restoration of a peaceful communal environment in Sri Lanka will require the establishment of rules to guide the demands for governmental resources by the various ethnic groups. The conflict in the country must be channelled into peaceful actions. This will require a very strong and concerted effort by the government to reestablish the rules of the game. At the moment, the Tamils do not have any significant input into policymaking. The system needs to be restructured in order to allow the Tamils this input. Until this restructuring is done, the communal situation in Sri Lanka will continue to remain unresolved.

Notes

1. See James Jupp, *Sri Lanka: Third World Democracy* (London: Frank Cass, 1979).

2. K. Sivathamby, "Some Aspects of the Social Composition of the Tamils of Sri Lanka," Social Scientists Association, eds., *Ethnicity and Social Change in Sri Lanka* (Colombo: Social Scientists Association, 1984), pp. 128-129.

3. In addition to these four ethnic groups, several small groups are found on the island. These groups are the Indian Moors, Malays, and Burghers. The Burghers are of mixed European, usually Dutch or Portuguese, and Sri Lankan extraction. During the colonial rule they were highly influential in government and commerce. This influence has declined in recent years.

4. G. G. Ponnambalam was not appointed to the cabinet until 1948, one year after its original formation.

5. Satchi Ponnambalam, *Sri Lanka: National Conflict and the Tamil Liberation Struggle* (London: Zed Books, 1984), p. 77.

6. A. Jeyaratnam Wilson, *Politics in Sri Lanka, 1947-1979* (London: Macmillan, 1979), p. 24.

7. Ibid.

8. Ibid.

9. Ibid., p. 25.

10. Ibid.

11. The agreement is also known as the Sirima-Shastri accord.

12. Shelton U. Kodikara, *Foreign Policy of Sri Lanka: A Third World Perspective* (New Delhi: Chanakya, 1982).

13. Wilson, *Politics in Sri Lanka*, p. 14.

14. See Robert N. Kearney, *Communalism and Language in the Politics of Ceylon* (Durham, N.C.: Duke University, 1967).

15. Ibid., p. 82.

16. Urmila Phadnis, *Religion and Politics in Sri Lanka* (New Delhi: Manohar, 1976), p. 272.

17. The 1965 coalition included sixty-six members of the UNP and the support of fourteen Federal party and three Tamil Congress members.

18. Phadnis, *Religion and Politics*, p. 273.

19. Wilson, *Politics in Sri Lanka*, pp. 220-221.

20. A. Jeyaratnam Wilson, *The Gaullist System in Asia: The Constitution of Sri Lanka (1978)* (London: Macmillan, 1980), pp. 119-120.

21. Kearney, *Communalism and Language*, p. 41.

22. C. R. De Silva, "Education," K. M. De Silva, ed., *Sri Lanka: A Survey* (Honolulu: University Press of Hawaii, 1977), p. 429.

23. Sunil Bastian, "University Admission and the National Question," Social Scientist's Association, *Ethnicity and Social Change.*

24. C. R. De Silva, "The Politics of University Admissions: A Review of Some Aspects of the Admissions Policy in Sri Lanka 1977-1978," *Sri Lanka Journal of Social Sciences* 1 (1978): 85-123.

25. The country is divided up into twenty-four administrative districts.

26. Bastian, "University Admission," p. 166.

27. It should be noted that there were four Tamil MPs from the east coast supporting the UNP government.

28. H. W. Abeynaike, *Ceylon Daily News Eighth Parliament of Sri Lanka, 1977* (Colombo: Associated Newspapers of Ceylon, 1978).

29. Abeynaike, *Ceylon Daily News*, p. 262.

30. See Robert C. Oberst, *Legislators and Representation in Sri Lanka: The Decentralization of Development Planning* (Boulder, Colo.: Westview Press, 1985).

31. Bruce Matthews, "District Development Councils in Sri Lanka," *Asian Survey* 22 (November 1984): 1117-1134.

32. The TULF and several of the leaders of the UNP did not believe that the plan could or would resolve Tamil demands. However, it did have the potential of providing Tamil regions with some local rule. See Parliamentary Debates (Hansard) 11, no. 7, cols. 480-481.

33. Wickrema Weerasooriya (Meeting with author in Colombo, July 5, 1984).

34. Paul Sieghart, *Sri Lanka: A Mounting Tragedy of Errors* (London: International Commission of Jurists, 1984), p. 32.

35. Ibid., p. 33.

36. *Island*, September 15, 1984.

37. *Island*, November 6, 1984.

38. Jay Rothman, "Majority Rule and Ethnic Conflict in Sri Lanka" (Unpublished paper presented at the first meeting of the Council for the Facilitation of International Conflict Resolution, University of Maryland, College Park, 1984).

39. T. D. S. A. Dissanayaka, *The Agony of Sri Lanka* (Colombo: Swastika Press, 1983).

7

Politics of Preference in the Caribbean: The Case of Guyana

RALPH R. PREMDAS

If the political allocative process in most developed countries is complex, then the process found in the typical Third World country is a veritable nightmare. At least in most industrially developed states, a body of shared values establishes the limits of discourse about basic issues of regime form and its system of distribution. However, in most states in the Third World, the social fabric is shattered by the pervasive phenomenon of multiethnicity and the assoicated absence of overarching agreements required to moderate competition for scarce resources.[1] Nearly every important decision made by the typical Third World government, which itself may be operating under the limitation of illegitimacy, tends to be interpreted through the prism of ethnicity. Each daily decision must reaffirm the faith of ethnic equity if legitimacy and democracy are to be preserved; otherwise, the threat of sabotage or secession is imminent. The fragile social fabric can easily succumb to destabilization and acts of disunity.[2]

The Guyana case illustrates these propositions and more. Guyana is a multiethnic state created almost two centuries ago by colonialism. Its six ethnic groups live on an enclave situated in the northeast shoulder of South America, but they are integrated functionally as part of the Caribbean culture. When Guyana was colonized, a new tier of political control was superimposed on the society. The subsequent importation of African slaves and Indian indentured laborers from the Old World to toil on cotton, coffee, and sugar plantations created a complex multiethnic, multitiered society from which communal interests evolved and imparted to Guyanese politics its enduring, defining characteristic.[3]

The politics of cultural pluralism in Guyana has been marked by ethnic competition for scarce resources in an environment of underdevelopment and poverty.[4] More than a decade ago Samuel Huntington underscored this theme generally in the Third World when he noted that "communal conflict, in contrast for instance to social revolution, has emerged as the dominant form of social strife."[5] In Guyana communal interests assumed preeminence from the inception of plantation society. More than two centuries later, in the immediate preindependence and postindependence periods, attempts were made to institute a system of justice consonant with the imperatives of ethnic arithmetic and communal demands. Because of interethnic leadership intransigence, however, the distribution of security, jobs, goods, services, and projects fell under the control of one or the other of the two major ethnic groups. Neither of the two trusted the other. Below the periodic rhetorical flourishes of commitment to intercommunal fellowship and unity that each group ritualistically proclaimed lurked an ingrained obsession with ethnic shares and fear of domination.

In this chapter I examine the politics of preference and distribution in Guyana, an ethnically divided state. The underlying assumption of this examination is that political behavior is sufficiently distinctive in unintegrated politics to warrant separate analytic treatment. Several notable models are available in the comparative politics literature to facilitate analysis of deeply divided societies. These models can be grouped around three ideas: hegemonic control; open competition; and segmental accommodation. A brief definition of each category is given below; however, none of them is adopted in its entirety in this study. Wherever useful and relevant, concepts from each have been applied to the data.

This study shows that in the same multiethnic state, drastic changes can occur in ethnic relations and in the politics of preference during different historical phases. In all multiethnic countries the dynamic of change demonstrates swings from one modal type of struggle for scarce resources to another, ranging from domination to competition to accommodative configurations. The process of change is continuous and ethnic preferences that prevail today in Lebanon, Belgium, Malaysia, Fiji, or Guyana may change radically in a short time. At any moment a regime may embody mixes of competition, control, or accommodation; indeed, the regime's policy may incorporate the forces of its transformation. Any new equilibrium can only be tentative. In this flux, the academic enterprise consists of analyzing historical data to identify the long-run, stable patterns of ethnic conflict, their impact on the distribution of governmental resources, and the forces of transformation in evidence from one stage to the next.

In Guyana the politics of ethnic preference moved through three phases, each bearing its defining core characteristics. In phase one, a multiethnic society was formed, but it was dominated by the colonial power so that most of the system's highly preferred values were monopolized by Europeans. After nearly a century the electoral franchise was gradually liberalized, and the seeds of the succeeding order were planted. In phase two the monopoly of

European dominance was broken and modified initially by an emergent nonwhite middle class. But this was only a preliminary gambit in a larger unfolding game where the colonial order was challenged and eventually expelled. Full-scale interethnic competition for the preferred values of government activity ensued. Intense conflict between the ethnic segments developed for power, jobs, projects, and security; this conflict was translated at the national level as competitive party politics. In phase three, one of the two major nonwhite ethnic groups seized power and applied the state apparatus and its full panoply of preferences to consolidate and perpetuate the group's control over the government.

In a curious twist of events, then, phases one and three completed a full circle: Each phase was structurally similar to the other and marked by ethnic control and dominance. The salient difference was that in phase one, colonial rule made no pretense of being a system of democracy and was not committed to a society based on egalitarian ideals. In phase three, however, ethnic dominance paraded under the banner of Marxism-Leninism, at once practicing ethnic chauvinism while invoking lofty humanistic values. If the central concern of phases one and three was control, then phase two's concern was open competition for resources. I shall examine the patterns in each phase to illustrate the characteristic features of government policies and ethnic preference. In what follows, then, two modal types of ethnic conflict for resources are discussed: monopoly hegemonic control and an open competitive market. The third variant, segmental accommodation, was ephemerally experienced in Guyana during the nationalist struggle for independence.

Monopoly Hegemonic Control

As defined by Rothchild, in a hegemonial system one ethnic segment dominates the others, wields preponderant coercive power, and arrogates to itself most of the benefits of the state.[6] Hegemonic control is facilitated by a centralized state apparatus in which a few grudging concessions of participation in decisionmaking are extended to excluded groups. Dominated ethnic groups are kept in their subordinate role by policies that formally or informally segregate them in discrete geographical and residential areas, limit their access to the strategic pillars of state power, and perpetuate their dependence on the ruling group for survival. M. G. Smith, like Furnivall before him, viewed ethnic domination and control as virtually inevitable in unintegrated multiracial states.[7]

Methods of hegemonial ethnic control may be relatively loose or rigorously regimented. Where control is loose, the dominant ethnic stratum tends to be accepted with little challenge to its hegemonic role by subordinate segments; the system of governmental allocation is rationalized by a widely accepted ideology of ethnic superiority. In the rigorously regimented order, as described by Ian Lustick, Sammy Smooha, Donald Rothchild, and Heribert Adam, a comprehensive set of repressive measures is erected to contain the political demands of subordinate segments.[8] The state is more steeply centralized, exclusion of the subordinate groups from power and privilege more complete, surveillance and terror more intensely utilized, and dependence, cooptation, and ethnic symbols more thoroughly manipulated to ensure survival of the control system. In effect, tight controls are required because legitimacy of the governing regime is not accepted but challenged.

In Guyana the period of European monopoly (1803-1891) corresponds to the loose variant of the ethnic hegemonic control model; the period from 1968 onward corresponds to the rigorously regimented variant. In the control model only selective sharing of resource with ethnic subordinates takes place, usually as an incentive for compliance with the system of ethnic hegemony. Bargaining is not the style of settling claims except when the system of ethnic dominance begins to crumble. To bargain with subordinate segments is to open the door to the loss of control of "the rules of the game."[9]

Open Competitive Market

Basically, in its ideal Weberian expression, the open competition market model embodies universalistic values stringently applied in a meritocratic order. Achievement criteria and not family or personal connections determine the distribution of government jobs and budgetary allocations. Electorally, in the competitive system, elections are conducted on a formula of first-past-the-post simple plurality. The winning party takes all in a zero-sum market struggle. In the government bureaucracy ascriptive criteria in assigning posts and promotions are ideally nonexistent. In practice, its ideals notwithstanding, competitive-universalistic models tend to incorporate aspects of ascription in resource and job allocation. Tests of achievement and performance, for instance, may reflect the mores of one section or class. Or open exceptions such as gender and age may be applied.

In Guyana a modified competitive system slowly emerged that was based on European concepts of achievement. Slowly, color and ancestry were relegated to secondary importance in the determination of state preferences. However, the roles of color, race, and personal connections were never completely set aside; thus, the emergent competitive system did not attain its fullest development in Guyana. After the independence movement split apart along ethnic lines, the public bureaucracy yielded to politicization. Equity in the distribution of jobs embodied in the concept of "representative bureaucracy" never took root although it was recommended by an international organization.[10]

Segmental Accommodation

In the segmental accommodation model, the communal segments seek a formula for sharing power and the benefits of official administration so as to maintain a minimum measure of democracy and order.   Arend Lijphart's consociational model is the most celebrated among the designs for accommodation in multiethnic states.[11]   Critics such as Brian Barry, Jurg Steiner, and Donald Rothchild have argued that Lijphart's proposal is too formal, complex, and rigid.[12]   Rothchild advocates a more informal bargaining arrangement that he labels hegemonial exchange, which stresses the role of sharing, protection, redistribution, and buffering. His framework relies heavily on the questionable assumption that ethnic demands can in practice be separated into negotiable objective interests and subjective nonnegotiable symbolic needs.[13] Further, Rothchild places too much reliance on the mechanism of bargaining thus minimizing the strength of substantive issues.   The former cannot be reduced to the latter.   Like Lijphart's consociational model, Rothchild's scheme could also be deemed overly complex if not too sanguine about the role of a rational formula in bringing stability and sanity to the communal conflicts in plural societies. Nevertheless, the Lijphart and Rothchild proposals offer useful insights into the complexities of ethnic conflict and accommodation.

Most formulations for interethnic accommodation focus on certain critical areas: recognition of each community's right to govern its internal communal affairs (segmental autonomy); symbolic and substantive participation of all ethnic segments in decisionmaking at the national level (coalition); quotas (proporz) in allocating government jobs (representative bureaucracy); and veto powers given each community over decisions affecting their vital interests (mutual veto). The fundamental objective of the various accommodation arrangements is to depoliticize aspects of the allocative process (Rothchild's objective negotiable interests) in a manner that ensures that no community obtains all or is denied all of the benefits of the state. This assumes that a system of equitable participation, accepted by the communal segments, will guarantee stability and a measure of democracy. In contrast, the zero-sum feature built into the market competitive model tends to lead to disorder and eventually to ethnic domination and even population expulsion and genocide. A sharing arrangement may avert intercommunal catastrophe. It can establish a middle ground between an outright repressive control system and an open, zero-sum, market competitive order. In Guyana a sort of accommodation between the major ethnic segments developed in the

Table 7.1 Allocation Patterns

	Bureaucratic Jobs	Budgetary Projects/Programs	Finance/Taxation	Security Forces	Input Representation
Control Model	Exclusion of ethnic rivals especially at senior administration levels.	Mainly located in areas and for functions benefiting dominant communal section.	Subordinate ethnic groups pay disproportionately larger amount for dominant group.	Rigorous exclusion of ethnic rivals especially in officer/command positions.	None
Competitive Model	Merit; universal application.	Determined by influence and pressure.	Determined by income categories.	Merit; universal application.	Persuasion; personal and party factors preeminent.
Consociation Model	Proportionality representative bureaucracy.	Formula for sharing; bargaining.	Formula for sharing; bargaining.	Proportionality.	Segmental autonomy and coalition.

electoral and parliamentary areas from 1950 to 1953 when the multiethnic independence movement was jointly led by Cheddi Jagan and Forbes Burnham. Again, in 1974 the two major communal parties were discussing a "peace plan." Even today there are proposals and counterproposals for a government of national unity. But none has been accepted. Ethnic dominance prevails.

Corresponding to each model is a pattern of preference in governmental allocations and a pattern of representation reflecting the underlying principles of control, competition, or consociation. Table 7.1 graphically shows the outline of this pattern.

Phase One: The Formation of a Segmented Society and European Monopoly Hegemonic Control

Guyana is often referred to as the "land of many peoples." The country, populated mainly by descendants of immigrants, comprises six ethnic groups—Africans, East Indians, Amerindians, Portuguese, Chinese, and Europeans. A significant "mixed" category also exists consisting of persons who have any combination or mixture of the above groups. Table 7.2 gives the ethnic breakdown of the population. Africans and Indians constitute more than 80 percent of the total, thereby imparting a bifurcated ethnic structure to the population. Nearly all of Guyana's people are concentrated on a 5 to 10 mile belt along the country's Atlantic coast. The ethnically heterogenous population is loosely integrated by a creole culture that has evolved during the last two hundred and fify years of Guyanese history. Nonetheless, strong social integrative institutions are few; they are rivalled by equally strong

Table 7.2   Ethnic Composition of Guyana's Population

Group	Size	%
East Indians	377,256	51.0
Africans	277,091	30.7
Amerindians	32,794	4.4
Portuguese	9,668	1.3
British	3,076	0.5
Chinese	4,674	0.6
Mixed	84,077	11.4

Source: Guyana Population Census 1970 (Georgetown: Government Printery, 1970).

subcultural patterns that threaten periodically to burst the society asunder at its ethnic seams.

The origins of Guyana's multiethnic structure go back to the first efforts at New World colonization attempted by Europeans. The area stretching from the Orinoco River to the Amazon, which includes the Guianas, came at one time or the other under the purview of French, Dutch, and British explorers. In the early seventeenth century the British started a settlement in Surinam, the French established two settlements in French Guiana, and the Dutch planted settlements at various points in what is now Guyana. The Dutch began plantation production in the seventeenth century; when they were evicted from the colony by the British in 1803, the dominant economic organization of the colony was the plantation. Importation of Africans, East Indians, Portuguese, Chinese, and poor whites to Guyana resulted from the nature of the plantation system, which to be viable required massive amounts of cheap labor.[14] By 1829, 230 sugar plantations and 174 coffee and cotton estates existed in Guyana.[15] Under British colonialism, cotton and coffee did not enjoy preferential prices, so they quickly succumbed to North American competition. Sugar production then became the dominant economic activity. Indeed, Guyana became little more than a huge sugar plantation.

In the Caribbean culture area, including British Guiana, the establishment of plantations was accomplished by the massive recruitment of African slaves. Resort to African sources of forced labor became necessary after the indigenous inhabitants, the Amerindians, had "succumbed to excessive labor demanded of them,"[16] while the poor whites who were indentured from Europe failed to meet the rigors of plantation life.[17] In 1807 the British slave trade with Africa was halted. Slavery in the British Caribbean, however, was not abolished until 1833.[18] Labor shortages that followed emancipation explain the addition of Chinese, Portuguese, and East Indians (from the Indian subcontinent) to the already existing ethnic groups in Guyana. Between 1835 and 1840 small batches of German, Portuguese, Irish, English, Indian, and Maltese laborers were recruited.[19] During 1853 Chinese were recruited. In the end, Asian Indians proved most adaptable, economical, and available, although Chinese and Portuguese immigrants trickled in for more than a half century. Between 1838 and 1917 approximately 238,960 indentured East Indian laborers arrived to work on the plantations.[20] At the expiration of their indentures nearly two-thirds opted to remain as free, permanent residents.[21]

The pattern of life of the ethnic groups in Guyana separated the communties into virtual cultural, residential, and occupational compartments, allowing for interaction mainly in economic and trade areas. The Europeans lived mainly in exclusive, guarded residential enclaves on sugar estates and urban areas. They were predominantly planters and settlers and controlled most of the colony's economic wealth and official political positions. Partly because of their economic and political power, a color-class stratification system evolved whereby

> things English and "white" were valued highly whilst things African and black were valued lowly. . . . The ability to speak properly, to dress properly, and to be able to read and write were all marks of prestige defined with reference to "English" culture. What gave the system its distinctive character was the element of color.[22]

In effect, in this first phase of history European ethnic superiority was established, and European preeminence in monopolizing the preferred values of society was being institutionalized—thus would emerge the basic outlines of a loose control system.

The year 1838 witnessed African exodus from the plantations.[23] At the end of the Free Village Movement, which lasted for a decade (1838-1848), more than one hundred villages were established.[24] By the end of the nineteenth century more than one-half of the African villagers would gravitate to urban centers where government jobs were available.[25] By the end of the first phase of European dominance, Africans held the position of advantage over other non-European groups. They became unbanished, educated, and acquired industrial skills and training. Africans dominated every department of the civil service by 1950,[26] while their portion of the population declined to 6.8 percent by 1960.[27]

Indians who remained in Guyana continued their close relationship with the plantations. Many were allotted land contiguous to the sugar estates in exchange for giving up their contractual right to return to India. A series of Indian villages sprang up within a radius of 15 miles of the plantations. Indians tended to work at first both on their private plots and on the plantations, but many progressively moved into full-time rice farming on private plots. By 1946 the Indian outflow from the sugar estates left only one-third as plantation residents; their urban presence was barely 10 percent.[28] In the 1960s, 25.5 percent of the Indian population was on sugar estates, 13.4 percent in urban centers, and the remaining 61.1 percent in villages.[29] Guyana's Indians then became predominantly rural dwellers serving either as sugar workers or farmers. They displayed distinctive patterns of cultural life initially reflecting residues of their Indian cultural heritage. After World War II, however, the Indian quest for civil service jobs required them to acculturate to English ways. Indians became a significant force in the 1950s and 1960s when their cultural adaptation brought them in competition with their African compatriots for scarce job opportunities.

The other ethnic elements in the population were small, but they, too, established their own residential and occupational niches. Amerindians were assigned to "reservations" mainly in the country's sparsely populated interior areas, while the Chinese and Portuguese gravitated to urban areas where the former engaged in service industries such as restaurants and the latter in the professions and business.[30]

Thus would a plural society be formed.[31] Slavery and indenture were the twin bases on which successful colonization of the climatically harsh tropical coasts occurred. A work force of culturally divergent immigrants was recruited to labor on plantations in the New World. Different patterns of residence, occupation, and cultural orientations by the imported groups reinforced original ethnic differences, thereby laying from the inception of settlement the foundations of Guyana's politics. By the beginning of the twentieth century certain features were clearly embedded in the social system. A communally oriented, multiethnic society was being fashioned. The control system was dominated by Europeans and an accompanying system of colonial laws and practices that institutionalized racial inequality along a color-class continuum. The wealth produced from the sugar plantations was repatriated to the metropolitan center, leaving very little for the plantation workers. African-Indian rivalry developed over the remnants of the colonial pie. Intercommunal struggle, however, would be restrained by the preponderantly rural-urban and occupational dichotomy that prevailed between the two major ethnic groups during the early colonial period.

In an interdependent communal order the political balance was held by a colonial government originating in conquest, maintained by coercion, and perpetuated by a color-class stratified order. The British who created the multiethnic social fabric served as the exclusive top tier in the stratified colonial hierarchy. Among the Europeans, however, a special subgroup, the planters, wielded dominant power in the Combined Court, the colonial decisionmaking body. Because of excessively high property and income requirements, the electorate was confined to the European planters. In the Combined Court the plantocracy controlled the purse string of British Guiana. "It determined the salaries of public officials, judges, civil servants. It decided whether or not money would be raised to maintain roads, construct sea defences, and extend the drainage systems. It determined how much money would be available for public health, welfare, and education."[32]

The area of public finance in particular displayed the prejudices of colonial administration. Prior to the emancipation of slavery, the state administrative machinery was simple because each plantation was "a little state in itself," and there was "little crime, no magistrates and no police." [33] Most state revenues were derived from a poll tax on slaves while planters paid an income tax of only 2 to 3 percent.[34] Once slavery was abolished, however, the plantocracy had to find a new source of revenues, and this was solved, as Alan Adamson pointed out, "by shifting the tax burden onto the Negro peasantry, the indentured immigrants and in a lesser degree the emerging Creole bourgeoisie."[35] Expenditures on public services such as health and education were negligible. After the abolition of slavery a significant part of government revenues was expended on sponsoring the importation of indentured laborers for the plantations. As the colonial society became more racially and economically complex, the Combined Court increased its budgetary expenditure on police, jails, and the judiciary from 3 percent in 1833 to about 25 percent in the 1850s.[36] Overall, then, in the loose control system the nonwhite population was not only exploited and made dependent on the superordinate planter group, but through a combination of laws, courts, and police enforcement, the basic structure of state domination and ethnic preference was maintained.

Phase Two: The Multiethnic Competitive Mode

While in phase one, Guyana's politics was characterized by European dominance; phase two witnessed a challenge to the old order. Persistent struggle during a half century (1891-1953) finally succeeded in evicting the old plantocracy from their positions of privilege. In the first phase, the rules of the game in the allocation of governmental resources were simple and hardly contested: The European conquerors by virtue of acquiring power from the Dutch in 1803 monopolized the benefits of state for themselves and engrafted a color-class stratification system to institutionalize their preeminence. In the second phase, the challengers came mainly from the nonwhite segments, and their associated interests differed radically from those of the plantocracy.

To be sure, the initial modification of the control system was gradual, but after World War II the old order rapidly eroded. A modified meritocracy was inaugurated, operating in a communal milieu with its intrinsic ethnic motifs and restraints. For the purpose of analysis, phase two is divided into two parts. The first part examines the limited changes that occurred when the constitutional order was liberalized and a stratum of nonwhite middle class persons acceded to influence in government and administration. The second part addresses the radical challenges to the colonial order that overturned it after World War II.

The Political Accession of the Nonwhite Middle Class

In 1891 Guyana experienced a major constitutional advance. After persistent pressure from the colony's emergent nonwhite middle class, the British colonial office liberalized franchise requirements to enlarge political participation. In the 1850s eligibility to vote required property worth at least $7,500 (BWI).[37] The electorate then consisted of only about 900 persons, all

Europeans, in a total population of about 130,000. In 1891 franchise restrictions were lowered to about $480.00 (BWI) and were even further liberalized about a decade later so that by 1915 the voting list showed that the nonwhite population had made impressive gains (see Table 7.3).

Table 7.3   The Electorate in 1915

Race	% of Male Population	% of Electorate	% Registered Voters
East Indians	51.8	6.4	0.6
Africans	42.3	62.7	6.8
Portuguese	2.9	11.4	17.7
European	1.7	17.0	46.1
Chinese	0.9	2.4	12.3

Source: Leo Despres, Cultural Pluralism and National Politics in British Guiana, (Chicago: Rand McNally, 1967), p. 40.

These figures show that a remarkable event of potentially revolutionary proportions had occurred by 1915—the African bourgeoisie had grown into the majority group in the electorate and had, in fact, come to control the financial affairs of the colony.[38] Cynthia Enloe commented on the impact that this control had on the allocation of public service jobs:

As early as 1925, of the persons employed in the colonial bureaucracy, 84.7% were listed as Negroes, while a mere 4% were listed as East Indians. This despite the fact that already the East Indians, brought to the colony by the ship load as indentured laborers to work the sugar plantations after slavery was abolished, amounted to 41.97% of the population, while Negroes represented only 39.36%. Europeans, Portuguese, and light-skinned persons of mixed parentage continued to dominate the upper reaches of the civil service, right up to the mid-1960s.[39]

Table 7.4 illustrates Enloe's points.

In other words, the European monopoly dominance had yielded to penetration and modification mainly by persons who were middle income Africans and mixed races. A fully competitive market model was still to emerge though, for color would continue to play a significant role in Guyana's political life until the mid-1950s. As one observer noted:

Even when non-whites were qualified professionally, they experienced difficulty in being recruited. This may be illustrated with reference to the medical field. Recruitment into the Colonial Medical Service was normally undertaken by the Colonial Office and it was not unusual for information to be requested on the racial antecedents of the applicants.[40]

By 1940 the non-white group, especially Africans and mixed races, was even making it up to the very top of the public service and into the select group of pensionable staff (see table 7.5).

Table 7.4 Ethnic Shares in the Public Service, 1925 (in percentages)

Race	% of Population	% in the Public Service
Europeans	1.11	3.0
Portuguese	3.08	0.2
Chinese	0.91	0.2
East Indians	41.97	4.0
Negroes	39.36	84.7
Mixed	10.28	7.3
Not stated	.22	0.6

Source: Daily Argosy (Guyana), August 13, 1925.

After emancipation it was the African communal section among the nonwhite society that took advantage of European education. In 1835 Christian denominational schools received a subsidy from the colonial government to provide limited public elementary education. (Secular schools did not exist.[41]) Most Indians saw the church-run schools as a cultural threat to their religious identity and therefore withheld their children. Further, Indians, most of whom engaged in full- or part-time farming, utilized their

Table 7.5 Ethnic Composition of Pensionable Civil Servants, 1940

Race	Department or Executive Heads		Pensionable Staff	
	N	%	N	%
Europeans	27	79.4	89	14.1
Africans	5	14.7	419	66.6
East Indians	0	0.0	63	10.0
Portuguese	2	5.9	40	6.4
Chinese and Others	0	0.0	18	2.9
Total	34	100.0	629	100.0

Source: Cheddi Jagan, The West on Trial: My Fight for Guyana's Freedom (Berlin, Seven Seas Publications, 1966) p. 163.

children in the fields. The upshot was that "by the end of the century, the Africans had come to dominate the public services at the national as well as the local level".[42]

Although a compulsory universal education ordinance was passed in 1876, it was not until the 1930s that Indians were compelled to send their children to Christian denominational schools.[43] Then, slowly but inexorably, Indians converged on the schools and in a reversal of their previous attitudes regarded the schools as an elixir to a new life free from the toil of agrarian drudgery. The repercussions of this new Indian position vis-à-vis education reverberated throughout the 1950s and afterward. Africans, mixed races, and others found in Indians new if not fierce competitors for limited job opportunities. Africans, in particular, faced the full brunt of this competitive assault, and this in turn unleashed an intense round of rivalry for the resources of the state. The European segment, already small, with the passage of time was eased out as a major force in the struggle for jobs. Africans and Indians confronted each other in ethnic competition that spilled over into party politics.[44] But Africans already had nearly a century's clear advantage, and this consequently placed them on the defensive. Indians were seen as the new challengers in the same way as the mixed races and Africans were seen by the Europeans at the turn of the twentieth century.

In 1928 the Colonial Office, acting under the pretense of the indebtedness of the Combined Court, suspended the 1891 constitution, which placed financial powers in the hands of the Black and mixed race middle class. A regressive crown colony system of government was imposed, which returned decisionmaking control to the colonial administration.[45] One positive feature of the constitutional change was the enfranchisement of women, but the old property and income qualifications for the vote remained very restrictive. Leadership and impetus for change after 1928 passed from the middle class black bourgeoisie to a multiracial and modernizing radical group that rejected piecemeal reform for a more fundamental rearrangement of the colonial order.[46] Trade unions emerged as the main mobilizer of popular sentiment.[47] A new era of politics was upon the colony. After World War II the political framework would alter and with it the nature of the politics of distribution.

Ethnic Conflict and the Politics of Decolonization

The unified multiracial independence movement that emerged in Guyana after World War II saw as its first task the elimination of colonial control and, with it, European dominance in the public service and society in general. The movement did not envisage a period of intense turmoil between Africans and Indians after the force of European presence waned. Although the control system was superseded by a relatively open market for state opportunities, the competition that ensued was cast in a zero-sum struggle between Africans and Indians.

The denial of adequate reforms in the colonial order after World War II invited the emergence of a radical response. In 1946 a Political Affairs Committee (PAC) was formed by Dr. Cheddi Jagan, a Marxist who had just returned from university training in the United States.[48] The PAC aimed at "establishing a strong, disciplined and enlightened party equipped with the theory of scientific socialism."[49] The PAC analyzed the colony's living conditions in class terms appealing mainly to workers and farmers of all ethnic groups.

Although the PAC was multiracial in composition, its leader, Dr. Jagan, was an East Indian—a fact that would compel the movement to recruit an African leader of equivalent standing after its losses in the 1947 general elections.[50] That search led to the selection of Forbes Burnham, an outstanding lawyer who had returned from London to Guyana in 1949. In January 1950 the PAC converted itself to the People's Progressive party (PPP) and reaffirmed its commitment to a socialist society.[51] New general elections were scheduled for April 1953 under a constitutional arrangement that conceded universal adult suffrage and a limited cabinet ministerial system. Full participation in collective decisionmaking was finally at hand. The PPP was victorious, winning eighteen out of twenty-four seats in the unicameral legislature. The only explanation for such an overwhelming victory was the extensive collaboration of African and Indian constituents inspired by the biracial leadership of Jagan and Burnham.[52] The period 1950-1953 was the Golden Age of racial harmony in Guyana. The control system had virtually collapsed while local leaders assumed power.

Within five months after assuming office the PPP suffered a major setback. During its one hundred thirty-three day rule, the PPP openly threatened to nationalize key foreign companies and radically rearrange the color-class system.[53] In response to the prodding of the plantocracy the British government suspended the constitution and evicted the PPP from office. In turn, this triggered a major crisis within the PPP as explanations were sought for the ouster. Two main factions surfaced, one supporting Jagan and the other Burnham. New elections were slated for 1957, and in the elections a more radical socialist Jaganite faction faced a moderate Burnhamite faction. Apart from their ideological stance, the Jagan and Burnham groupings obtained support mainly from Indian and African constitutents respectively. In the elections, at the grassroots, racial appeals were widely used, and the crosscommunal goodwill between Africans and Indians was shattered. Jagan won the elections, but as premier of Guyana he was now presiding over a state whose communal fabric was inflamed by electoral politics that pitted one ethnic segment against the other.[54]

Between 1957 and 1963 unprecedented racial turmoil racked Guyana and resulted in the removal of Jagan from power and the acquisition of leadership by Burnham. Burnham criticized Jagan's party for its pro-Indian government and its discrimination against Afro-Guyanese.[55] Burnham's party, the People's National Congress (PNC), collaborated with a third splinter party, the United Force (UF), headed by Portuguese businessman Peter D'aguiar who appealed mainly to Europeans, Portuguese, Chinese, mixed races, Amerindians, and a small group of middle class Africans and Indians.

In the 1961 general elections Jagan's PPP defeated both Burnham's PNC and D'aguiar's UF under the old first-past-the-post simple plurality electoral system. Jagan had obtained a disproportionately higher number of seats measured against his percentage of the popular votes. This fact served as the excuse that prompted the Opposition into a sustained set of severe attacks, strikes, demonstrations, and disruptions intended to destabilize the Jagan government and enable the British Colonial Office to alter the electoral system to one of proportional representation.[56] With Jagan's group holding slightly less than 50 percent of the adult votes, Burnham and D'aguiar barely defeated Jagan's PPP in the 1964 elections. Ehtnic strife grew to fearsome proportions. At one point virtual civil war ensued, and mixed Indian-African villages became places of terror where British troops were required to maintain communal peace.[57]

The role of ethnic competition is worth brief analysis because it entailed the use of the public bureaucracy as a major instrument in the removal of a government. The joint biracial leadership of the independence movement by Jagan and Burnham concealed the fact that the government bureaucracy had come to be dominated by Africans. The public and teaching services had emerged as the largest employers in the country, and, more importantly, they were staffed by the best educated and organized persons in the nonwhite population. If any regime wished to govern peacefully, it could not incur the wrath of the public bureaucracy. In Guyana's communal context this basic fact of power became imbued with racial motivations. When Jagan and Burnham were together, the public service cooperated. Competition for state job opportunities was substantially based on merit. But after the eviction of the unified independence movement from office and the rise of racially based parties, the bureaucracy assumed an active interventionist role in partisan politics.

> After the split in the national government, it was the Negro section of the population that was more advantageously placed in control of the machinery of government. This was seen in the fact that, although the Jaganite faction of the PPP defeated the Burnhamite faction at the elections held in 1957 and participated in the government as the majority party, it was by no means in a position of strength. Quite apart from operating in a colonial situation in which the British

government possessed wide powers of control over the governmental machinery, after a time the Jaganite regime became keenly aware of its lack of support from some of the crucial institutions and groups in the public bureaucracy. The People's National Congress (the Burnhamite faction) though not in government, was nevertheless in a position to embarrass and frustrate it.[58]

Jagan was in a quandary. Although he professed to be a socialist and recruited a racially mixed cabinet, he still had to meet some of the demands for jobs, services, and projects by Indian political constituents. The Jagan regime, coming to power in 1957, therefore embarked on a set of policies that sought to eliminate Christian control of schools and to orient economic planning in favor of rural industries.[59] Burnham's party protested vigorously against the "agricultural bent" of the PPP's policies, charging the Jaganites with running an Indian "Coolie government" and "a Rice Government."[60] The Jagan government also sought to rectify the ethnic imbalance in recruitment of the public service. In particular, Jagan feared the fact that the stability of his government depended heavily on an African-dominated police force.

In 1961 the Jagan government persuaded the British to accept that the victor in the 1961 elections would lead the country into independence. This was a most crucial fact, for the party in power after independence could redefine the rules of the game and remain in power indefinitely.   For the highly politicized and insecure Indian and African segments, the 1961 elections could mean the indefinite domination of one group by the other.[61] It was on this vital issue that the African-dominated public service would be courted, politicized, and mobilized against the Jagan government. Two major unions, the Civil Service Association (CSA) and the Federation of Unions of Government employees (FUGE), both African controlled, represented public servants.   Demonstrations and strikes in 1962 and 1964 against the Jagan regime witnessed the conversion of a neutral civil service into a politicized instrument of power in ethnically motivated partisan politics.

The events between 1962 and 1964 which all but brought down the Jagan government was dramatic illustration of this [politicization of the public service].   The PNC opposition was effectively using institutions over which it had control or influence in an attempt to embarrass and ultimately defeat the government—a fact of which it made no secret—and the Civil Service Association (C.S.A.) was one such institution.   The political nature of the C.S.A.'s involvement could also be seen in part from the fact that although many of the issues remained unresolved after the change of government in 1964, no similar action has so far been taken by the C.S.A. against the PNC government.[62]

The Burnham government that succeeded Jagan in 1964 itself would suffer from similar boycotts and crippling strikes, but this time the mobilizer would be the Jagan forces who in opposition deployed the sugar industry unions, which were overwhelmingly Indian dominated. The fact that Africans resided mainly in the urban areas, especially in Georgetown, and Indians in the rural areas, partly restrained the interracial conflict. However, few racially interlocking endeavors existed to provide meaningful moderation in the conflict. Communal strife consequently became polarized, a special variant of intransigence locked in an uncompromising zero-sum struggle.[63]

It would be difficult to predict exactly what alterations in the state bureaucracy and in the allocation of resources might have occurred under the racially unified PPP government of 1953. One could legitimately expect the allocation of government expenditures would have been diverted away from serving the interests of the plantocracy to serving the interests of the nonwhite working class. In their brief one hundred thirty-three day interregnum, the PPP had already signalled its intention to dismantle the monopolistic power of the sugar planters. But apart from seeking to reorient broad governmental programs away from the European minority interests, the PPP government had hardly undertaken the task of redefining the role of the bureaucracy to reconcile the communal structure of the society with the regime's egalitarian values.

Table 7.6   Racial Composition of Staff Employed in all Ministries and Departments in British Guiana

	Negro	Indian	European	Portuguese	Mixed	Chinese	Amerindian
Senior staff, i.e., senior clerk level up.	335	227	37	20	255	68	1
Clerical service below senior clerk level.	697	543	1	17	222	23	5
Others below senior clerk level.	6327	3830	2	69	843	68	282
Total	7359	4600	40	106	1320	159	288
Percent of total	53.05	33.16	0.29	0.76	9.52	1.15	2.08

Source: Report of the British Guiana Commission of Inquiry (International Commission of Jurists, Geneva, 1965), p. 84.

Hence, no formula for interethnic sharing of the benefits of government administration and programs was enunciated. Consequently, the drift characteristic of the latter part of the previous period prevailed. This essentially meant that a modified meritocracy practiced according to European values persisted. In practical terms, those who acquired English ways and schooling obtained a head start over those who lagged. When Jagan and Burnham parted company and formed their own parties, the communal conflict spilled over into the government administrative machinery. Upon capturing power in 1957 the Jaganite faction sought to rectify the racial imbalance in the public service. The Geneva-based International Commission of Jurists (ICJ) was invited to do a survey of the problem (see Table 7.6 for the results of the commission's survey).

Clearly, Indians, who constituted about 51 percent of the population, obtained only about 33 percent of the jobs, while Africans and mixed races, who formed about 40 percent of the population, obtained about 53 percent of the available jobs. Europeans still controlled about five times as many jobs relative to their ratio in the population, and these jobs were among the most senior positions.

In part, the political contest waged among the racially divided population was not only about jobs and government allocations, but more significantly about averting ethnic domination. Consequently, in a tense situation of all-out communal confrontation, the ethnic composition of the police and coercive forces came to play a pivotal role. More so then in any other government institution, the ICJ found the gravest imbalance here (tables 7.7 and 7.8 demonstrate this imbalance).

These tables show that in the security forces Indians constituted 20 percent and Africans and mixed races about 78 percent of those employed. Professor Enloe offered an historical explanation for the imbalance: "Police were recruited overwhelmingly from Africans, presumably because they were numerous in the towns and because they met the physical requirements such as height and chest measurement which smaller Indian frames could not."[64] Overall, in the public service including the police and security divisions, no principle of sharing or proportionality operated. As Europeans left the country, the contest for jobs was in the open competitive market among the nonwhite communal segments. At an early part of Guyana's history, Indo-African conflict was contained by the fact that these communal segments lived apart. But toward the turn of the century Indians began coming to towns to compete for jobs and scarce urban-based opportunities. The conflict between these two groups, then, at least in part, has an objective basis in the fight for scarce resources. Table 7.9 illustrates Guyana's demographic settlement and shows that by 1960 Indians had become nearly one-fourth of the urban population. There they would seek out skills and training and thus further intensify the conditions of the interethnic conflict.

If Africans dominated public service jobs, then Indians did so in agriculture and business. Table 7.10 summarizes several critical aspects of racial distribution in employment: first, African domination of public service departments; second, Indian domination in rural land development; and third, Indian challenge in local government and teachers services. These figures are

Table   7.7   Racial Composition of the Security Forces in British Guiana

	Negro	Indian	European	Portuguese	Mixed	Others
Police force	2122	710	7	28	149	45
Volunteer force	507	51	6	4	3	3
Special service unit	72	72	-	-	2	-
Total	2701	833	13	32	154	48
Percent of total	73.5	19.9	0.3	0.8	4.2	1.3

Source: Report of the British Guiana Commission of Inquiry (International Commission of Jurists, Geneva), p. 49.

Table 7.8   Distribution of Security Forces by Rank and Race in British Guiana, 1965 (in percent)

	Negro	Indian	European	Portuguese	Mixed	Others
Police force						
Officers	80.3	9.1	1.2	1.0	7.9	0.5
Constables	72.8	21.9	---	0.1	4.3	0.9
Volunteer force						
Officers	83.9	5.8	4.4	1.5	2.9	1.5
Lance Corporals & Privates	89.5	9.8	---	0.5	0.2	---
Special service unit						
Officers	50.0	50.0	---	---	---	---
Constables	51.3	47.0	---	---	1.7	---
Special constabulary						
Officers	55.2	13.8	---	13.8	17.2	---
Constables	74.2	21.9	0.2	0.2	3.4	---
Prisons						
Officers	81.8	---	---	---	18.8	---
Prison officers	83.9	16.1	---	---	---	---
Fire Brigade						
Officers	85.2	3.7	---	1.8	9.2	---
Firemen	61.1	21.4	---	1.6	15.9	---
Total						
Officers	79.4	9.4	1.6	1.6	7.5	0.6
Others	75.1	20.6	---	0.2	3.5	0.5

Source: Report of the British Guiana Commission of Inquiry (International Commission of Jurists, 1965), p. 172.

all related in turn to the ethnic composition of the population and the urban-rural settlement patterns. In brief, greater Indian participation in the public service and the movement of Indians to urban areas triggered intense ethnic competition for economic opportunities, but without a restraining sharing formula such as proportionality, the contest became politicized and violent.

Table 7.9 Distribution of Population by Race in Sugar Estates, Villages, and Urban Centers of British Guiana, 1891–1960 (in percent)

Year of Census	Negro	Indian	White	Portuguese	Mixed	Chinese	Other
Sugar estates							
1891	14.44	79.36	0.93	1.12	2.42	1.59	0.14
1921	13.96	81.77	0.72	0.39	2.29	0.76	0.12
1960	14.74	80.45	0.58	0.18	3.35	0.38	0.31
Villages							
1891	61.20	26.70	0.33	4.31	6.11	1.03	0.32
1921	49.86	41.16	0.22	2.15	5.48	0.77	0.36
Urban Centers							
1891	47.19	8.44	5.02	10.23	27.03	1.50	0.59
1921	50.59	11.34	3.45	8.54	24.08	1.60	0.40
1946	54.43	15.68	1.68	6.04	19.57	2.20	0.39
1960	49.00	22.13	1.22	3.78	21.72	1.81	0.34

Source: Report of the British Guiana Commission of Inquiry (International Commission of Jurists, 1965), p. 164.

The Postindependence Racially Repressive Control System

After Jagan was ousted from power in 1964, the new coalition government led by Forbes Burnham appointed and accepted the recommendations of the International Commission of Jurists to rectify the ethnic "imbalance" in the public services. In a number of areas in particular, affirmative action was prescribed to offset the overrepresentation of Africans and mixed races. R. S. Milne has noted, for example, that "the Commission recommended that for the next five years 75% of the recruits to the police force should be Indian and the government accepted this principle."[65]

If the new regime had honored its commitment to establish an equitable balance in the public services and to restore racial harmony by implementing racially nondiscriminatory programs, then Guyana would have embarked on a future of ethnic stability. For a while during the life of the coalition government (1964-1968) when Burnham's political partner, Portuguese businessman Peter D'aguiar, retained much influence in government policies, the rhetoric of ethnic balance was still credible. But the dissolution of the coalition in 1968 and the seizure of power by Burnham's party radically altered the prospect of ethnic parity. A new era of ethnic domination was

Table 7.10 Total Racial Distribution in the Security Forces, the Civil Service, Government Agencies and Undertakings, and Areas of Government Responsibility (in percent)

Body	European %	Portuguese %	Indian %	Negro %	Amerindian %	Mixed %	Chinese %	Others %
Security forces	.35	.8	19.9	73.5	1.1	4.19	.16	---
Civil service	.29	.76	33.16	53.05	2.08	9.52	1.15	---
Government agencies and undertakings	.39	1.05	27.17	62.49	.14	8.02	.91	---
Local government	.06	.57	49.68	38.89	.11	10.46	.23	---
Teachers in primary education	---	1.72	41.27	53.87	1.06	1.46	.58	.04
Land development	---	.4	85.49	13.06	.17	.66	.11	.11
Percentage of total	.22	.88	39.97	50.64	1.16	6.35	.75	.03
Percentage of total population	.57	1.49	47.79	32.83	---	11.99	.73	4.59[a]
Percentage of urban population	1.22	3.78	22.13	49.00	---	21.72	1.81	0.34[a]
Percentage of rural population	.3[b]	---	58.3	26.2	6.3	8.0	.3	.6

Source: Report of the British Guiana Commission of Inquiry (International Commission of Jurists, 1965).

[a] Includes Amerindians.

[b] Includes Portuguese.

launched making the preindependence colonial practices of racial repression appear minor by comparison.[66] The fundamental imbalance in ethnic representation that prevailed at independence remained in place throughout Burnham's reign and thereafter. In effect, in this period of Guyanese history, one nonwhite communal group repressed another. The color-class system of social differentiation was replaced by a new system of domination. No accommodative formula such as consociational democracy emerged to restrain communal chauvinism and moderate ethnic competition.

When the new government of Forbes Burnham acceded to power in 1964, three major objectives informed the coalition regime's platform. First, Burnham's main interest was to protect his communal section from ethnic domination. Second, Burnham's coalition partner, Peter D'aguiar, who mainly represented the small residual non-African and non-Indian communal groups, sought to protect private property from nationalization and preserve the status quo with its entrenched color-based system of social stratification. Third, the United States, which assisted the coalition government in acquiring power, was concerned with extinguishing all socialist and communist influences in Guyana.[67]

The first item on the new government's agenda was to restore domestic tranquility in the wake of the virtual ethnic civil war that erupted in Guyana during the previous three years. But this inevitably meant that Jagan's Indian-based party, the PPP (Jagan retained the old 1953 PPP label for his faction, while Burnham named his faction the People's National Congress, or PNC), bore the brunt of the government's attack. A new control system, more comprehensive and draconian than its moribund plantation antecedent, was devised. Under a National Security Act and a state of emergency, Jagan's party activists were ruthlessly suppressed; many were arrested and held in detention for long periods of time without trial. The communal factor inevitably pervaded the entire law enforcement exercise and cast a dark shadow of suspicion over the government's motives. It was during this period, in 1965, that the Guyana Defense Force (GDF) was formed; it would add to the ruling regime's coercive capabilities. Like the police force, the GDF was recruited mainly from the African communal section.[68] In the end, this recruitment pattern would provide a powerful base not only for the protection of the African community from ethnic domination, but also for the maintenance of the African-led government in power.

To reconstruct Guyana from the ravages of the previous years' ethnic confrontation, the PNC regime realized that multiracial participation was necessary if only because the vital agricultural sector of the economy was under Indian control.[69] Burnham pleaded for cooperation and appointed a few Indians to his cabinet. But like Jagan, who had made similar calls for multiracial cooperation, Burnham learned that appeals to race during election campaigns, even though covert and subtle, were not easily forgotten.

Further, the party in power was captive to its communalist base. Followers demanded patronage at the expense of a vanquished ethnic enemy. To deny them would be to risk losing political support; to cater to them would result in the further alienation of the opposition communal group. The communal monster surreptitiously invoked to obtain votes and manipulated to maintain power would return to haunt the government that acquired power.

To Jagan, the Burnham-D'aguiar government was illegitimate. He refused to cooperate with the government and instead continued to call strikes, demonstrations, and protests. Burnham was not happy with D'aguiar, his coalition partner, who controlled the Ministry of Finance and restrained the PNC from liberally rewarding its communal supporters. About six months before the 1968 general elections, the PNC engineered a number of parliamentary defections from the PPP and gained a majority in the National Assembly and sole control of the government. It then reconstituted the electoral commission with its own partisan sympathizers and tampered with the electoral machinery. In what would be established incontrovertibly as rigged elections involving tens of thousands of fictitious votes, the PNC won an absolute majority of seats in the 1968 elections.[70] The electoral fraud was perpetrated under the supervision of politicized and communally lopsided police and military forces.

The "seizure of power" in 1968 was a watershed in ethnic relations in Guyana. In a racially plural society, the PNC representing a minority African group (32 percent) grabbed the government. To avert internal disruption the PNC government purged the critical pillars of its power—the coercive forces and the civil service—of most of their non-African elements. The control system was being tightened and made increasingly reliant on naked force and terror for its survival. The ethnic imbalance in the public service was exacerbated, and the regime refused to permit impartial examination of its employment record. Regime legitimacy was now lost, and the state coercive machinery was the main guardian of PNC's power. To be sure, the PNC government continued formally to espouse the ideals of racial equality and did recruit a number of prominent Indians to highly visible positions. Where communal malcontents did not strike and demonstrate, many migrated to Europe and North America. This was especially true in the case of Europeans, Chinese, and Portuguese. Table 7.11 shows the massive migration of these groups from Guyana, leaving a society predominantly polarized between Africans and Indians.

When Burnham seized power in 1968, he realized that the economy was essentially controlled by his political opponents. For his control system to survive, he needed to rectify this problem in his favor, preferably to reverse the roles. Gradually he abandoned the capitalist structure of the economy, which favored businessmen, big property owners, and land cultivators, and whose membership was mainly non-African.[71] Burnham's own survival depended on his addressing the needs of his communal constituents. Toward the end of 1969, then, the PNC regime adopted a socialist framework for Guyana's reconstruction and in 1970 declared Guyana a "cooperative republic."[72]

Table 7.11 Composition of Population by Race (in percent)

Year	Amerindian	Chinese	East Indian	African	Mixed	Portuguese	European	Other	Total
1891	----	1.4	38.9	42.7	10.7	4.5	1.7	0.1	100
1921	3.1	0.9	42.0	39.4	10.3	3.1	1.1	0.2	100
1946	4.3	0.9	43.5	38.2	10.0	2.3	0.7	0.1	100
1960	4.5	0.7	47.8	32.8	12.0	1.5	0.6	0.1	100
1970	4.4	0.6	51.0	30.7	11.4	1.3	0.5	0.1	100

Source: Census Bulletin No. 2, Population Census 1970 (Georgetown, 1970).

The economy was heretofore to be founded on cooperatives as the main instrument of production, distribution, and consumption. Thereafter, the regime, due to a variety of circumstances that have been recounted elsewhere, floundered from crisis to crisis, lost U.S. support, and suffered from persistent boycotts by the non-African population, particularly Indian sugar and rice farmers.[73] It ran a gauntlet besieged by high unemployment (20-30 percent), double-digit inflation, prohibitive fuel costs, demonstration, boycotts, and strikes. A vicious cycle of poverty was created by a pattern of polarized and unstable ethnic politics intermixed with socialist ideological and programmatic justifications.

Between 1971 and 1976 the government nationalized nearly all foreign firms, thereby bringing 80 percent of the economy under state control.[74] This unwieldy public sector provided the job opportunities necessary to quell the increasing demands of PNC supporters for patronage.[75] When the Burnham regime nationalized the economy, this grossly enlarged the state bureaucratic apparatus. Government ministries increased from twelve in 1968 to twenty-one in 1977. State corporations proliferated, but most were placed under an umbrella state agency called GUYSTAC, which controlled twenty-nine corporations and several companies valued at more than $500 million(G).[76] The government also ran five banks, three bauxite companies, and the gigantic sugar corporation that at one time dominated the country's entire economy and occupied its best cultivable lands.[77]

Burnham himself admitted that "we don't believe in the neutrality of the Civil Service."[78] He argued that the neutrality concept was a colonial anachronism irrelevant to Guyana's socialist revolution. But the bulging public bureaucracy was not transformed into socialist organizations.

Evidence that bourgeois rule persists in Guyana is found most abundantly in the nationalized sector. In all state-owned enterprises, traditional hierarchical methods of decision-making remained firmly in place. In none of the nationalized industries has meaningful workers' participation in decision-making been institutionalised.[79]

There is no question, however, that the country's economy had been radically altered. According to Marxist scholar Jay Mandle, Guyana's rulers were not socialist but racialist in attitude and ideology:

The older colonial ruling class and its business firms have been banished and decision-making power now rests with a local elite of state and cooperative-based managers. In the Guyanese context, this assumes the form of the emergence of an urban Afro-Guyanese leadership under the auspices of the People's National Congress.[80]

Precise figures on the relative ethnic distribution of employees in the Guyana public service were hard to come by after 1970. Doubtlessly, the African segment had attained unprecedented representation in the public bureaucracy. Preference policies for Afro-Guyanese were jusitified as necessary correctives to previous anti-African bias.

Discrimination in favor of Afro-Guyanese in the public corporations and other quasi-governmental services is a response to discrimination against Afro-Guyanese in other areas such as businesses, banks, and medical appointments in some hospitals. In this view, preference for Africans in the expanding public and quasi-public sector acts as a counterweight to the imbalance in the private sector, thus producing some kind of overall balance.[81]

The police, security, and armed forces, in particular, were expanded to protect the besieged PNC government. In 1964, the police and auxiliary armed forces numbered about 3,770; by 1977 they were estimated to be 21,751.[82] In 1964 there was one military person to 284 civilians; in 1976 there was one for every 37 citizens.[83] The budgetary allocation for the military rose from 0.21 percent in 1965 to 8 percent in 1973 and then to 14.2 percent in 1976. That is, the increase has been more than 4,000 percent.[84] More than any other public service department, the police and coercive forces were overwhelmed by Afro-Guyanese. Burnham named himself chairman of the Defense Board where he took personal control over promotions and appointments.[85] The main assignment of the armed forces was to supplement the police constabulary in maintaining law and order.

For a regime to maintain and extend Guyana's economic development, it would require programs that encouraged agricultural production. Guyana lacks even a minor industrial capacity, and its mining sector is small. The country's capacity to feed itself depends on agricultural production. Sugar production is the backbone of the economic system as a whole, and sugar workers are mainly Indians. In the mid-1970s the sugar companies, all foreign owned, were nationalized. The next most significant agricultural industry was rice, and this was almost wholly under Indian peasant production. When Jagan was in power he provided several programs, such as credits, subsidies, marketing, technical assistance, and drainage and irrigation, to the rice industry. Hence, the PNC labelled the Jagan regime a "rice government" partisan to Indian communal interests. When the PNC acceded to power, the rice growers were victimized through the elimination of most state subsidies. Rice production plummeted to half its original size. The Government's Rice Marketing Board, which had a monopoly in purchasing the farmers' rice, was reorganized and staffed with PNC personnel. Rice farmers, under Jagan's instruction, boycotted rice production and created grave shortages in the country.

Like the sugar industry, rice became a political and ethnic football. The PNC government wanted to eliminate its dependence on Indian agriculturalists for much of the country's food. In 1970, then, under its announced policy of "cooperative socialism," the PNC attempted to locate landless Afro-Guyanese on state lands previously leased to Indian farmers. The Indian stranglehold on peasant agriculture provided Jagan's PPP with a powerful base of support. The PNC's strategy for redistributing land and subsidies failed because rice cultivation required years of experience for success. Despite the PNC's attempts to victimize Indian rice farmers, the PNC continued to appeal to these very farmers to produce. But their cooperation was not forthcoming:

> Fundamentally at issue here is the nature of the PNC government. Briefly put, it is a regime which is manager-dominated, urban and predominantly Afro-Guyanese. The peasant and agricultural section of the population—largely of Indo-Guyanese descent—is inadequately represented within the government ranks. As a result, the ruling party and the government is poorly equipped either to mobilize the rural labor force or to call upon its good-will in attempting to transform agriculture.[86]

When the Burnham regime declared Guyana a cooperative republic the cooperative was intended to give the African section meaningful power and participation in the country's economy.[87] Several cooperatives were established to compete with the remaining private sector enterprises, but, most importantly, in practice the cooperative provided a formidable ideological justification for what was in fact an attempt to wrest control over critical parts of the economy from the non-African population. For the most part the cooperatives established after Burnham's accession to power failed because of inefficiency and corruption. This factor has largely been responsible for the decline in living standards in the country as a whole. Party and ethnicity variables have combined to deny the African section of the population the economic promise of participation and power that the cooperative program envisaged.

The overall policy output of the PNC regime, even if it were to be interpreted foremost in socialist terms, pointed indisputably to ethnic favoritism and preference. The polarization of the races was probably attributable as much to ethnic chauvinism among PNC activists as to PPP boycotts and strikes against the government. The economic situation deteriorated so badly that toward the end of the 1970s everyone was adversely affected, regardless of ethnic membership. Strikes and demonstrations and other challenges to Burnham's power increasingly came from all ethnic segments. The arsenal of coercive powers previously used against Indians was now used against African dissidents also.

The judiciary also came under the PNC regime's direct influence. The appointment of judges and magistrates was routinely based on party loyalty.[88] Thus, the use of the courts to challenge the legality and constitutionality of the regime's decisions was futile. In 1978 the government altered the constitution so that the appointment of judges and magistrates fell under the purview of President Burnham. The new constitutional system inaugurated an executive presidency that was given to Burnham. The judicial system, then, became integrated into the regime's coercive and control arsenal to be used against political dissidents.

The trade union sector remained problematic for the regime. Partly because of the structure of the economy and the history of ethnic residential and occupational patterns, agricultural workers and their unions fell under Jagan's control. Even where Jagan's forces were suppressed, rural workers adamantly remained under his sway. Although the PNC government had become accustomed to opposition-inspired sugar strikes, it was not able to cope with similar actions emanating from its own community. Burnham's repressive regime was presiding over an economy that had deteriorated so badly that large numbers of its African supporters had also become disenchanted. To combat this problem, the regime resorted to assassination of some opposition activists including Dr. Walter Rodney, the Afro-Guyanese Marxist scholar who was particularly effective in mobilizing African workers against the regime.[89] The regime could not afford this breach in its communal ranks. To minimize this possibility, the PNC regime passed new legislation in 1984 that made it difficult legally for state workers and civil servants to go on strike.

Conclusion

The politics of preference in an ethnically divided state skirts at all times the fundamental systemic issues of legitimacy, unity, and stability. The more politicized the population, the more likely it is to perceive political problemsolving through the prism of ethnicity. What complicates the allocative process is the varying conceptions of equity that each community may espouse. Clearly, an accommodative solution is hard to reach, and even if arrived at, it may not easily survive changes in demography, new claims, and grievances. Any governing regime in a multiethhnic state runs the risk of charges of communal prejudice in collective decisionmaking. In an environment of poverty, this problem is further accentuated.

Unlike a hegemonial control system, an accommodative governmental arrangement in a democratic order is immensely more difficult to forge and sustain. The constraints of poverty apart, special qualities in leadership are required to maintain a sharing outlook and a pragmatic approach to issues that are often imbued with emotive symbolism. Faced with rising expectations, a limited and underdeveloped resource base, and incessant claims for ethnic distributive justice, most Third World states succumb to the temptation of repressive rule. A control system appears easier to run.

In Guyana the regime of President Burnham and that of his successors (after Burnham's death in late 1985) failed to reflect in their decisionmaking and administration the sociocultural composition of an ethnically divided society. The nationalization of the economy exacerbated the issue of ethnic preference because it created a congested area of ethnic competition and overexposed the government to criticism and acts of noncooperation. The ruling regime responded to challenges by imposing further controls, which incurred more noncompliance and thus required greater budgetary allocations for security. This cycle points to self-destruction. In Third World states, as in Guyana, the control system of administration misallocates scarce resources and in the long run can only perpetuate conditions of poverty and intensify ethnic rivalry for scarce resources.

Notes

1. See Crawford Young, *The Politics of Cultural Pluralism* (Madison: University of Wisconsin Press, 1976).
2. See Alvin Rabushka and Howard Shepsle, *Politics in Plural Societies: A Theory of Democratic Instability* (Colombus, Ohio: Bobbs Merrill, 1972).
3. R. T. Smith, *British Guiana* (London: Oxford University Press, 1962); and Leo Despres, *Cultural Pluralism and National Politics in British Guiana* (Chicago: Rand McNally, 1967).

4. Cynthia Enloe, *Conflict and Political Development* (Boston: Little, Brown, 1973); and Leo Despres, "Ethnicity and Resource Allocation in Guyanese Society," Leo Depres, ed., *Ethnicity and Resource Allocation in Plural Societies* (The Hague: Moughton, 1975).

5. Samuel Huntington, "Foreword," E. A. Nordlinger, *Conflict Regulation in Divided Societies*, Harvard University Center for International Affairs, Occasional Paper no. 29 (Cambridge, Mass.: Harvard University, 1972).

6. See "Group Demands" in Chapter 2 of this volume.

7. M. G. Smith, "Institutional and Political Conditions of Pluralism," L. Kuper and M. G. Smith, eds., *Pluralism in Africa* (Berkeley: University of California Press, 1965), pp. 26-63.

8. I. Lustick, "Stability in Deeply Divided Societies: Consociationalism Versus Control," *World Politics* 31, no. 3 (April 1979); S. Smooha, "Control of Minorities in Israel and Northern Ireland," *Comparative Studies in History and Society* 22, no. 2 (April 1980); H. Adam, *Modernising Racial Domination* (Berkeley: University of California Press, 1971); and Rothchild (Chapter 2 of this volume). See also P. Hintzen and R. Premdas, "Guyana: Coercion and Control in Political Change," *Journal of Inter-American Studies and World Affairs* 24, no. 3 (August 1982).

9. R. S. Milne, *Politics in Ethnically Bipolar States* (Vancouver: University of British Columbia Press, 1982), p. 176.

10. For a discussion of "representative bureaucracy," see Milton J. Esman, "Public Administration and the Struggle for Shares in Ethnically and Racially Plural Societies" (Paper delivered at the annual meeting of the American Political Science Association, New York, 31 August - 3 September, 1978).

11. A. Lijphart, *Democracy in Plural Societies* (New Haven, Conn.: Yale University Press, 1977).

12. B. Barry, "The Consociational Model and Its Dangers," *European Journal of Political Research* 3, no. 4 (December 1970); J. Steiner, "The Principles of Majority and Proportionality," *British Journal of Political Science* 2, no. 1 (January 1971); and Rothchild, Chapter 2, this volume.

13. Rothchild, Chapter 2 of this volume.

14. Eric Williams, *Capitalism and Slavery* (London: Andre Deutsch, 1964).

15. Despres, *Cultural Pluralism*, p. 45.

16. Williams, *Capitalism and Slavery*, p. 7.

17. James Rodway, *Guiana: British, Dutch, and French* (London: T. Fisher and Unwin, 1912), p. 224.

18. Alan Young, *The Approaches to Local Self-Government in British Guiana* (London: Longmans, Green, 1958), p. 7.

19. Smith, *Pluralism in Africa*, pp. 43-44.

20. Dwarka Nath, *A History of Indians in British Guiana* (London: Thomas Nelson and Sons, 1950), pp. 179-180.

21. Chandra Jayawardena, *Conflict and Solidarity on a Guiana Plantation* (London: Athlone Press, 1963), p. 14.

22. Smith, *Pluralism in Africa*, pp. 41-42.

23. Rawle Farley, "The Rise of the Peasantry in British Guiana," *Social and Economic Studies* 2, no. 4 (June 1954): 95.

24. Young, *The Approaches to Local Self-Government*, p. 23.

25. Ibid.

26. *Report of the British Guiana Commission of Inquiry on Racial Problems in the Public Service* (Geneva: International Commission of Jurists, 1965), p. 164. (Hereafter referred to as the *ICJ Report.*)

27. Ibid.

28. G. W. Roberts, "Some Observations on the Population of British Guiana," *Population Studies* 2 (September 1948): 186-187.

29. *ICJ Report,* p. 165.

30. Smith, *Pluralism in Africa,* pp. 42-44.

31. See J. S. Furnivall, *Colonial Policy and Practice* (London: Cambridge University Press, 1948), pp. 304-312.   The "plural society" concept is elaborated by M. G. Smith, ibid.

32. Depres, *Cultural Pluralism,* p. 37.

33. Alan H. Adamson, *Sugar Without Slaves* (New Haven, Conn.: Yale University Press, 1972), p. 241.

34. Ibid.

35. Ibid., p. 242.

36. Despres, *Cultural Pluralism,* p. 39.

37. Ibid., p. 40.

38. Cecil Clementi, *A Constitutional History of British Guiana* (London: 1937), p. 369.

39. C. Enloe, "Civilian Control of the Military: Implications in the Plural Societies of Guyana and Malaysia" (Paper presented at the Interdisciplinary Seminar on Armed Forces and Society, SUNY-Buffalo, October 18-19, 1974, mimeograph), p. 27.

40. H. Lutchman, "Race and Bureaucracy in Guyana," *Journal of Comparative Administration* 4, no. 2 (August 1972): 230.

41. For the historical background to educational development in Guyana, see M. K. Bacchus, *Education and Socio-Cultural Integration in a Plural Society* (Montreal: McGill University Press, 1970).

42. Raj K. Vasil, *Politics in Bi-Racial Societies* (New Delhi: Vikas Publishing, 1984), p. 69.

43. Bacchus, *Education and Socio-Cultural Integration.*

44. See Ralph R. Premdas, *Racial Politics in Guyana* (Denver, Colo.: University of Denver Press, 1973); J. E. Greene, *Race vs. Politics in Guyana* (ISER-UWI Mona, Jamaica: 1974); and Peter Newman, *British Guiana: Problems of Cohesion in an Immigrant Society* (London: Oxford University Press, 1964).

45. Paul Singh, *Guyana: Socialism in a Plural Society* (London: Fabian Society, 1972).

46. See Ralph R. Premdas, "The Rise of the First Mass-Based Multi-Racial Party in Guyana," *Caribbean Quarterly* 20 (September-December 1974).

47. Ashton Chase, *A History of Trade Unionism in Guyana* (Georgetown: New Guiana Co., 1964).

48. Cheddi Jagan, *Forbidden Freedom: The Story of British Guiana* (London: Lawrence and Wishart, 1954).

49. "The Aims of the Political Affairs Committee," *The PAC Bulletin,* Nov. 6, 1946, p. 1.

50. Premdas, "The Rise of the First Mass-Based Multi-Racial Party," pp. 10-13.

51. "Aims and Programme of the People's Progressive Party," *Thunder* 1, no. 4, (April 1950), pp. 6-7.

52. Premdas, "The Rise of the First Mass-Based Multi-Racial Party," pp. 10-15.

53. Ashton Chase, *133 Days Towards Freedom in Guyana* (Georgetown: New Guiana Co., 1953).

54. See Ralph R. Premdas, "Election and Political Campaigns in a Racially Bifurcated State," *Journal of Inter-American Studies and World Affairs* 12 (August 1972).

55. See "Money Being Spent on Majority Party's Stronghold," *New Nation*, Jan. 24, 1959; and "We Want Nationalism Not Sectionalism," *New Nation*, Feb. 1, 1958.

56. See Arthur Schlesinger, Jr., *A Thousand Days* (New York: Houghton Mifflin, 1965), p. 779.

57. See Ralph R. Premdas, "Guyana: Violence and Democracy in a Communal State," *Plural Societies* 12, nos. 3-4 (Autumn-Winter 1981); and Peter Simms, *Trouble in Guyana* (London: Allen and Unwin, 1966).

58. Lutchman, "Race and Bureaucracy," p. 242.

59. See R. Hope and W. C. David, "Planning For Development in Guyana: The Experience from 1945 to 1973," *Inter-American Economic Affairs* (Spring 1974).

60. See Ralph R. Premdas, "Competitive Party Organizations and Political Integration in a Racially Fragmented State: The Case of Guyana," *Caribbean Studies* 12, no. 4 (January 1973), especially footnotes 30 and 32.

61. Despres, *Cultural Pluralism and National Policies in British Guiana*; also see Ralph R. Premdas, "Guyana: Communal Conflict, Socialism, and Political Reconciliation," *Inter-American Affairs* 30, no. 8 (Spring 1977).

62. Lutchman, "Race and Bureaucracy," p. 242. Also see *Report of the Commission of Inquiry into the Disturbances in British Guiana in Feb. 1962* (London: HMSO, 2849, 1965); and Ralph R. Premdas, "Guyana: Destabilisation in the Western Hemisphere," *Caribbean Quarterly* 25, no. 3 (March 1980).

63. See Milne, *Politics in Ethnically Bipolar States.*

64. Enloe, "Civilian Control of the Military," p. 27.

65. Milne, *Politics in Ethnically Bipolar States*, p. 146.

66. See Percy Hintzen and Ralph Premdas, "Guyana: Coercion and Control in Political Change," *Journal of Inter-American Studies and World Affairs* 24, no. 3 (August 1982).

67. Drew Pearson, "U.S. Faces Line Holding Decision," *Washington Post*, May 31, 1964; Ralph R. Premdas, "Guyana: Socialist Reconstruction or Political Opportunism," *Journal of Inter-American Studies and World Affairs* 20, no. 2 (May 1978); and Ralph Premdas, "Guyana's Foreign Policy: Ideology and Change," *World Affairs* (Fall 1982).

68. Enloe, "Civilian Control of the Military"; see also her *Ethnic Soldiers* (Harmondsworth, England: Penguin, 1979).

69. See A. Kundu, "Rice in the British Caribbean Islands and British Guiana 1950-75," *Social and Economic Studies* 13, no. 2 (June 1964); also Eric R. Hanley, "Rice, Politics and Development in Guyana," I. Oxall et al., eds., *Beyond the Sociology of Development* (London: Routledge and Kegan Paul, 1975), pp. 131-154.

70. Adrian Mitchell, "Jagan and Burnham: It's Polling Day Tomorrow. Have Guyanese Elections Already Been Decided in Britain?" *The Sunday Times* (London), Dec. 15, 1968.

71. Jay Mandle, "Continuity and Change in Guyanese Underdevelopment," *Monthly Review* 21, no. 2 (June 1976).

72. See Forbes Burnham, *A Destiny to Mould* (London: Longman Caribbean, 1970); and F. Burnham, *Towards a Cooperative Republic* (Georgetown: Chronicle Publishers, 1969).

73. Premdas, "Guyana: Socialist Reconstruction or Political Opportunism?"

74. Ibid.

75. Percy Hintzen, "The Dynamics of Ethnicity, Class, and International Capitalist Penetration in Political Economy: Guyana and Trinidad" (Paper presented to the American Political Science Association, August 31-September 3, 1979).

76. Hintzen, "Guyana: Coercion and Control."

77. Ibid.; also see "Farewell to Bookers Empire," *Caribbean Contact* (March 1976): 10.

78. S. Narine, "Public Servants Not Forced to Join PNC," *Graphic* (Guyana), Dec. 20, 1974, p. 1.

79. Mandle, "Continuity and Change," p. 6.

80. Ibid., p. 11.

81. Milne, *Politics in Ethnically Bipolar States*, p. 147.

82. See George K. Danns, "Militarisation and Development: An Experiment in Nation-Building in Guyana," *Transition* (Guyana) 1, no. 1 (January 1978).

83. Ibid.

84. See James A. Sackey, "Dependence, Underdevelopment and Socialist-Oriented Transformation in Guyana," *Inter-American Affairs* 33, no. 1 (Summer 1979).

85. See Enloe, "Civilian Control of the Military."

86. Jay Mandle, "The Post-Colonial Mode of Production in Guyana" (Temple University, Department of Economics, 1979, mimeographed).

87. Milne, "Continuity and Change," p. 147.

88. See David DeCaries, "Intense Political Pressures on Guyana's Judicial System," *Caribbean Contact* (June 1979).

89. Ralph Premdas, "Communal Politics: Rodney's Guyana Revisited" *Revista Americana* (February 1985).

Contributors

Charles H. Kennedy is Assistant Professor of Politics at Wake Forest University. He previously taught at Bowdoin College and held a Senior Fulbright Research Fellowship in Pakistan. His research interests include bureaucracy, policy, and Islamic jurisprudence. His publications include *Bureaucracy in Pakistan* (Karachi: Oxford University Press, 1986) and he has contributed to a number of books and journals.

Gordon P. Means is Professor of Political Science at McMaster University in Hamilton, Ontario. He has engaged in field research in Malaysia, Indonesia, and India, and he counts among his current research interests the politics of ethnic and tribal minorities, and development policies and strategies in developing areas. He is author of *Malaysian Politics* (London: Hodder Stoughton, 1976); editor of *Development and Underdevelopment in Southeast Asia* (Ottawa: Canadian Council for Southeast Asian Studies, 1976), and *The Past in Southeast Asias Present* (Ottawa: Canadian Council for Southeast Asia Studies, 1977); and has contributed to other books and journals.

R. S. Milne is Professor Emeritus (Political Science) of the University of British Columbia. He is a Fellow of the Royal Society of Canada. He previously taught at Bristol University, University of Wellington (New Zealand), University of the Philippines, Institute of Social Studies, The Hague, and Singapore University. He is author, co-author or editor of over a dozen books and author of about eighty articles. His most recent books include: *Politics in Ethically Bipolar States: Guyana, Malaysia and Fiji* (Vancouver: University of British Columbia Press, 1981); (with Diane K. Mauzy) *Malaysia: Tradition, Modernity, and Islam* (Boulder, Colorado: Westview Press, 1986).

Neil Nevitte is Associate Professor of Political Science at the University of Calgary, Alberta. He previously taught at Harvard University and at the University of Leeds. His research interests include minority nationalist movements and minority-state relations. His publications include *Minorities and the Canadian State* (Oakville, Ontario: Mosaic Press, 1985) and *The Future of North America: Canada, the United States and Quebec Nationalism* (Cambridge, Massachusetts: Harvard University Press, 1979) as contributing co-editor, and he has published in a number of journals.

Robert Oberst is Assistant Professor of Political Science at Nebraska Wesleyan University. He is the author of *Legislators and Representation in Sri Lanka: The Decentralization of Development Planning* (Boulder, Colorado: Westview Press, 1985) and he has contributed articles to such journals as *Asian Survey, Pacific Affairs,* and *Public Administration and Development.*

Ralph P. Premdas is Visiting Professor of Political Science at McGill University. He has taught previously at the University of Guyana and the University of California at Berkeley. He is the author of *Racial Politics in Guyana* (Denver, Colorado: University of Denver Press, 1973) and several articles and monographs on Guyana's society and politics.

Donald Rothchild is Professor of Political Science at the University of California, Davis. He has also served as a visiting professor at universities in Uganda, Kenya, Zambia, and Ghana. He is the author of a number of articles and books, including *Racial Bargaining in Independent Kenya* (London: Oxford University Press, 1973), *Scarcity, Choice, and Public Policy in Middle Africa* (Berkeley; University of California Press, 1978), and *State Versus Ethnic Claims: African Policy Dilemmas* (Boulder, Colorado: Westview Press, 1983).

Index